1975

Agora Paperback

GENERAL EDITOR: ALLAN

ot

On Tyranny

On Tyranny

REVISED AND ENLARGED

BY LEO STRAUSS

Cornell Paperbacks

CORNELL UNIVERSITY PRESS

ITHACA, NEW YORK

FOREWORD

Agora Paperback Editions is enriched by this edition of Leo Strauss' classic interpretation of a classic text. Professor Strauss has singlehandedly revived the serious study of ancient political thought and shown that it is not merely an object for historical curiosity but is relevant to our most vital present interests. Central to this study is the concern for the texts that convey the teaching of the classical philosophers; it is well that Mr. Strauss' only book devoted to the interpretation of a single Greek text be available to the public. The wisdom of the ancients reveals itself only to those who have the proper dispositions. These dispositions are encouraged by this book, which is a model of the care and respect necessary to the interpreter. It does not so much present a doctrine as prepare the way for a quest.

This edition includes a literal translation of the *Hiero* designed to allow the reader to follow Mr. Strauss' argument. His interpretation is based on a close textual analysis which takes seriously every detail of Xenophon's presentation. None of the available translations was based on such premises. In them much of the essential detail disappears, with the result that the reader is unable to understand Mr. Strauss' references; by themselves, such translations make it impossible to discover Xenophon's teaching—let alone judge it. A new translation was commissioned, and, although Mr. Strauss is not responsible for it, the editors hope that it reflects Mr. Strauss' care and will make it feasible for the reader to exercise a similar care.

We have also included in this volume the debate carried on by Leo Strauss and Alexandre Kojève concerning the adequacy of the Xenophontic understanding of tyranny. This is one of the few truly philosophic confrontations in recent times in which the participants understand the issues and one another and present clear alternatives. M. Kojève is the profoundest modern student of Hegel and hence represents the most serious stratum of that historical or historicist understanding of things human and political criticized in this book; it is as a response to this view that Professor Strauss proposes the classical teaching. Mr. Strauss has suggested that this historicist view has been the dominant one since the end of the eighteenth century, although its foundations and its consequences are seldom adequately reasoned. M. Kojève does have such an understanding and is able to present it intransigently. This is, therefore, a confrontation of positions on the level of the real issues—argued with an intimate knowledge of the teachings and a clear grasp of the phenomena. The question debated is whether human nature is unchanging and whether philosophy can move from the historic to the permanent.

Despite the fact that M. Kojève is the author of the best book yet written on Hegel (*Introduction à la Lecture de Hegel*, Gallimard, Paris, 1947), both he and his book are virtually unknown in America. It is hoped that this first translation of his work into English will begin to correct this ignorance, for he is an important interpreter of modern thought. He has had a decisive, if often hidden, influence on contemporary French thought; although his popular reputation does not rival that of those who have most profited from him, his contribution is recognized on the Continent by those who know. He is largely responsible for his own anonymity; he writes little, has little respect for schools, doubts the possibility of instructing men at large, and despises fame. But he alone dared to contend that the properly understood Hegelian system is the true and final philosophic teaching at a time when there was practically universal agreement that Hegel's system had been refuted by Schelling, Kierkegaard, and Nietzsche, to say nothing of natural science and history; he restored the original Hegel in contradistinction both to the traditional Hegelianism of the late nineteenth century and to "neo-Hegelianism."

The few men who read him or studied with him saw the force of his mind and brought his views into currency; one might add that they were not always too generous in acknowledging their source. M. Kojève is of Russian origin and studied in Berlin after the Russian Revolution. He went to Paris in the early thirties and taught a course on the Phenomenology of the Mind at the École Pratique de Hautes Études from 1933 to 1939. It was attended by many men who have since become eminent in French letters; his book consists of the notes from that course assembled by the novelist Raymond Queneau. Other than a few articles in *Critique* and *Les Temps Modernes*, this is all he has published. For the last fifteen years M. Kojève has been spending the public part of his life in the appropriate Hegelian role of civil servant; he is one of the chief planners for the Common Market in the French Ministry of Economic Affairs. He is, as he says, presiding over the end of history. His vast learning is used only on Sundays in writing what he calls his "posthumous works"; this undertaking is intended to be a comprehensive history of philosophy. Given the title, it is not appropriate to await its appearance too impatiently. We must therefore make do with reflection on what he has already given us.

ALLAN BLOOM

General Editor, Agora Paperback Editions

CONTENTS

On Tyranny

XENOPHON'S

Hiero
or Tyrannicus

◘ ◘ ◘

I

(1) Simonides the poet once came to visit Hiero the tyrant. After they both had found leisure, Simonides said,

"Would you be willing to tell me something, Hiero, which you probably know better than I?"

"And what kind of thing is it," said Hiero, "which I myself would know better than so wise a man as you?"

(2) "I know for my part," he said, "that you have been a private man and are now a tyrant. It is likely, then, that since you have experienced both, you also know better than I how the tyrannical and the private life differ in human pleasures and pains."

(3) "Then why don't you remind me of something in private life," said Hiero, "since, now at least, you are still a private man? For in this way I think I would best be able to show you what is different in each."

(4) So Simonides spoke in this way: "Well then, as for private men, Hiero, I believe I have observed them pleased and distressed through their eyes, by sights; through their ears, by sounds; through their nose, by odors; through their mouth, by meats and drinks;

Translated by Marvin Kendrick.

and as to the things of Aphrodite through what, of course, we all know. (5) As to what is cold and hot, hard and soft, light and heavy, when we distinguish between them, we seem to me to be pleased and pained by them with our entire body. And we seem to me to be pleased and pained by what is good and bad sometimes through the soul alone, and at other times through the soul and the body in common. (6) That we are pleased by sleep I think myself I perceive, but how, by what, and when—of this I believe I am somehow more ignorant," he said. "And perhaps it is not to be wondered that things in waking give us clearer perceptions than do things in sleep."

(7) Now to this Hiero replied: "Then I for one, Simonides," he said, "would certainly be unable to say how the tyrant can perceive anything other than these things you yourself have mentioned. So that up to this point at least I do not know whether the tyrannical life differs at all from the private life."

(8) Simonides spoke. "But in this way it does differ," he said, "[the tyrant's] pleasure is multiplied many times over through each of these means, and he has far fewer pains."

"That is not so, Simonides," Hiero said. "Know well tyrants have much fewer pleasures than private men who live on moderate means, and they have far more and greater pains."

(9) "What you say is incredible," said Simonides. "For if this is the case, why would many desire to be tyrant, and this on the part of reputedly very able men? And why would all envy the tyrants?"

(10) "By Zeus," said Hiero, "because they speculate about it, although they are inexperienced in the deeds of both lives. I will try to teach you that I speak the truth, beginning with sight; for I seem to recall you also began speaking there.

(11) "In the first place, when I reason on it, I find that tyrants are at a disadvantage in the spectacles which impress us through vision. For one thing, there are different things in different countries worth seeing. Private men go to each of these places, and to whatever cities they please, for the sake of spectacles. And they go to the common festivals, where the things which human beings hold most worth seeing are brought together. (12) But tyrants have little share in viewing these, for it is not safe for them to go where they are not going to be stronger than those who will be present. Nor is what they possess at home secure enough for them

to entrust it to others and go abroad. For there is the fear that they will at the same time be deprived of their rule and become powerless to take vengeance on those who have committed the injustice.

(13) "Perhaps, then, you may say, 'But surely [sights] of this kind come to them, even when they remain at home.' By Zeus, yes, Simonides, but only few of many; and these, being of such a kind, are sold to tyrants at such a price that those who display anything at all expect to leave, receiving from the tyrant in a moment an amount multiplied many times over what they possess from all human beings besides in their entire lifetime."

(14) And Simonides said, "But if you are worse off with respect to spectacles, you at least gain the advantage through hearing; since you never lack praise, the sweetest sound. For all who are in your presence praise everything you say and everything you do. You in turn are out of the range of abuse, the harshest of things to hear; for no one within sight of a tyrant is willing to accuse him."

(15) Hiero spoke. "What pleasure," he said, "do you think a tyrant gets from those who say nothing bad, when he knows clearly every thought these silent men have is bad for him? Or what pleasure do you think he gets from those who praise him, when he suspects them of bestowing their praise for the sake of flattery?"

(16) And Simonides said, "By Zeus, this I certainly grant you, Hiero: the sweetest praise comes from the freest men. But, you see, you still would not persuade any human being that you do not get much more pleasure from that which nourishes us humans."

(17) "I know, at least, Simonides," he said, "that the majority judge we drink and eat with more pleasure than private men, believing they themselves would dine more pleasantly on the dish served to us than the one served to them; for what surpasses the ordinary causes the pleasures. (18) For this reason all human beings save tyrants anticipate feasts with delight. For [tyrants'] tables are always prepared for them in such abundance that they can hold nothing more at feasts. So, first, in this pleasure of hope [tyrants] are worse off than private men." (19) "Next," he said, "I know well that you are experienced in this: the more someone is served with an amount beyond what is sufficient, the more quickly he is struck with satiety of eating. So in the duration of pleasure too, one who is served many dishes fares worse than those who live in a moderate way."

(20) "But, by Zeus," Simonides said, "so long as the appetite admits, those who are nourished by richer dishes have much more pleasure than those served cheaper fare."

(21) "Then do you think, Simonides," said Hiero, "that the man who gets the most pleasure from each act also has the most love for it?"

"Certainly," he said.

"Well then, do you see tyrants going to their fare with any more pleasure than private men to theirs?"

"No, by Zeus," he said, "I certainly do not, but, as it would seem to many, even more sourly."

(22) "For why else," said Hiero, "do you see so many contrived dishes served to tyrants: sharp, bitter, sour, and the like?"

"Certainly," Simonides said, "and they seem to me very unnatural for human beings."

(23) "Do you think these foods," said Hiero, "anything else but objects of desire to a soft soul weakened by luxury? Since I myself know well, and presumably you know too, that those who eat with pleasure need none of these sophistries."

(24) "Well, and what is more," said Simonides, "as for these expensive scents you anoint yourself with, I suppose those near you enjoy them more than you yourselves do; just as a man who has eaten does not himself perceive graceless odors as much as those near him."

(25) "Moreover," said Hiero, "so with respect to food, the one who always has all kinds takes none of it with longing. But the one who lacks something takes his fill with delight whenever it comes to sight before him."

(26) "Your enjoyment of what is of Aphrodite alone," said Simonides, "comes dangerously close to producing the desire for tyrany. For there it is possible for you to have intercourse with the fairest you see."

(27) "But now," said Hiero, "you have mentioned the very thing—know well—in which, if at all, we are at a greater disadvantage than private men. For as regards marriage, first there is marriage with those superior in wealth and power, which I presume is held to be the noblest, and to confer a certain pleasurable distinction on the bridegroom. Secondly, there is marriage with equals. But marriage with those who are lower is considered very dishonor-

able and useless. (28) Well then, unless the tyrant marries a foreign woman, necessity compels him to marry an inferior, so that what would content him is not readily accessible to him. Furthermore, it is attentions from the proudest women which give the most pleasure, whereas attentions from slaves, even when they are available, do not content at all, and rather cause violent anger and pain if anything is neglected.

(29) "But in the pleasures of Aphrodite with boys the tyrant comes off still much worse than in those with women for begetting offspring. For I presume we all know these pleasures of Aphrodite give much greater enjoyment when accompanied with love. (30) But love in turn is least of all willing to arise in the tyrant, for love takes pleasure in longing not for what is at hand, but for what is hoped for. Then, just as a man without experience of thirst engages in drinking, so too the man without experience of love is without experience of the sweetest pleasures of Aphrodite." So Hiero spoke.

(31) Simonides laughed at this and said, "What do you mean, Hiero? So you deny that love of boys arises naturally in a tyrant? How could you, in that case, love Dailochus, the one they call the fairest?"

(32) "By Zeus, Simonides," he said, "it is not because I particularly desire to get what seems available in him, but to win what is very ill-suited for a tyrant. (33) Because I love Dailochus for that very thing which nature perhaps compels a human being to want from the fair, and it is this I love to win; but I desire very deeply to win it with love* and from one who is willing; and I think I desire less to take it from him by force than to do myself an injury. (34) I believe myself that to take from an unwilling enemy is the most pleasant of all things, but I think the sweetest favors are from willing boys. (35) For instance, the glances of one who loves back are sweet; the questions are sweet and sweet the answers; but fights and quarrels are the most pleasant and provocative. (36) It certainly seems to me," he said, "that pleasure taken from unwilling boys is more an act of robbery than of Aphrodite. Although the profit and vexation to his private enemy give a certain pleasure to the robber,

* Here φιλία, love returned on the part of the beloved. Hiero maintains a distinction throughout this passage (29–end) between the ἔρως (erotic or passionate love) which is not engendered on his part and the φιλία (love, liking, friendship) which is not returned by the beloved. The parallel to μετὰ φιλίας is μετ᾽ ἔρωτος in 29 *supra*.

yet to take pleasure in the pain of whomever one loves, to kiss and be hated, to touch and be loathed—must this not by now be a distressing and pitiful affliction? (37) To the private man it is immediately a sign that the beloved grants favors from love when he renders some service, because the private man knows his beloved serves under no compulsion. But it is never possible for the tyrant to trust that he is loved. (38) For we know as a matter of course that those who serve through fear try by every means in their power to make themselves appear to be like friends by the services of friends. And what is more, plots against tyrants spring from none more than from those who most pretend to love them."

II

(1) To this Simonides said, "Well, these disadvantages you mention seem to me at least to be very trivial. For I see many," he said, "reputed to be manly men, who willingly suffer disadvantages in food, drink, and delicacies, and who even refrain from sex. (2) But you tyrants far surpass private men surely in the following. You contrive great enterprises; you execute them swiftly; you have the most possessions in superfluity; you own horses surpassing in virtue, arms surpassing in beauty, superior adornment for your women, the most magnificent houses, and these furnished with what is of the most value; moreover, the servants you possess are the best in their numbers and their knowledge; and you are the ones most capable of harming your private enemies and benefiting your friends."

(3) To this Hiero said, "I do not wonder at all that the multitude of human beings are utterly deceived by tyranny, Simonides. For the crowd seems to me to form the opinion from what they see that certain men are happy or wretched. (4) Now tyranny displays openly, evident for all to see, the possessions which are held to be of much value. But it keeps what is harsh hidden in the tyrants' souls, where human happiness and unhappiness lie concealed. (5) That this escapes the notice of the multitude is, as I said, not a wonder to me. But that you [wise] are ignorant of this, you who are reputed to get a finer view of most matters through your understanding than through your eyes, this I do hold to be a wonder. (6) But I myself know clearly from experience, Simonides, and I tell you that tyrants share least in the highest goods, and for the most part possess the greatest evils. (7) Take this for example: if peace is held to be a

great good for human beings, for tyrants there is the least share in it; and if war is a great evil, in this tyrants get the largest share. (8) For, to begin with, it is possible for private men, unless their city is engaged in fighting a common war, to take a journey wherever they wish, without being afraid that someone will kill them. But the tyrants, all of them, proceed everywhere as through hostile territory. They themselves at least think it necessary to go armed and always to be surrounded by an armed bodyguard. (9) Moreover, if private men go on an expedition somewhere into enemy country, they believe they are safe at least after they have returned home. But the tyrants know that when they reach their own city they are then in the midst of the largest number of their enemies. (10) Again, if others who are stronger attack the city, and those outside the wall, being weaker, think they are in danger, all believe they have been rendered safe, at least after they have come within the fortifications. The tyrant, however, not even when he passes inside his house is free from danger; he thinks it is there that he must be particularly on his guard. (11) Furthermore, for private men, relief from war is brought about both by treaties and by peace. Whereas for tyrants peace is never made with those subject to their tyranny; nor could the tyrant be confident trusting for a moment to a treaty.

(12) "There are also wars, of course, which the cities as well as the tyrants wage against those they have formerly subjected by force. Now in these wars, everything hard which the man in the cities undergoes, the tyrant too undergoes. (13) For both must be armed, must be on their guard, and run risks; and if, being beaten, they suffer some harm, each suffers pain from these wars. (14) Up to this point, then, the wars of both are equal. But when it comes to the pleasures which the men in the cities get from fighting the cities, these the tyrants cease to have. (15) For surely when the cities overpower their opponents in a battle, it is not easy to express how much pleasure [the men] get from routing the enemy; how much from the pursuit; how much from killing their enemies; how they exult in the deed; how they claim a brilliant reputation for themselves; and how they take delight in believing they have augmented their city. (16) Each one pretends that he shared in the planning and killed the most; and it is hard to find where they do not make some false additions, claiming they killed more than all

who really died. So noble a thing does a great victory seem to them.

(17) "But when the tyrant suspects certain men of plotting against him, and, perceiving that they are in fact plotting, puts them to death, he knows that he does not augment the whole city; he knows without a doubt that he will rule fewer men, and he cannot be glad; he does not pride himself on the deed, but rather minimizes what has happened as much as he can, and while he does it he makes the apology that he has done it without committing injustice. Thus what he has done does not seem noble even to him. (18) And when they whom he feared are dead he is not any bolder, but is still more on his guard than before. So, then, the tyrant spends his life fighting the kind of war which I myself am showing you."

III

(1) "Now consider friendship in its turn, and how the tyrants partake of it. First let us reflect whether friendship is a great good for human beings. (2) For surely it is the case with a man who is loved by someone that the one who loves him gladly sees him present; gladly benefits him; longs for him when he leaves; welcomes him returning again; takes pleasure with him in the goods which are his; and comes to his aid if he sees him fallen into any trouble.

(3) "Moreover, it has not escaped the notice of the cities that friendship is the greatest and most pleasant human good. At any rate, many of the cities have an established custom that only adulterers may be slain with impunity, and manifestly because they believe adulterers are the destroyers of wives' friendship for their husbands. (4) Since when, by some concurrence of circumstances, a wife has been seduced, her husband honors her no less for this provided he is of the opinion that her friendship continues uncorrupted.

(5) "I myself judge being loved a good so great that I believe benefits actually come of themselves to the one who is loved, both from gods and men. (6) Yet in this kind of possession too, tyrants are at a disadvantage beyond all others.

"But if you wish to know, Simonides, that I speak the truth, reflect on this consideration. (7) For surely the firmest friendships are held to be those of parents for children, and children for their parents, brothers for their brothers, wives for their husbands, and comrades for comrades. (8) If, then, you are willing to reflect thoughtfully on it, you will find that private men are loved chiefly by these, whereas many tyrants have killed their own children, and many have themselves perished at the hands of their children; that many brothers in tyrannies have become one another's murderers; and that many tyrants have been brought to ruin both by their wives and by comrades whom they thought were most their friends. (9) How, then, is it possible to conceive that those who are thus hated by such as are inclined by nature and compelled by law to love them, can be loved by anyone else?

IV

(1) "Again, take trust also, who can share least in this and not suffer disadvantage in a great good? For what kind of companionship is sweet without mutual trust? What kind of intimacy is delightful to man and wife without trust? Or what kind of servant is pleasing if he is not trusted? (2) Now of this trusting someone, a tyrant has the least share; inasmuch as he not only spends his life without trusting his food and drink, but it is even a practice tyrants have, before they begin sacrifice to the gods, to first bid the attendants taste it, because of their distrust that even in that they may eat or drink something bad.

(3) "Fatherlands in their turn, are of the highest value to other human beings. For citizens act as a bodyguard to one another against slaves, and against evil-doers, without pay, so that no citizen will meet a violent death. (4) And they have advanced so far in watchfulness that many have made a law that even the accomplice of a slayer is not free from taint. Thus, because of the fatherlands, each of the citizens lives his life in safety. (5) But in this too it is the reverse for the tyrants. For instead of avenging them, the cities greatly honor the one who kills the tyrant; and instead of excluding the killer from sacred rites, as they do the murderers of private men, the cities erect in their temples statues of those who have committed such an act.

(6) "And if you think that because the tyrant has more possessions than private men he gets more pleasure from them, this is not the case either, Simonides. But just as athletes do not enjoy proving stronger than [untrained] private men, but are annoyed when they prove weaker than their opponents, so the tyrant gets no pleasure from appearing to have more than private men, but suffers pain when

he has less than other tyrants. For these he regards as rivals for his own wealth.

(7) "Nor does something of what he desires come more quickly to the tyrant than to the private man. For the private man desires a house, or a field, or a domestic slave; but the tyrant desires cities, extensive territory, harbors, or mighty citadels, which are things much harder and more dangerous to win than the objects desired by private men.

(8) "And, furthermore, you will see but few private men as poor as many tyrants. For what is a large and sufficient amount is not judged by an enumeration, but with a view to its use. Accordingly, an amount which exceeds what is sufficient is large, but what falls short of sufficiency is small. (9) Now for the tyrant a multiplicity of possessions is less adequate for his necessary expenditures than for the private man. For private men can cut their daily expenditure in any way they wish, but the tyrants cannot, because their largest and most necessary expenses go to guard their lives. And to curtail these would be their utter destruction.

(10) "Next, why would someone pity as poor all those who can get what they need by just means? And who would not justly call wretched and poor all those who are compelled by their need to live by contriving something evil and degrading? (11) Now the tyrants are compelled most of the time to plunder unjustly both temples and human beings, because they always need additional money to meet their necessary expenses. For, as if there were a perpetual war on, [tyrants] are compelled to support an army or perish."

V

(1) "I will tell you of another harsh affliction, Simonides, which the tyrants have. For although they recognize the decent, the wise, and the just, no less than private men [the tyrants] fear rather than admire them. They fear the brave because they might dare something for the sake of freedom; the wise, because they might contrive something; and the just, because the multitude might desire to be ruled by them. (2) When, because of their fear, they do away secretly with such men, who is left for them to use save the unjust, the incontinent, and the slavish? The unjust are trusted because they are afraid, just as the tyrants are, that some day the cities, becoming

free, will become their masters. The incontinent are trusted because they are at liberty for the present, and the slavish because not even they deem themselves worthy to be free. This affliction, then, seems harsh to me: to think some are good men, and yet to be compelled to make use of the others.

(3) "Moreover, the tyrant also is compelled to be a lover of the city; for without the city he would not be able either to preserve himself or to be happy. Yet tyranny compels [the tyrants] to run down even their own fatherlands. For they do not rejoice in making the citizens either brave or well-armed. Rather they take pleasure in making strangers more formidable than the citizens, and these strangers they use as bodyguards. (4) Furthermore, when good seasons come and there is an abundance of good things, not even then does the tyrant rejoice with them. For [tyrants] think that as men are more in want, they are more submissive for being used."

VI

(1) "I wish, Simonides," he said, "to make clear to you those pleasures which I enjoyed when I was a private man; now, since I became a tyrant, I perceive that I am deprived of them. (2) I was together with companions of my own age, taking pleasure in them, and they in me; I was a companion to myself when I desired peace and tranquility; I lived amid banquets, often until I forgot everything harsh in human life, and often until my soul was completely absorbed in song, festivity, and dancing, and often until there was desire in common between me and those who were present. (3) Now I am deprived of those who take pleasure in me, because I have slaves instead of friends for comrades. I myself am deprived of pleasant intimacy with them, because I see in them no good will for me. And I guard against drunkenness and sleep as if I were in an ambush. (4) To fear the crowd, yet to fear solitude; to fear being without a guard, and to fear the very men who are guarding; to be unwilling to have unarmed men about me, yet not gladly to see them armed—how could this fail to be a painful condition? (5) Furthermore, to trust strangers more than citizens, barbarians more than Greeks; to desire to keep the free slaves, and be compelled to make the slaves free—do not all these things seem to you signs of a soul distracted by fears?

(6) "But fear when in the soul is not only painful itself, it also

becomes the spoiler of all the pleasures it accompanies. (7) If you are experienced in warfare, Simonides, and have ever before now been posted near the enemy line, recall what sort of food you took at that time, and what sort of sleep you had. (8) The kind of pain you suffered then is the kind the tyrants have, only far more violent. For the tyrants believe they see enemies not only in front of them, but on every side."

(9) After he heard this, Simonides interrupted and said, "I think you put some things extremely well. For war is a fearful thing. But nevertheless, Hiero, we at any rate post guards, when we are on a campaign, and take our share of food and sleep heartily."

(10) And Hiero said, "Yes, by Zeus, Simonides, for the laws stand watch over the guards, so that they fear for themselves and in your behalf. But the tyrants hire guards, like harvesters, for pay. (11) And surely the guards, if they ought to be capable of doing anything, ought to be faithful. Yet one faithful man is much harder to find than a great many workers for whatever kind of task you wish, especially when those doing the guarding are only present for the sake of money, and when they may get in a moment much more by killing the tyrant than all they earn from him being his guards for a long time.

(12) "As to why you were jealous of us, because we are most able to benefit our friends, and because we, above all men, master our private enemies, this is not the case either. (13) For as to friends, how would you believe that you ever confer a benefit, when you know well that the one who receives the most from you would the most gladly get out of your sight as quickly as possible? For whatever it is he receives from a tyrant, no one believes it his own until he is beyond the tyrant's power to command. (14) As for private enemies in their turn, how would you say the tyrants have the most ability to master them, when they know well their private enemies are all those subject to their tyranny, and when it is not possible either to kill all these outright or to put them in chains? For who then would be left for [the tyrant] to rule? But knowing that they are his enemies, he must at the same time guard against, and be compelled to make use of, these very men.

(15) "Know well, Simonides, that those whom they fear among the citizens they find it hard to see alive, and yet hard to kill. It is just as if there were a good horse who yet gives rise to the fear that

he might do some irreparable harm; a man would find it hard to kill him because of his virtue, yet hard to manage him alive, being constantly alert against his working irreparable harm in the midst of danger. (16) So too with respect to as many other possessions as are hard to manage but useful; all alike give pain to their possessors, and to those who are rid of them."

VII

(1) When he heard these things from [Hiero], Simonides spoke. "Apparently," he said, "honor is a great thing, and human beings undergo all toil and endure all danger striving for it. (2) You [tyrants] too, apparently, although tyranny has as many difficulties as you say, nevertheless rush into it headlong in order that you may be honored, and in order that all—all who are present—may serve you in all your commands without excuses, admire you, rise from their seats, give way in the streets, and always defer to you both in their words and their actions. For it is such things that the subjects of tyrants do, and always do for anyone else they happen to honor.

(3) "I myself think, Hiero, that a real man differs from the other animals in this striving for honor. Since, after all, all animals alike seem to take pleasure in food, drink, sleep, and sex. But ambition does not arise naturally either in animals without reason or in all human beings. Those in whom love of honor and praise arises by nature are the ones who already far surpass the brutes, and who are also believed to be no longer human beings merely, but real men. (4) Accordingly, it seems to me that you probably endure all these things you bear in the tyranny because you are honored beyond all other human beings. For no human pleasure appears nearer the divine than the enjoyment of honors."

(5) To this Hiero said, "But, Simonides, even the honors of the tyrants appear to me of a kind similar to that which I showed their sex to be. (6) For services from those who do not love in return we do not hold to be favors to us, and sex which is forced does not appear pleasant either. In the same way, services from those under fear are not honors. (7) For must we say that those who are forced to rise from their chairs stand up to honor those who are treating them unjustly, or that those who give way in the streets to the stronger yield to honor those who are treating them unjustly?

(8) "The many give gifts to those they hate, especially when

they fear they may suffer some harm from them. But this, I think, would probably be considered an act of slavery. Whereas I believe for my part that honors derive from acts the opposite of this. (9) For when human beings, considering a real man able to be their benefactor, and believing that they enjoy his goods, for this reason have him on their lips in praise; when each one sees him as his own private good; when they willingly give way to him in the streets and rise from their chairs out of liking and not fear; when they crown him for his public virtue and beneficence, and willingly bestow gifts on him; these men who serve him in this way, I believe, honor him truly; and the one deemed worthy of these things I believe to be honored in reality. I myself count blessed the one so honored. (10) For I perceive that he is not plotted against, but rather that he causes anxiety lest he suffer harm, and that he lives his life—happy, without fear, without envy, and without danger. But the tyrant, Simonides, know well, lives night and day as one condemned by all human beings to die for his injustice."

(11) When Simonides heard all this through to the end, he said, "But why, Hiero, if being a tyrant is so wretched, and you realize this, do you not rid yourself of so great an evil, and why did no one else ever willingly let a tyranny go, who once acquired it?"

(12) "Because," he said, "in this too is tyranny most miserable, Simonides: it is not possible to be rid of it either. For how would some tyrant ever be able to repay in full the money of those he has dispossessed, or suffer in turn the chains he has loaded on them, or how supply in requital enough lives to die for those he has put to death? (13) Rather, if it profits any other man, Simonides, to hang himself, know," he said, "that I myself find this most profits the tyrant. He alone, whether he keeps his troubles or lays them aside, gains no advantage."

VIII

(1) Simonides took him up and said, "Well, Hiero, I do not wonder that you are for the moment out of heart with tyranny; since, desiring to be loved by human beings, you believe that tyranny is an obstacle in the way of your attaining this. However, I think myself able to teach you that ruling does not at all prevent your being loved, and that it even has the advantage of private life in this respect. (2) While examining whether this is of itself the

case, let us not yet inquire whether because of his greater potential the ruler also would be able to grant more favors; but rather, if the private man and the tyrant do similar things, consider which of the two wins more gratitude by means of equal favors. I will begin with the simplest examples. (3) First, suppose the ruler and the private man, when they see someone, address him in a friendly way. In this case, from which man do you believe the greeting gives the hearer more pleasure? Again, suppose both praise the same man; from which of them do you think the praise brings greater pleasure? Suppose each, when he offers sacrifice, honors the same man; from which of the two do you think the honor would obtain more gratitude? (4) Suppose they alike attend a sick person; is it not obvious that attentions from the most powerful produce the greatest cheer? Suppose, then, they make equal gifts; is it not clear, in this case too, that favors of half the value from the most powerful are worth more than the whole of a grant from the private man? (5) Indeed, I myself hold that even from gods a certain honor and grace attend a man who rules. For not only does ruling make a real man nobler, but this same man is also nobler to our view when he rules than when he lives privately; and we delight more in discoursing with those preeminent in honor than with those equal to us.

(6) "As for boys, with regard to whom you found the most fault with tyranny, they are least offended at the old age of one who rules, and they pay least attention to the ugliness of whomever they happen to be intimate with. For his being honored itself helps most to dignify him, so that his offensiveness disappears, and what is noble appears more resplendent.

(7) "Since, then, you [tyrants] obtain greater thanks by means of equal services, must it not be fitting, when you are able to confer benefits by accomplishing many times more things and are able to make many times more gifts, that you also be loved far more than the private men?"

(8) Hiero answered at once, "No, by Zeus, Simonides," he said, "because we are compelled to do the things for which human beings are hated much more than private men. (9) We must exact money if we are to have the means to spend on our needs; we must compel [men] to guard the things which need guarding; we must punish the unjust; we must restrain those who wish to be insolent; and when the moment comes to set out with all speed on an expedition

by land or sea, we must not entrust the business to the sluggards. (10) Moreover, the man who is a tyrant needs mercenaries. And no burden weighs heavier on the citizens than that. For the citizens believe that tyrants keep these mercenaries not to share equal honors with themselves, but to get the advantage by supporting them."

IX

(1) To this in its turn Simonides said, "Well, I do not deny that all these matters require attention, Hiero. Some cares seem to me, however, to lead to much hatred, whereas others seem to be mutually very gratifying. (2) For to teach what is morally best, and to praise and honor the man who achieves this in the noblest way, is a concern which itself gives rise to mutual regard; whereas to rebuke the one who is slack in doing something, to coerce, to punish, to correct— these things necessarily give rise more to mutual enmity. (3) Accordingly I say that the man who rules ought to command others to punish the one who requires coercion, but that he ought to award the prizes himself. What occurs at present confirms that this is a good arrangement. (4) For whenever we wish our choruses to compete, the *Archon* offers the prizes, but he orders the managers of each chorus to assemble them, and others to instruct them and to apply coercion to those who are at all slack in performing. Accordingly, what gives rise to gratitude in these contests comes about at once through the *Archon*, and what is the contrary comes about through others. (5) Now what prevents the other political things from also being managed in this way? For all the cities are apportioned up, some according to tribes, some according to divisions, others according to companies, and rulers are put in charge of each section. (6) If someone should offer prizes to these sections, like choruses, for good arms, good discipline, horsemanship, bravery in war, and justice in contracts, it is likely that all these things, through emulation, would be practiced intently. (7) Yes, and, by Zeus, they would set out on an expedition with more speed wherever required, striving for honor; they would contribute money more promptly when the moment for this came; and farming, certainly the most useful thing of all, but the least accustomed to being managed by emulation, would itself greatly improve, if someone should offer prizes by fields or villages to those who best cultivate the ground; and many good things would be accomplished by those among the

citizens who turn to it vigorously. (8) For the revenues would increase, and moderation would follow much more closely upon the absence of leisure. And as for evil doings, they arise less naturally in those who are busy.

(9) "If imports are of any benefit to a city, the one honored the most for engaging in this would also bring together more importers. And if it should become apparent that the man who invents some painless revenue for the city will be honored, reflection itself would not be left uncultivated. (10) To sum it up, if it should become clear with respect to all matters that the man who introduces something beneficial will not go unrewarded, he would stimulate many to engage in reflecting on something good. And whenever many are concerned with what is useful, this is necessarily discovered and perfected all the more.

(11) "But if you are afraid, Hiero, that when prizes are offered among many, correspondingly many expenses will arise, keep in mind that no articles of commerce are cheaper than what human beings purchase by means of prizes. Do you see that in contests of horsemanship, gymnastic, and choruses small prizes bring forth great expenditures, much toil, and much care from human beings?"

X

(1) And Hiero said, "Well, Simonides, you seem to me to speak well as far as these matters go; but have you anything to say regarding the mercenaries, so that I may not incur hatred because of them? Or do you mean that once a ruler wins friendship he will no longer need a bodyguard at all?"

(2) "By Zeus, certainly he will need it," said Simonides. "For I know that it is inbred in some human beings, just as in horses, to be insolent in proportion as the needs they have are more fully satisfied. (3) The fear inspired by the bodyguard would make such men more moderate. And as for the gentlemen, there is nothing, it seems to me, by means of which you would confer so great services on them as by the mercenaries. (4) For surely you support them as guards for yourself; but before now many masters have died violently at the hands of their slaves. If, then, one—and this the first—of the mercenaries' orders should be, that as the bodyguard of all the citizens they were, whenever they perceived a thing of this kind, to go to the aid of all—and if they were ordered to guard against the evil-doers we

all know arise in cities—the citizens would know they were helped by them. (5) In addition to this, these [mercenaries] would probably best be able to provide confidence and safety for the husbandmen and property of herds and flocks in the country, alike for your own privately and for those throughout the country. They are capable, moreover, of providing the citizens with leisure to concern themselves with their private property, by guarding the positions of advantage. (6) Furthermore, as regards the secret and surprise attacks of enemies, who would be readier either to perceive them in advance or to prevent them than those who are always under arms and disciplined? Surely on a campaign, what is more useful to citizens than mercenaries? For [mercenaries] are likely to be readier to toil, run risks, and stand guard for the citizens. (7) As for the neighboring cities, is there not a necessity, brought about by those who are constantly under arms, for them especially to desire peace? For being disciplined the mercenaries would best be able to preserve what belongs to their friends and to destroy what belongs to their enemies. Surely when the citizens realize that these mercenaries do no harm at all to one who commits no injustice; that they restrain those who wish to do evil; that they come to the aid of those who are unjustly wronged; and that they take counsel for and incur danger in behalf of the citizens—must they not necessarily spend very gladly for their upkeep? After all, men support guards privately, and for lesser objects than these."

XI

(1) "You must not, Hiero, shrink from spending from your private possessions for the common good. For it seems to me that what a man as tyrant lays out for the city is spent more on what is necessary than what he lays out for his private [estate]. Let us examine each detail point by point. (2) First, which do you think would dignify you more, a house embellished at tremendous cost, or the whole city furnished with walls, temples, colonnades, market places, and harbors? (3) As for arms, which of the two would appear more formidable to your enemies, yourself fitted out in the most splendid arms, or your entire city well armed? (4) Take revenues; in which way do you think they would become greater, if you should keep your private property alone productive, or if you should contrive to make the property of all the citizens so? (5) And

regarding the pursuit believed to be the most noble and magnificent
of all, the raising of chariot horses, in which way do you think there
would be greater dignity, if you yourself should raise the most teams
among the Greeks and send them to the games, or if the most
breeders, and the most in competition, should be from your city?
And as for winning victories, which do you hold the nobler way,
by the virtue of your team, or by the happiness of the city which
you rule? (6) I myself say that it is not fitting for a man who is a
tyrant even to compete against private men. For, winning the victory, you would not be admired, but envied, as meeting the cost by
means of many estates, and, losing, you would be ridiculed most of
all.

(7) "But I tell you, Hiero, that the contest is against others who
rule cities; if you make the city you rule the happiest of these, know
well that you are victorious in the most noble and magnificent
contest among human beings. (8) First, you would at once secure
the love of your subjects, which is the very thing you happen to
desire. Further, not one man would herald your victory, but all
human beings would sing of your virtue. (9) Being an object of
attention you would be cherished not only by private men, but by
many cities; marveled at not only in private, but in public among all
as well; (10) it would be possible for you, as far as safety is concerned, to travel wherever you wish, for the sake of viewing the
sights; and it would be possible for you to do this remaining here.
For there would be a continual festival by you of those wishing to
display whatever wise, beautiful, or good thing they had, and of
those desiring to serve you as well. (11) Every man present would be
your ally, and every man absent would desire to see you. Therefore,
you would not only be liked, you would be loved by human beings;
as for the fair, you would not need to test them, but to endure being
tested by them; as for fear, you would have none, but you would
cause fear in others that you might suffer some harm; (12) you
would have willing men obeying you, and you would see them
willingly take thought for you; if there should be some danger, you
would see not only allies, but also champions, and those eager; being
deemed worthy of many gifts, you will not be at a loss for someone
well disposed with whom to share them, with all men rejoicing at
your good things and all fighting for those which are yours just as

if they were their own. (13) For treasuries, furthermore, you would have all the wealth of your friends.

"But enrich your friends with confidence, Hiero; for you will enrich yourself. Augment the city, for you will attach power to yourself. Acquire allies for it. (14) Consider the fatherland to be your estate, the citizens your comrades, friends your own children, your sons the same as your life, and try to win victory by benefiting all these. For if you master your friends in beneficence, your enemies will be utterly unable to resist you. And if you do all these things, know well, of all the things among human beings you will acquire the noblest and most blessed possession; for being happy, you will not be envied."

On Tyranny

The habit of writing against the government had, of itself, an unfavorable effect on the character. For whoever was in the habit of writing against the government was in the habit of breaking the law; and the habit of breaking even an unreasonable law tends to make men altogether lawless. . . .

From the day on which the emancipation of our literature was accomplished, the purification of our literature began. . . . During a hundred and sixty years the liberty of our press has been constantly becoming more and more entire; and during those hundred and sixty years the restraint imposed on writers by the general feeling of readers has been constantly becoming more and more strict. . . . At this day foreigners, who dare not print a word reflecting on the government under which they live, are at a loss to understand how it happens that the freest press in Europe is the most prudish.

MACAULAY

INTRODUCTION

IT IS PROPER that I should indicate my reasons for submitting this detailed analysis of a forgotten dialogue on tyranny to the consideration of political scientists.

Tyranny is a danger coeval with political life. The analysis of tyranny is therefore as old as political science itself. The analysis of tyranny that was made by the first political scientists was so clear, so comprehensive, and so unforgettably expressed that it was remembered and understood by generations which did not have any direct experience of actual tyranny. On the other hand, when we were brought face to face with tyranny—with a kind of tyranny that surpassed the boldest imagination of the most powerful thinkers of the past—our political science failed to recognize it. It is not surprising then that many of our contemporaries, disappointed or repelled by present-day analyses of present-day tyranny, were relieved when they rediscovered the pages in which Plato and other classical thinkers seemed to have interpreted for us the horrors of the twentieth century. What is surprising is that the renewed general interest in authentic interpretation of the phenomenon of tyranny did not lead to renewed interest, general or scholarly, in the only writing of the classical period which is explicitly devoted to the discussion of tyranny and its implications, and to nothing else, and which has never been subjected to comprehensive analysis: Xenophon's *Hiero*.

Not much observation and reflection is needed to realize that there is an essential difference between the tyranny analyzed by the classics and that of our age. In contradistinction to classical tyranny, present-day tyranny has at its disposal "technology" as well as "ideologies"; more generally expressed, it presupposes the existence of "science," i.e., of a particular interpretation, or kind, of science. Conversely, classical tyranny, unlike modern tyranny, was confronted, actually or potentially, by a science which was not meant to be applied to "the conquest of nature" or to be popularized and diffused. But in noting this one implicitly grants that one cannot understand modern tyranny in its specific character before one has understood the elementary and in a sense natural form of tyranny which is premodern tyranny. This basic stratum of modern tyranny remains, for all practical purposes, unintelligible to us if we do not have recourse to the political science of the classics.

It is no accident that present-day political science has failed to grasp tyranny as what it really is. Our political science is haunted by the belief that "value judgments" are inadmissible in scientific considerations, and to call a regime tyrannical clearly amounts to pronouncing a "value judgment." The political scientist who accepts this view of science will speak of the mass-state, of dictatorship, of totalitarianism, of authoritarianism, and so on, and as a citizen he may wholeheartedly condemn these things; but as a political scientist he is forced to reject the notion of tyranny as "mythical." One cannot overcome this limitation without reflecting on the basis, or the origin, of present-day political science. Present-day political science often traces its origin to Machiavelli. There is truth in this contention. To say nothing of broader considerations, Machiavelli's *Prince* (as distinguished from his *Discourses on Livy*) is characterized by the deliberate indifference to the distinction between king and tyrant; the *Prince* presupposes the tacit rejection of that traditional distinction.[1] Machiavelli was fully aware that by conceiving the view expounded in the *Prince* he was breaking away from the whole tradition of political science; or, to apply to the *Prince* an expression which he uses when speaking of his *Discourses*, that he was taking a road which had not yet been followed by anyone.[2] To understand the basic premise of present-day political science, one would have to understand the meaning of the epoch-making change effected by Machiavelli; for that change consisted in the discovery of the continent on which all specifically modern political thought, and hence especially present-day political science, is at home.

It is precisely when trying to bring to light the deepest roots of modern political thought that one will find it to be very useful, not to say indispensable, to devote some attention to the *Hiero*. One cannot understand the meaning of Machiavelli's achievement if one does not confront his teaching with the traditional teaching he rejects. As regards the *Prince* in particular, which is deservedly his most famous work, one has to confront its teaching with that of the traditional mirrors of princes. But in doing this one must beware of the temptation to try to be wiser, or rather more learned, than Machiavelli wants his readers to be, by attaching undue importance to medieval and early modern mirrors of princes which Machiavelli never stoops to mention by name. Instead one should concentrate on the only mirror of princes to which he emphatically refers and which is, as one would expect, the classic and the fountainhead of this whole genre: Xenophon's *Education of Cyrus*.[3] This work has never been studied by modern historians with even a small fraction of the care and concentration it merits and which is needed if it is to disclose its meaning. The *Education of Cyrus* may be said to be devoted to the perfect king in contradistinction to the tyrant, whereas the *Prince* is characterized by the deliberate disregard of the difference between king and tyrant. There is only one earlier work on tyranny to which Machiavelli emphatically refers: Xenophon's *Hiero*.[4] The analysis of the *Hiero* leads to the conclusion that the teaching of that dialogue comes as near to the teaching of the *Prince* as the teaching of any Socratic could possibly come. By confronting the teaching of the *Prince* with that transmitted through the *Hiero*,

one can grasp most clearly the subtlest and indeed the decisive difference between Socratic political science and Machiavellian political
science. If it is true that all premodern political science rests on
the foundations laid by Socrates, whereas all specifically modern
political science rests on the foundations laid by Machiavelli, one
may also say that the *Hiero* marks the point of closest contact between premodern and modern political science.[5]

As regards the manner in which I have treated my subject, I
have been mindful that there are two opposed ways in which one
can study the thought of the past. Many present-day scholars start
from the historicist assumption, namely, that all human thought
is "historical" or that the foundations of human thought are laid
by specific experiences which are not, as a matter of principle,
coeval with human thought as such. Yet there is a fatal disproportion
between historicism and true historical understanding. The goal of
the historian of thought is to understand the thought of the past "as
it really has been," i.e., to understand it as exactly as possible as it
was actually understood by its authors. But the historicist approaches
the thought of the past on the basis of the historicist assumption
which was wholly alien to the thought of the past. He is therefore
compelled to attempt to understand the thought of the past better
than it understood itself before he has understood it exactly as it
understood itself. In one way or the other, his presentation will be a
questionable mixture of interpretation and critique. It is the beginning of historical understanding, its necessary and, one is tempted
to add, its sufficient condition that one realizes the problematic
character of historicism. For one cannot realize it without becoming
seriously interested in an impartial confrontation of the historicist
approach that prevails today with the nonhistoricist approach of the
past. And such a confrontation in its turn requires that the nonhistoricist thought of the past be understood on its own terms, and
not in the way in which it presents itself within the horizon of
historicism.

In accordance with this principle, I have tried to understand
Xenophon's thought as exactly as I could. I have not tried to relate
his thought to his "historical situation" because this is not the natural
way of reading the work of a wise man; and, in addition, Xenophon
never indicated that he wanted to be understood that way. I assumed
that Xenophon, being an able writer, gave us to the best of his

powers the information required for understanding his work. I have relied therefore as much as possible on what he himself says, directly or indirectly, and as little as possible on extraneous information, to say nothing of modern hypotheses. Distrustful of all conventions, however trivial, which are likely to do harm to matters of importance, I went so far as to omit the angular brackets with which modern scholars are in the habit of adorning their citations of certain ancient writings. It goes without saying that I never believed that my mind was moving in a larger "circle of ideas" than Xenophon's mind.

The neglect of the *Hiero* (as well as of the *Education of Cyrus*) is no doubt partly due to the fashionable underestimation and even contempt of Xenophon's intellectual powers. Until the end of the eighteenth century, he was generally considered a wise man and a classic in the precise sense. In the nineteenth and twentieth centuries, he is compared as a philosopher to Plato, and found wanting; he is compared as a historian to Thucydides, and found wanting. One need not, as well one might, take issue with the views of philosophy and of history which are presupposed in these comparisons. One merely has to raise the question whether Xenophon wanted to be understood primarily as a philosopher or as a historian. In the manuscripts of his works, he is frequently designated as "the orator Xenophon." It is reasonable to assume that the temporary eclipse of Xenophon—just as the temporary eclipse of Livy and of Cicero—has been due to a decline in the understanding of the significance of rhetoric: both the peculiar "idealism" and the peculiar "realism" of the nineteenth century were guided by the modern concept of "Art" and for that reason were unable to understand the crucial significance of the lowly art of rhetoric. While they could thus find a place for Plato and Thucydides, they completely failed duly to appreciate Xenophon.

Xenophon's rhetoric is not ordinary rhetoric; it is Socratic rhetoric. The character of Socratic rhetoric does not become sufficiently clear from the judiciously scattered remarks on the subject that occur in Plato's and Xenophon's writings, but only from detailed analyses of its products. The most perfect product of Socratic rhetoric is the dialogue. The form of Plato's dialogues has been discussed frequently, but no one would claim that the problem of the Platonic dialogue has been solved. Modern analyses are, as a rule, vitiated by the estheticist prejudice of the interpreters. Yet Plato's expulsion of the poets from his best city should have sufficed for discouraging any estheticist approach. It would seem that the attempt to clarify the meaning of the dialogue should start from an analysis of Xenophon's dialogue. Xenophon uses far fewer devices than Plato uses even in his simplest works. By understanding the art of Xenophon, one will realize certain minimum requirements that one must fulfill when interpreting any Platonic dialogue, requirements which today are so little fulfilled that they are hardly known.

The dialogue that deserves the name communicates the thought of the author in an indirect or oblique way. Thus the danger of arbitrary interpretation might well seem to be overwhelming. The danger can be overcome only if the greatest possible attention is paid to every detail, and especially to the unthematic details, and if the function of Socratic rhetoric is never lost sight of.

Socratic rhetoric is meant to be an ·indispensable instrument of philosophy. Its purpose is to lead potential philosophers to philosophy both by training them and by liberating them from the charms which obstruct the philosophic effort, as well as to prevent the access to philosophy of those who are not fit for it. Socratic rhetoric is emphatically just. It is animated by the spirit of social responsibility. It is based on the premise that there is a disproportion between the intransigent quest for truth and the requirements of society, or that not all truths are always harmless. Society will always try to tyrannize thought. Socratic rhetoric is the classic means for ever again frustrating these attempts. This highest kind of rhetoric did not die with the immediate pupils of Socrates. Many monographs bear witness to the fact that great thinkers of later times have used a kind of caution or thrift in communicating their thought to posterity which is no longer appreciated: it ceased to be appreciated at about the same time at which historicism emerged, at about the end of the eighteenth century.

The experience of the present generation has taught us to read the great political literature of the past with different eyes and with different expectations. The lesson may not be without value for our political orientation. We are now brought face to face with a tyranny which holds out the threat of becoming, thanks to "the conquest of nature" and in particular of human nature, what no earlier tyranny ever became: perpetual and universal. Confronted by the appalling alternative that man, or human thought, must be collectivized either by one stroke and without mercy or else by slow and gentle processes, we are forced to wonder how we could escape from this dilemma. We reconsider therefore the elementary and unobtrusive conditions of human freedom.

The historical form in which this reflection is here presented is perhaps not inappropriate. The manifest and deliberate collectivization or coordination of thought is being prepared in a hidden and frequently quite unconscious way by the spread of the teaching that all human thought is collective independently of any human effort directed to this end, because all human thought is historical. There seems to be no more appropriate way of combating this teaching than the study of history.

As has been indicated, one must have some patience if one wants to grasp the meaning of the *Hiero*. The patience of the interpreter does not make superfluous the patience of the reader of the interpretation. In explaining writings like the *Hiero,* one has to engage in long-winded and sometimes repetitious considerations which can arrest attention only if one sees their purpose, and it is necessary that this purpose should reveal itself in its proper place, which cannot be at the beginning. If one wants to establish the precise meaning of a subtle hint, one must proceed in a way which comes dangerously close to the loathsome business of explaining a joke. The charm produced by Xenophon's unobtrusive art is destroyed, at least for a moment, if that art is made obtrusive by the interpretation. Still, I believe that I have not dotted all the *i*'s. One can only hope that the time will again come when Xenophon's art will be understood by a generation which, properly trained in their youth, will no longer need cumbersome introductions like the present study.

◨ ◨ ◨

I

THE PROBLEM

THE INTENTION of the *Hiero* is nowhere stated by the author. Being an account of a conversation between the poet Simonides and the tyrant Hiero, the work consists almost exclusively of the utterances, recorded in direct speech, of these two characters. The author limits himself to describing at the beginning in sixteen words the circumstances in which the conversation took place, and to linking with each other, or separating from each other, the statements of the two interlocutors by such expressions as "Simonides said" and "Hiero answered."

The intention of the work does not become manifest at once from the content. The work consists of two main parts of very unequal length, the first part making up about five sevenths of the whole. In the first part (ch. 1–7), Hiero proves to Simonides that the life of a tyrant, as compared with the life of a private man, is so unhappy that the tyrant can hardly do better than to hang himself. In the second part (ch. 8–11), Simonides proves to Hiero that the tyrant could be the happiest of men. The first part seems to be directed against the popular prejudice that the life of a tyrant is more pleasant than private life. The second part, however, seems to establish the view that the life of a beneficent tyrant is superior, in the most important respect, to private life.[1] At first glance, the work as a whole clearly conveys the message that the life of a beneficent tyrant is highly desirable. But it is not clear what that message means since we do not know to what type of men it is addressed. If we assume that the work is addressed to tyrants, its intention is to exhort them to exercise their rule in a spirit of shrewd benevolence. Yet only a very small part of its readers can be supposed to be actual tyrants. The work as a whole may therefore have to be taken as a recommendation addressed to properly equipped young men who are pondering what way of life they should choose—a recommendation to strive for tyrannical power, not indeed to gratify their desires, but to gain the love and admiration of all men by deeds of benevolence on the greatest possible scale.[2] Socrates, the teacher of Xenophon, was suspected of teaching his companions to be "tyrannical":[3] Xenophon lays himself open to the same suspicion.

Yet it is not Xenophon but Simonides who proves that a beneficent tyrant will reach the summit of happiness, and one cannot identify without further consideration the author's views with those of one of his characters. The fact that Simonides is called "wise" by Hiero[4] does not prove anything, since we do not know what Xenophon thought of Hiero's competence. But even if we assume that Simonides is simply the mouthpiece of Xenophon, great difficulties remain, for Simonides' thesis is ambiguous. It is addressed to a tyrant who is out of heart with tyranny, who has just declared that a tyrant can hardly do better than to hang himself. Does it not serve the purpose of comforting the sad tyrant, and does not the intention to comfort detract from the sincerity of a speech?[5] Is any speech addressed to a tyrant by a man who is in the tyrant's power likely to be a sincere speech?[6]

II

THE TITLE AND THE FORM

WHILE PRACTICALLY EVERYTHING said in the *Hiero* is said by Xenophon's characters, Xenophon himself takes full responsibility for the title of the work.[1] The title is Ἱέρων ἢ Τυραννικός. No other work contained in the *Corpus Xenophonteum* has a title consisting of both a proper name and an adjective referring to the subject. The first part of the title is reminiscent of the title of the *Agesilaus*. The *Agesilaus* deals with an outstanding Greek king, just as the *Hiero* deals with an outstanding Greek tyrant. Proper names of individuals also occur in the titles of the *Cyri Institutio*, the *Cyri Expeditio*, and the *Apologia Socratis*. Agesilaus, the two Cyruses, and Socrates seem to be the men Xenophon admired most. But the two Cyruses were not Greek, and Socrates was not a ruler: the *Agesilaus* and the *Hiero*, the only writings of Xenophon the titles of which contain proper names of individuals in the nominative, are the only writings of Xenophon which may be said to be devoted to Greek rulers.

The second part of the title reminds one of the titles of the *Hipparchicus*, the *Oeconomicus*, and the *Cynegeticus*. These three writings serve the purpose of teaching skills befitting gentlemen: the skill of a commander of cavalry, the skill of managing one's estate, and the skill of hunting.[2] Accordingly, one should expect that the purpose of the *Tyrannicus* is to teach the skill of the tyrant, the σοφία (or τέχνη) τυραννική;[3] and in fact Simonides does therein teach Hiero how best to exercise tyrannical rule.

There is only one work of Xenophon apart from the *Hiero* which has an alternative title: the Πόροι ἢ περὶ προσόδων (*Ways and Means*). The purpose of that work is to show the (democratic) rulers of Athens how they could become more just by showing them how they could overcome the necessity under which they found themselves of acting unjustly.[4] That is to say, its purpose is to show how the democratic order of Athens could be improved without being fundamentally changed. Similarly, Simonides shows the tyrannical ruler of Syracuse how he could overcome the necessity of acting unjustly under which he found himself without abandoning tyrannical rule as such.[5] Xenophon, the pupil of Socrates, seems to have considered both democracy and tyranny faulty regimes.[6] The *Ways and Means* and the *Hiero* are the only works of Xenophon which are devoted to the question of how a given political order (πολιτεία) of a faulty character could be corrected without being transformed into a good political order.

Xenophon could easily have explained in direct terms the conditional character of the policy recommended in the *Hiero*. Had he done so, however, he might have conveyed the impression that he was not absolutely opposed to tyranny. But "the cities," and especially Athens, were absolutely opposed to tyranny.[7] Besides, one of the charges brought against Socrates was that he taught his pupils to be "tyrannical." Reasons such as these explain why Xenophon presented his reflections on the improvement of tyrannical rule (and therewith on the stabilization of such rule), as distinguished from his reflections on the improvement of the Athenian regime, in the form of a dialogue in which he does not participate in any way: the *Hiero* is the only work of Xenophon in which the author, when speaking in his own name, never uses the first person, whereas the *Ways and Means* is the only work of Xenophon whose very opening word is an emphatic *I*. The reasons indicated explain besides why the fairly brief suggestions for the improvement of tyrannical rule are prefaced by a considerably more extensive discourse which expounds the undesirable character of tyranny in the strongest possible terms.

The *Hiero* consists almost exclusively of utterances of men other than the author. There is only one other work of Xenophon which has that character: the *Oeconomicus*. In the *Oeconomicus*, too, the author "hides himself"[8] almost completely. The *Oeconom-*

icus is a dialogue between Socrates and another Athenian on the management of the household. According to Socrates, there does not seem to be an essential difference between the art of managing the household and that of managing the affairs of the city: both are called by him "the royal art."[9] Hence it can only be due to secondary considerations that the dialogue which is destined to teach that art is called *Oeconomicus*, and not *Politicus* or *Basilicus*. There is ample evidence to show that the *Oeconomicus*, while apparently devoted to the economic art only, actually deals with the royal art as such.[10] It is then permissible to describe the relation of Xenophon's two dialogues as that of a *Basilicus* to a *Tyrannicus*: the two dialogues deal with *the* two types of monarchic rule.[11] Since the economist is a ruler, the *Oeconomicus* is, just as the *Hiero*, a dialogue between a wise man (Socrates)[12] and a ruler (the potential economist Critobulus and the actual economist Ischomachus). But whereas the wise man and the rulers of the *Oeconomicus* are Athenians, the wise man and the ruler of the *Hiero* are not. And whereas the wise man and the potential ruler of the *Oeconomicus* were friends of Xenophon, and Xenophon himself was present at their conversation, the wise man and the ruler of the *Hiero* were dead long before Xenophon's time. It was evidently impossible to assign the "tyrannical" teaching to Socrates. But the reason was not that there was any scarcity of actual or potential tyrants in the entourage of Socrates. Rather the reverse. Nothing would have been easier for Xenophon than to arrange a conversation on how to rule well as a tyrant between Socrates and Charmides or Critias[13] or Alcibiades. So doing, though—giving Socrates such a role in such a context—he would have destroyed the basis of his own defense of Socrates. It is for this reason that the place occupied in the *Oeconomicus* by Socrates is occupied in the *Hiero* by another wise man. After having chosen Simonides, Xenophon was free to present him as engaged in a conversation with the Athenian tyrant Hipparchus;[14] but he apparently wished to avoid any connection between the topics "tyranny" and "Athens."

One cannot help wondering why Xenophon chose Simonides as a chief character in preference to certain other wise men who were known to have conversed with tyrants.[15] A clue is offered by the parallelism between the *Hiero* and the *Oeconomicus*. The royal art is morally superior to the tyrannical art. Socrates, who teaches the royal or economic art, has perfect self-control as regards the pleasures deriving from wealth.[16] Simonides, who teaches the tyrannical art, was famous for his greed.[17] Socrates, who teaches the economic or royal art, was not himself an economist because he was not interested in increasing his property; accordingly, his teaching consists largely of giving to a potential economist an account of a conversation which he once had with an actual economist.[18] Simonides, who teaches the tyrannical art, and therewith at least some rudiments of the economic art as well,[19] without any assistance, *was* an "economist."

In the light of the parallelism between the *Oeconomicus* and the *Hiero,* our previous explanation of the fact that Xenophon presented the "tyrannical" teaching in the form of a dialogue proves to be insufficient. With a view to that parallelism, we have to raise the more comprehensive question as to why the *Oeconomicus* and the *Hiero,* as distinguished from Xenophon's two other technical writings, the *Hipparchicus* and the *Cynegeticus,* are written in the form not of treatises, nor even of stories, but of dialogues. The subjects of the two former works, we shall venture to say, are of a higher order, or are more philosophic than those of the two latter. Accordingly, their treatment too should be more philosophic. From Xenophon's point of view, philosophic treatment is conversational treatment. Conversational teaching of the skill of ruling has these two particular advantages. First, it necessitates the confrontation of a wise man (the teacher) and a ruler (the pupil). Besides, it compels the reader to wonder whether the lessons given by the wise man to the ruler bore fruit, because it compels the author to leave unanswered that question which is nothing less than a special form of the fundamental question of the relation of theory and practice, or of knowledge and virtue.

The second advantage of conversational teaching is particularly striking in the *Hiero.* Whereas the proof of the unhappiness of the unjust tyrant is emphatically based on experience,[20] the proof of the happiness of the beneficent tyrant is not: that happiness is merely promised—by a poet. The reader is left wondering whether experience offered a single instance of a tyrant who was happy because he was virtuous.[21] The corresponding question forced upon the reader of the *Oeconomicus* is answered, if not by the *Oeconomicus* itself, by the *Cyropaedia* and the *Agesilaus.* But the question of the actual happiness of the virtuous tyrant is left open by the *Corpus Xenophonteum* as a whole. And whereas the *Cyropaedia* and the *Agesilaus* set the happiness of the virtuous kings Cyrus and Agesilaus beyond any imaginable doubt by showing or at least intimating how they died, the *Hiero*, owing to its form, cannot throw any light on the end of the tyrant Hiero.[22]

We hope to have explained why Xenophon presents the "tyrannical" teaching in the form of a conversation between Simonides and a non-Athenian tyrant. An adequate understanding of that teaching requires more than an understanding of its content. One must also consider the form in which it is presented, for otherwise one cannot realize the place which it occupies, according to the author, within the whole of wisdom. The form in which it is presented characterizes it as a philosophic teaching of the sort that a truly wise man would not care to present in his own name. Moreover, by throwing some light on the procedure of the wise man who stoops to present the "tyrannical" teaching in his own name, i.e., of Simonides, the author shows us how that teaching should be presented to its ultimate addressee, the tyrant.

□ □ □

III

THE SETTING

a. The characters and their intentions

"SIMONIDES THE POET came once upon a time to Hiero the tyrant. After both had found leisure, Simonides said. . . ." This is all that Xenophon says thematically and explicitly about the situation in which the conversation took place. "Simonides came to Hiero": Hiero did not come to Simonides. Tyrants do not like to travel to foreign parts,[1] and, as Simonides seems to have said to Hiero's wife, the wise are spending their time at the doors of the rich and not *vice versa*.[2] Simonides came to Hiero "once upon a time": he was merely visiting Hiero; those coming to display before the tyrant something wise or beautiful or good prefer to go away as soon as they have received their reward.[3] The conversation opens "after both had found leisure" and, we may add, when they were alone: it does not open immediately on Simonides' arrival. It appears in the course of the conversation that prior to the conversation Hiero had acquired a definite opinion of Simonides' qualities, and Simonides had made some observations about Hiero. It is not impossible that the business which each had before both found leisure was a business which they had with each other. At any rate, they were not complete strangers to each other at the moment when the conversation starts. Their knowledge of, or their opinions about, each other might even explain why they engage in a leisurely conversation at all, as well as how they behave during their conversation from its very beginning.

It is Simonides who opens the conversation. What is his purpose? He starts with the question whether Hiero would be willing to explain to him something which he is likely to know better than the poet. The polite question which he addresses to a tyrant who is not his ruler keeps in the appropriate middle between the informal request, so frequently used by Socrates in particular, "Tell me," or the polite request, "I want very much to learn," on the one hand, and the deferential question addressed by Socrates to tyrants who were his rulers (the "legislators" Critias and Charicles), "Is it permitted to inquire. . .?" on the other.[4] By his question, Simonides presents himself as a wise man who, always desirous to learn, wishes to avail himself of the opportunity of learning something from Hiero. He thus assigns to Hiero the position of a man who is, in a certain respect, wiser, a greater authority than he is himself. Hiero, fully aware of how wise Simonides is, has not the slightest notion as to what sort of thing he could know better than a man of Simonides' wisdom. Simonides explains to him that since he, Hiero, was born a private man and is now a tyrant, he is, on the basis of his experience of both conditions, likely to know better than Simonides in what way the life of a tyrant and that of private men differ with regard to human enjoyments and pains.[5] The choice of the topic is perfect. A comparison of a tyrant's life and private life is the only comprehensive, or "wise," topic in the discussion of which a wise man can with some plausibility be presented as inferior to a tyrant who once had been a private man and who is not wise. Moreover, the point of view which, as Simonides suggests, should guide the comparison—pleasure–pain as distinguished from virtue–vice—seems to be characteristic of tyrants as distinguished from kings.[6] Simonides seems then to open the conversation with the intention of learning something from Hiero, or of getting some first-hand information from an authority on the subject which he proposes.

Yet the reason with which he justifies his question in the eyes of Hiero is only a probable one. It leaves out of consideration the decisive contribution of judgment, or wisdom, to the correct evaluation of experiences.[7] Moreover, the question itself is not of such a nature that peculiar experiences which a wise man may or may not have had (such as those which only an actual tyrant can have had) could contribute significantly to its complete answer. It rather belongs to the kind of question to which the wise man as such (and only the wise man as such) necessarily possesses the complete answer. Simonides' question concerning the manner of difference between the tyrant's life and private life in regard to pleasures and pains is identical, in the context, with the question as to which of the two ways of life is more desirable; for "pleasure–pain" is the only ultimate criterion of preference which is thematically considered. The initial question is rendered more specific by the assertion which Simonides makes soon afterward that the tyrant's life knows many more pleasures of all kinds and many fewer pains of all kinds than private life, in other words, that tyrannical life is more desirable than private life.[8] Even Hiero states that Simonides' assertion is surprising in the mouth of a reputedly wise man: a wise man should be able to judge of the happiness or misery of the tyrant's life without ever having had the actual experience of tyrannical life.[9] The question as to whether, or how far, tyrannical life is more desirable than private life, and in particular whether, or how far, it is more desirable from the point of view of pleasure, is no longer a question for a man who has acquired wisdom.[10] If Simonides was a wise man, he must then have had a motive other than eagerness to learn for inquiring with Hiero about that subject.

Hiero expresses the view that Simonides is a wise man, a man much wiser than he himself is. This assertion is borne out to a certain extent by the action of the dialogue, by which Simonides is shown to be able to teach Hiero the art of ruling as a tyrant. While Simonides is thus shown to be wiser than Hiero, it is by no means certain that Xenophon considered him simply wise. What Xenophon thought of Simonides' wisdom can be definitely established only by a comparison of Simonides with Socrates, whom Xenophon certainly considered wise. It is possible, however, to reach a provisional conclusion on the basis of the parallelism of the *Hiero* and the *Oeconomicus* as well as of the following consideration: If Simonides was wise, he had conversational skill; i.e., he could do what he liked with any interlocutor,[11] or he could lead any conversation to the end which he desired. His conversation with Hiero leads up to such suggestions about the improvement of tyrannical rule as a wise man could be expected to make to a tyrant toward whom he is well disposed. We shall then assume that the wise Simonides opens the conversation intending to be of some benefit to Hiero, perhaps in order to be benefited in turn or to benefit the tyrant's subjects. During his stay with Hiero, Simonides had observed several things about the ruler—some concerning his appetite, some concerning his amours;[12] and Simonides knew that Hiero was making certain grave mistakes, such as his participating at the Olympic and Pythian games.[13] To express this more generally, Simonides knew that Hiero was not a perfect ruler. He decided to teach him how to rule well as a tyrant. More specifically, he considered it advisable to warn him against certain grave mistakes. But, to say nothing of common politeness, no one wishes to rebuke, or to speak against, a tyrant in his presence.[14] Simonides had, then, by the least offensive means to reduce the tyrant to a mood in which the latter would be pleased to listen attentively to, and even to ask for, the poet's advice. He had at the same time, or by the same action, to convince Hiero of his competence to give sound advice to a tyrant.

Before Simonides can teach Hiero how to rule as a tyrant, he has to make him aware, or to remind him, of the difficulties with which he is beset and which he cannot overcome, of the shortcomings of his rule, and indeed of his whole life. To be made aware by someone else of one's own shortcomings means, for most people, to be humbled by the censor. Simonides has to humble the tyrant; he has to reduce him to a condition of inferiority; or, to describe Simonides' intention in the light of the aim apparently achieved by him, he has to dishearten the tyrant. Moreover, if he intends to use Hiero's recognition of his shortcomings as the starting point for his teaching, he has to induce Hiero expressly to grant all the relevant unpleasant facts about his life. The least he can do, in order to avoid unnecessary offense, is to talk, not about Hiero's life, but about a more general, a less offensive, subject. To begin with, we shall assume that when starting a conversation with Hiero about the relative desirability of the life of the tyrant and private life, he is guided by the intention to dishearten the tyrant by a comparison of the life of the tyrant, and therewith of Hiero's own life, with private life.

To reach this immediate aim in the least offensive manner, Simonides has to create a situation in which not he, but the tyrant himself, explains the shortcomings of his life, or of tyrannical life in general, and a situation in which, moreover, the tyrant does this normally unpleasant work not only spontaneously but even gladly. The artifice by means of which Simonides brings about this result consists in his giving to Hiero an opportunity of vindicating his superiority while demonstrating his inferiority. He starts the conversation by presenting himself explicitly as a man who has to learn from Hiero, or who is, in a certain respect, less wise than Hiero, or by assuming the role of the pupil. Thereafter, he makes himself the spokesman of the opinion that tyrannical life is more desirable than private life, i.e., of the crude opinion about tyranny which is characteristic of the unwise, of the multitude, or the vulgar.[15] He thus presents himself tacitly, and therefore all the more effectively, as a man who is absolutely less wise than Hiero. He thus tempts Hiero to assume the role of the teacher.[16] He succeeds in seducing him into refuting the vulgar opinion, and thus into proving that tyrannical life, and hence his own life, is extremely unhappy. Hiero vindicates his superiority by winning his argument, which, so far as its content is concerned, would be merely depressing for him: by proving that he is extremely unhappy, he proves that he is wiser than the wise Simonides. Yet his victory is his defeat. By appealing to the tyrant's interest in superiority, or desire for victory, Simonides brings about the tyrant's spontaneous and almost joyful recognition of all the shortcomings of his life and therewith a situation in which the offering of advice is the act, not of an awkward schoolmaster, but of a humane poet. And besides, in the moment that Hiero becomes aware of his having walked straight into the trap which Simonides had so ingeniously and so charmingly set for him, he will be more convinced than ever before of Simonides' wisdom.

Before Simonides starts teaching Hiero, in other words, in the largest part of the *Hiero* (ch. 1–7), he presents himself to Hiero as less wise than he really is. In the first part of the *Hiero*, Simonides hides his wisdom. He does not merely report the vulgar opinion about tyranny, he does not merely hand it over to Hiero for its refutation by asking him what he thinks about it; he actually adopts it. Hiero is justifiably under the impression that Simonides is ignorant of or deceived about the nature of tyrannical life.[17] Thus the question arises as to why Simonides' artifice does not defeat his purpose: why can Hiero still take him seriously? Why does he not consider him a fool, a foolish follower of the opinions of the vulgar?

The situation in which the conversation takes place remains wholly obscure as long as this difficulty is not satisfactorily explained.

The difficulty would be insoluble if to be vulgar merely meant to be simply foolish or unwise. The vulgar opinion about tyranny can be summarized as follows: Tyranny is bad for the city but good for the tyrant, for the tyrannical life is the most enjoyable and desirable way of life.[18] This opinion is founded on the basic premise of the vulgar mind that bodily pleasures and wealth or power are more important than virtue. The vulgar opinion is contested, not only by the wise, but above all by the gentlemen. According to the opinion of the perfect gentleman, tyranny is bad, not only for the city, but above all for the tyrant himself.[19] By adopting the vulgar view, Simonides tacitly rejects the gentleman's view. Could he not be a gentleman? Could he lack the moderation, the self-restraint of the gentleman? Could he be dangerous? Whether this suspicion arises evidently depends on what opinion is held by Hiero about the relation of "wise" and "gentlemen." But if it arises, the theoretical and somewhat playful discussion will transform itself into a conflict.

The ironic element of Simonides' procedure would endanger the achievement of his serious purpose if it did not arouse a deeper emotion in the soul of the tyrant than the somewhat whimsical desire to win a dialectical victory. The manner in which he understands, and reacts to, Simonides' question and assertion is bound to be determined by his view of Simonides' qualities and of his intention. He considers Simonides a wise man. His attitude toward Simonides will then be a special case of his attitude toward wise men in general. He says that tyrants fear the wise. His attitude toward Simonides must be understood accordingly: "Instead of admiring" him, he fears him.[20] Considering the fact that Simonides is a stranger in Hiero's city, and therefore not likely to be really dangerous to Hiero's rule,[21] we prefer to say that his admiration for Simonides is mitigated by some fear, by some fear *in statu nascendi*, i.e., by distrust. He does not trust people in any case; he will be particularly distrustful in his dealings with a man of unusually great abilities. Hence he is not likely to be perfectly frank. He is likely to be as reserved as Simonides, although for somewhat different reasons.[22] Their conversation is likely to take place in an atmosphere of limited straightforwardness.

The tyrant's fear of the wise is a specific one. This crucial fact is explained by Hiero in what is even literally the central passage of the *Hiero*.[23] He fears the brave because they might take risks for the sake of freedom. He fears the just because the multitude might desire to be ruled by them. As regards the wise, he fears that "they might contrive something." He fears, then, the brave and the just because their virtues or virtuous actions might bring about the restoration of freedom or at least of nontyrannical government. This much, and not more, is explained by Hiero in unequivocal terms. He does not say explicitly what kind of danger he apprehends from the wise: Does he fear that they might contrive something for the sake of freedom or of just government, or does he fear that they might contrive something for some other purpose?[24] Hiero's explicit statement leaves unanswered the crucial question, Why does the tyrant fear the wise?

The most cautious explanation of Hiero's silence would be the suggestion that he does not know what the wise intend. Having once been a private man, a private citizen, a subject of a tyrant, he knows and understands the goals of the brave and the just as well as they themselves do. But he has never been a wise man: he does not know wisdom from his own experience. He realizes that wisdom is a virtue, a power, hence a limit to the tyrant's power, and therefore a danger to the tyrant's rule. He realizes, besides, that wisdom is something different from courage and justice. But he does not clearly grasp the specific and positive character of wisdom: wisdom is more elusive than courage and justice. Perhaps it would not be too much to say that for the tyrant wisdom, as distinguished from courage and justice, is something uncanny. At any rate, his fear of the wise is an indeterminate fear, in some cases (as in the case of Hiero's fear of Simonides) hardly more than a vague, but strong, uneasiness.

This attitude toward the wise is characteristic not only of tyrants. The fate of Socrates must be presumed always to have been present to Xenophon's mind. It confirmed the view that wise men are apt to be envied by men who are less wise or altogether unwise, and that they are exposed to all sorts of vague suspicion on the part of "the many." Xenophon himself suggested that the same experience which Socrates had had under a democracy could have been had by him under a monarchy: wise men are apt to be envied, or suspected, by monarchs as well as by ordinary citizens.[25] The distrust of the wise, which proceeds from lack of understanding of wisdom, is characteristic of the vulgar, of tyrants and nontyrants alike. Hiero's attitude toward the wise bears at least some resemblance to the vulgar attitude.

The fate of Socrates showed that those who do not understand the nature of wisdom are apt to mistake the wise man for the sophist. Both the wise man and the sophist are in a sense possessors of wisdom. But whereas the sophist prostitutes wisdom for base purposes, and especially for money, the wise man makes the most noble or moral use of wisdom.[26] The wise man is a gentleman, whereas the sophist is servile. The error of mistaking the wise man for the sophist is made possible by the ambiguity of "gentlemanliness." In common parlance, "gentleman" designates a just and brave man, a good citizen, who as such is not necessarily a wise man. Ischomachus, that perfectly respectable man whom Xenophon confronts with Socrates, is called a gentleman by everyone, by men and women, by strangers and citizens. In the Socratic meaning of the term, the gentleman is identical with the wise man.[27] The essence of wisdom, or what distinguishes wisdom from ordinary gentlemanliness, escapes the vulgar, who may thus be led to believe in an opposition between wisdom and the only gentlemanliness known to them: they may doubt the gentlemanliness of the wise. They will see this much, that wisdom is the ability to contrive the acquisition of that possession which is most valuable and therefore most difficult to obtain. But believing that the tyrannical life is the most enjoyable and therefore the most desirable possession, they will be inclined to identify wisdom with the ability to become a tyrant or to remain a tyrant. Those who succeeded in acquiring tyrannical power, and in preserving it for ever so short a time, are admired as wise and lucky men: the specific ability which enables a man to become, and to remain, a tyrant is popularly identified with wisdom. On the other hand, if a wise man manifestly abstains from striving for tyrannical power, he may still be suspected of teaching his friends to be "tyrannical."[28] On the basis of the vulgar notion of wisdom, the conclusion is plausible that a wise man would aspire to tyranny or, if he is already a tyrant, that he would attempt to preserve his position.

Let us now return to Hiero's statement about the various types of human excellence. The brave would take risks for the sake of freedom; the just would be desired as rulers by the multitude. The brave as brave would not be desired as rulers, and the just as just would not rebel. As clearly as the brave as brave are distinguished from the just as just, the wise as wise are distinguished from both the brave and the just. Would the wise take risks for the sake of freedom? Did Socrates, as distinguished from Thrasybulus, take such risks? While blaming "somewhere" the practices of Critias and his fellows, and while refusing to obey their unjust commands, he did not work for their overthrow.[29] Would the wise be desired as rulers by the multitude? Was Socrates desired as a ruler by the multitude? One has no right to assume that Hiero's view of wisdom and justice is identical with Xenophon's. The context suggests that, according to Hiero, the wise as wise have a purpose different from those of the brave and of the just, or, if courage and justice combined are the essence of gentlemanliness, that the wise man is not necessarily a gentleman. The context suggests that the wise have another goal than the typical enemies of tyranny, who are concerned with restoring freedom and "possession of good laws."[30] This suggestion is far from being contradicted by Simonides, who avoids in his teaching the very terms "freedom" and "law." There is only one reasonable alternative: the tyrant fears the wise man because he might attempt to overthrow the tyrant, not in order to restore nontyrannical government, but to become a tyrant himself or because he might advise a pupil or friend of his as to how he could become a tyrant by overthrowing the actual tyrant. Hiero's central statement does not exclude but rather suggests the vulgar view of wisdom;[31] it does not exclude but rather suggests the view that the wise man is a potential tyrant.[32]

Hiero is somehow aware of the fact that wise men do not judge of happiness or misery on the basis of outward appearance because they know that the seat of happiness and misery is in the souls of men. It therefore seems surprising to him that Simonides should identify, for all practical purposes, happiness with wealth and power, and ultimately with the tyrannical life. He does not say, however, that Simonides, being a wise man, cannot possibly mean what he says, or that he must be joking. On the contrary, he takes Simonides' assertion most seriously. He does not consider it incredible or impossible that a wise man should hold the view adopted

by Simonides.[33] He does not consider it impossible because he
believes that only the experience of a tyrant can establish with final
certainty whether tyrannical life is, or is not, more desirable than
private life.[34] He does not really know the purpose of the wise.
He is then not convinced that the wise man is a potential tyrant.
Nor is he convinced of the contrary. He oscillates between two
diametrically opposed views, between the vulgar view and the wise
view of wisdom. Which of the two opposed views he will take in
a given case will depend on the behavior of the wise individual
with whom he converses. Regarding Simonides, the question is
decided by the fact that he adopts the vulgar opinion according to
which the tyrannical life is more desirable than private life. At
least in his conversation with Simonides, Hiero will be disturbed by
the suspicion that the wise man may be a potential tyrant, or a
potential adviser of possible rivals of Hiero.[35]

Hiero's fear or distrust of Simonides originates in his attitude
toward wise men and would exist regardless of the topic of their
conversation. But if there were any one topic which could ag-
gravate Hiero's suspicion of Simonides, it is that topic which the
wise man in fact proposed—a topic relating to the object with
regard to which the tyrants fear the wise. In addition, Simonides
explicitly says that all men regard tyrants with a mixture of admiration and envy, or that they are jealous of tyrants, and Hiero
understands the bearing of this statement sufficiently to apply it to
Simonides by speaking of Simonides himself being jealous of
tyrants.[36] Hiero does not possess that true understanding of the
nature of wisdom which alone could protect him from being
suspicious of Simonides' question about the relative desirability of
tyrannical and private life. Lacking such understanding, Hiero
cannot be certain that the question might not serve the very practical purpose of eliciting some first-hand information from the tyrant
about a condition of which the poet is jealous or to which he is
aspiring for himself or someone else. His fear or distrust of Simonides will be a fear or distrust strengthened and rendered definite
by Simonides' apparently believing that the tyrannical life is more
desirable than private life. Simonides' apparently frank confession
of his preference will seem to Hiero to supply him with an opportunity of getting rid of his uneasiness. His whole answer will serve

the very practical purpose of dissuading Simonides from looking at tyrants with a mixture of admiration and envy.

By playing upon this intention of Hiero,[37] Simonides compels him to use the strongest possible language against tyranny and thus finally to declare his bankruptcy, therewith handing over the leadership in the conversation to Simonides. Simonides' intention to dishearten Hiero and Hiero's intention to dissuade Simonides from admiring or envying tyrants produce by their cooperation the result primarily intended by Simonides, viz., a situation in which Hiero has no choice but to listen to Simonides' advice.

In order to provoke Hiero's passionate reaction, Simonides has to overstate the case for tyranny. When reading all his statements by themselves, one is struck by the fact that there are indeed some passages in which he, more or less compelled by Hiero's arguments, grants that tyranny has its drawbacks, whereas one finds more passages in which he spontaneously and strongly asserts its advantages. The statements of Simonides on tyranny would justify Hiero in thinking that Simonides is envious of tyrants. Yet the ironic character of Simonides' praise of tyranny as such (as distinguished from his praise of beneficent tyranny in the second part of the *Hiero*) can hardly escape the notice of any reader. For instance, when he asserts that tyrants derive greater pleasure from sounds than private men because they constantly hear the most pleasant kind of sound— viz., praise—he is not ignorant of the fact that the praise bestowed upon tyrants by their entourage is not genuine praise.[38] On the other hand, Hiero is interested in overstating the case against tyranny. This point requires some discussion since the explicit indictment of tyranny in the *Hiero* is entrusted exclusively to Hiero, and therefore the understanding of the tendency of the *Hiero* as a whole depends decisively on the correct appreciation of Hiero's utterances on the subject.

It is certainly inadmissible to take for granted that Hiero simply voices Xenophon's considered judgment on tyranny: Hiero is not Xenophon. Besides, there is some specific evidence which goes to show that Hiero's indictment of tyranny is, according to Xenophon's view, exaggerated. Hiero asserts that "*the* cities magnificently honor the tyrannicide"; Xenophon, however, tells us that those murderers of Jason who survived were honored "in *most* of the Greek cities" to which they came.[39] Hiero asserts that the tyrants "know well that *all* their subjects are their enemies"; Xenophon, however, tells us that the subjects of the tyrant Euphron considered him their benefactor and revered him highly.[40] Hiero describes the tyrant as deprived of all pleasures of gay companionship; Xenophon, however, describes the tyrant Astyages as securely enjoying those pleasures to the full.[41] Yet Hiero may have said more against tyranny than Xenophon would grant; he may still have said exactly what he himself thought about the subject on the basis of his bitter experiences. Now, no reader however careful of the speeches of Hiero can possibly know anything of the expression of Hiero's face, of his gestures, and of the inflections of his voice. He is then not in the best position to detect which words of Hiero's rang true and which rang false. One of the many advantages of a dialogue one character of which is a wise man is that it puts at the disposal of the reader the wise man's discriminating observations concerning the different degree of reliability of the various utterances which flow with an equal ease, but not necessarily with an equal degree of conviction, from his companion's mouth. When reading the *Hiero* cursorily, one is bound to feel that Hiero is worried particularly by the tyrant's lack of friendship, confidence, patriotism, and true honor as well as by the constant danger of assassination. Yet Xenophon's Simonides, who is our sole authority for the adequate interpretation of the speeches of Xenophon's Hiero, was definitely not under the impression that Hiero's greatest sorrow was caused by the lack of the noble things mentioned, or by those agonies of perpetual and limitless fear which he describes in so edifying a manner. He has not the slightest doubt that Hiero has blamed tyranny most of all with a view to the fact that the tyrant is deprived of the sweetest pleasures of homosexual love, i.e., of pleasures which Simonides himself declares to be of minor importance.[42] Simonides is then not greatly impressed by Hiero's indictment of tyranny. That indictment, however touching or eloquent, has therefore to be read with a great deal of reasonable distrust.

When proving that private men derive greater pleasure from victory than tyrants, Hiero compares the victory of the citizens over their foreign enemies with the victory of the tyrant over his subjects: the citizens consider their victory something noble, and they are proud of it and boast of it, whereas the tyrant cannot be proud of his victory, or boast of it, or consider it noble.[43] Hiero fails to mention not only the victory of a party in a civil war but above all the victory of the citizens governed or led by their tyrannical ruler over their foreign enemies: he forgets his own victory in the battle of Cumae. He fails to consider the obvious possibility that a tyrant, who takes the chief responsibility for the outcome of a war, might be more gratified by victory than might the ordinary citizen; for it was the prudent counsel and efficient leadership of the tyrant that brought about the happy issue, while the ordinary citizen never can have had more than a small share in the deliberations concerning the war. Hiero fails to consider that this great pleasure might fully compensate the tyrant for the lack of many lesser pleasures.

We may speak of a twofold meaning of the indictment of tyranny which forms the first and by far the largest part of the *Hiero*. According to its obvious meaning, it amounts to the strongest possible indictment of tyranny: the greatest possible authority on the subject, a tyrant who as such speaks from experience, shows that tyranny is bad even from the point of view of tyrants, even from the point of view of the pleasures of the tyrant.[44] This meaning is obvious; one merely has to read the first part of the *Hiero*, which consists chiefly of speeches of Hiero to this effect, in order to grasp it. A less obvious meaning of the first part of the *Hiero* comes into sight as soon as one considers its conversational setting— the fact that the distrustful tyrant is speaking *pro domo*—and, going one step further in the same direction, when one considers the facts recorded in Xenophon's historical work (the *Hellenica*). These considerations lead one to a more qualified indictment of tyranny, or to a more truthful account of tyranny, or to the wise view of tyranny. This means that in order to grasp Xenophon's view of tyranny as distinguished from Hiero's utterances about tyranny, one has to consider Hiero's "speeches" in the light of the more trustworthy "deeds" or "actions" or "facts,"[45] and in particular that most important of "facts," the conversational setting of the *Hiero*. To the two meanings correspond then two types of reading, and ultimately two types of men. It was with a view to this difference between types of men and a corresponding difference between types of speaking that Socrates liked to quote the verses from the *Iliad* in which Odysseus is described as using different language when speaking to outstanding men on the one hand, and when speaking to the common people on the other;[46] and that he distinguished the superficial understanding of Homer on the part of the rhapsodes from that understanding which grasps the poet's "insinuations."[47] The superficial understanding is not simply wrong, since it grasps the obvious meaning which is as much intended by the author as is the deeper meaning. To describe in one sentence the art employed by Xenophon in the first part of the *Hiero*, we may say that by choosing a conversational setting in which the strongest possible indictment of tyranny becomes necessary, he intimates the limited validity of that indictment.[48]

b. The action of the dialogue

No genuine communication could develop if Hiero were animated exclusively by distrust of Simonides, or if Simonides did not succeed in gaining the tyrant's confidence to some extent. At the beginning of the conversation he reassures Hiero by declaring his willingness to learn from Hiero, i.e., to trust him in what he is going to say about the relative desirability of tyrannical and private life. The first section of the dialogue (ch. 1) is characterized by the interplay of Simonides' intention to reassure Hiero with his intention to dishearten him. That interplay ceases as soon as Hiero is completely committed to the continuance of the conversation. From that moment Simonides limits himself to provoking Hiero to express his unqualified indictment of tyranny.

Hiero, perhaps offended by Simonides' inevitable reference to his pretyrannical past and at the same time desirous to know more about Simonides' intentions and his preferences, emphasizes how remote he considers that past by asking Simonides to remind him of the pleasures and pains of private men: he pretends to have forgotten them.[1] In this context he mentions the fact that Simonides is "at present still a private man." Simonides seems to accept the challenge for a moment. At any rate, he makes to begin with a distinction between himself and private men ("I seem to have observed that private men enjoy . . ."); but he soon drops that odious distinction by identifying himself unreservedly with the private men ("We seem to enjoy . . .").[2] In complying with Hiero's request, Simonides enumerates various groups of pleasurable and painful things. The enumeration is in a sense complete: it covers the pleasures and pains of the body, those of the soul, and those common to body and soul.

Otherwise, it is most surprising. While it is unnecessarily detailed as regards the pleasures and pains of the body, it does not give any details whatsoever as regards the other kinds of pleasure and pain mentioned. It is reasonable to assume that the selection is made, at least partly, *ad hominem*, or that it is meant to prepare a discussion which serves a specific practical purpose. Simonides enumerates seven groups of things which are sometimes pleasant and sometimes painful for private men, and one which is always pleasant for them: that which is always pleasant for them is sleep—which the tyrant, haunted by fears of all kinds, must strive to avoid.[3] This example seems to show that the purpose of Simonides' enumeration is to remind the tyrant of the pleasures of which he is supposed to be deprived, and thus to induce him to make clear to himself the misery of tyrannical life. It is for this reason, one might surmise to begin with, that the enumeration puts the emphasis on the pleasures of the body,[4] i.e., on those pleasures the enjoyment of which is not characteristic of actual or potential tyrants. However, if Simonides' chief intention had been to remind Hiero of the pleasures of which he is actually or supposedly deprived, he would not have dropped the topic "sleep" in the discussion which immediately follows (in ch. 1). Furthermore, Simonides' initial enumeration fails to have any depressing effect on Hiero. It seems therefore preferable to say that his emphasizing the pleasures of the body in the initial enumeration is chiefly due to his intention to reassure Hiero. Emphasizing these pleasures, he creates the impression that he is himself chiefly interested in them. But men chiefly interested in bodily pleasures are not likely to aspire to any ruling position.[5]

Hiero is satisfied with Simonides' enumeration. He gives Simonides to understand that it exhausts the types of pleasure and pain experienced by tyrants as well as by private men. Simonides strikes the first obvious note of dissonance by asserting that the life of a tyrant contains many more pleasures of all kinds and many fewer pains of all kinds than private life. Hiero's immediate answer is still restrained. He does not assert that tyrannical life is inferior to private life as such; he merely says that tyrannical life is inferior to the life of private men of moderate means.[6] He admits by implication that the condition of tyrants is preferable to that of poor men. Yet poverty and wealth are to be measured, not by number, but with a view to use, or to need.[7] At least from this point of view, Simonides may be poor and hence justified in being jealous of tyrants. At any rate, he now reveals that he looks at tyrants with a mixture of admiration and envy and that he might belong to the "many who are reputed to be most able men" who desire to be tyrants. The tension increases. Hiero strengthens his reply, which is more emphatic than any previous utterance of his, by an oath, and he expresses his intention to teach Simonides the truth about the relative desirability of tyrannical and private life.[8] Speaking as a teacher, he embarks upon a discussion of the various kinds of bodily pleasure which keeps in the main to the order followed by Simonides in his initial enumeration.[9] Hiero now tries to prove the thesis that tyrannical life is inferior, not merely to a specific private life, but to private life as such.[10]

The discussion of bodily pleasures (1.10–38) reveals the preferences of the two interlocutors in an indirect way.[11] According to Hiero, the inferiority of tyranny shows itself most clearly with regard to the pleasures of sex, and especially of homosexuality.[12] The only proper name occurring in the *Hiero* (apart from those of Simonides, Hiero, Zeus, and the Greeks), i.e., the only concrete reference to Hiero's life, as well as Hiero's second emphatic oath (which is his last emphatic oath), occurs in the passage dealing with homosexual ·love.[13] Simonides is particularly vocal regarding the pleasures of hearing, i.e., the pleasures of hearing praise, and, above all, regarding the pleasures of food. His most emphatic assertion, occurring in the discussion of bodily pleasures, concerns food.[14] Two of his five "by Zeus" occur in the passage dealing with food.[15] That passage is the only part of the *Hiero* where the conversation takes on the character of a lively discussion, and in fact of a Socratic elenchus (with Hiero in the role of Socrates): Hiero is compelled, point by point, to refute Simonides' assertion that tyrants derive greater pleasure from food than private men.[16] Only in reading the discussion concerning food does one get the impression that Hiero has to overcome a serious resistance on the part of Simonides: four times he appeals from Simonides' assertion to Simonides' experience, observation, or knowledge. How much Hiero is aware of this state of things is shown by the fact that after Simonides had already abandoned the subject, Hiero once more returns to it in order to leave no doubt whatsoever in Simonides' mind as to the inferiority of tyrannical life in the matter of the pleasures of the table: he does not rest until Simonides has granted that, as regards these pleasures, tyrants are worse off than private men.[17] As an explanation we suggest that Simonides wants to reassure Hiero by presenting himself as a man chiefly interested in food, or in "good living" in general, or by ironically overstating his actual liking for "good living."[18]

At the end of the discussion of the bodily pleasures, we seem to have reached the end of the whole conversation. Simonides had originally enumerated eight groups of pleasurable or painful things: (1) sights, (2) sounds, (3) odors, (4) food and drink, (5) sex, (6) objects perceived by the whole body, (7) good and bad things, and (8) sleep. After four of them (sights, sounds, food and drink, odors) have been discussed, he says that the pleasures of sex seem to be the only motive which excites in tyrants the desire for tyrannical rule.[19] By implication, he thus dismisses as irrelevant three of the four groups of pleasant or painful things which had not thereto been discussed (objects perceived by the whole body, good and bad things, sleep). Hence, he narrows down the whole question of the relative desirability of tyrannical and private life to the question, Do tyrants or private men enjoy to a higher degree the pleasures of sex? So doing, he completely reassures Hiero: he practically capitulates. For of nothing is Hiero more convinced than of this, that precisely as regards the pleasures of sex, tyrants are most evidently worse off than private men. He is so much convinced of the truth of his thesis and of the decisive character of the argument by which he upholds it that he can speak later on of his having "demonstrated" to Simonides the true character of a tyrant's amatory pleasures.[20] At the end of the discussion of sex, i.e., at the end of the discussion of the bodily pleasures, Hiero has proved to Simonides what the latter had admitted to be the only point which still needed proof if Hiero's general thesis were to be established securely. On the level of the surface argument the discussion has reached its end. The discussion would have reached its end as well if Simonides had no other intention than to find out what Hiero's greatest worries are, or to remind him of the pleasures from the lack of which he suffers most, or to give him an opportunity of speaking freely of what disturbs him most. All these aims have been reached at the end of the discussion of sex: Hiero is concerned most of all with the tyrant's lack of the sweetest pleasures of homosexual love,[21] and the later discussion is devoted to entirely different subjects. On the other hand, the continuation of the conversation is evidently necessary if

Simonides' intention is to defeat Hiero by playing upon the tyrant's fear of the wise.

The first round ends, so it seems, with a complete victory for Hiero. He has proved his thesis without saying too much against tyranny and therewith against himself. Now the struggle begins in earnest. In the preceding part of the conversation, Simonides' expressions of jealousy of the tyrants had been mitigated, if not altogether retracted, by his emphasis on the pleasures of the body. Now he declares in glaring contrast to all that has gone before, and in particular to what he has said about the unique significance of the pleasures of sex, that the whole preceding discussion is irrelevant, because it dealt only with what he believes to be very minor matters: many of those who are reputed to be (real) men ($\mathring{\alpha}\nu\delta\rho\epsilon\varsigma$)[22] just despise the bodily pleasures; they aspire to greater things, namely, to power and wealth; it is in relation to wealth and power that tyrannical life is manifestly superior to private life. In the preceding part of the conversation, Simonides had tacitly identified himself with the vulgar; now he tactitly makes a distinction between himself and the vulgar. But the nonvulgar type to which he tacitly claims to belong is not the type of the "gentleman" but of the "real man."[23] While elaborating the thesis that tyrannical life brings greater wealth and power than private life, he supplements his initial enumeration of pleasurable and painful things (in which the "good or bad" things have almost disappeared amid the throng of objects of bodily pleasure) by an enumeration of the elements of power and wealth. In doing this he seems to imply that power and wealth are unambiguously "good" and in fact the only things that matter.[24] Since Simonides knows that Hiero considers him a real man, and since he declares explicitly that he himself considers the bodily pleasures as of very minor importance, Simonides thus intimates[25] an unequivocal taste for tyranny. In enumerating the various elements of power and wealth, he reveals his taste more specifically, and more subtly, by what he mentions and by what he fails to mention.[26]

From this moment the conversation changes its character in a surprising manner. Whereas Simonides had been fairly vocal during the rather short discussion of the bodily pleasures (his contribution consisting of about 218 words out of 1058), he is almost completely silent during the much more extensive discussion of the good or bad things (his contribution consisting of 28 words out of about 2000).

Besides, the discussion of the bodily pleasures had kept, in the main, to the items and the sequence suggested in Simonides' initial enumeration, and this had been due largely to Simonides' almost continuous interference with Hiero's exposition. But now, in the discussion of the good or bad things, Hiero deviates considerably, not to say completely, from Simonides' enumeration of these things and their sequence by introducing topics which had barely been hinted at by Simonides.[27] The purpose of Hiero's procedure is evident. In the first place, he can refute only with difficulty the cautious assertion to which the wise Simonides had limited himself,[28] that the tyrant possesses greater power and wealth than private men. Above all, he is very anxious to push "wealth" into the background in favor of the other good things because wealth is so highly desired by "real men" of the type of Simonides as well as by the actual tyrant himself.[29] The topics not mentioned by Simonides but introduced by Hiero are: peace and war, friendship,[30] confidence, fatherland, good men, city and citizens, fear and protection. Simonides' declaration asserting the superiority of tyrants as regards power and wealth provokes Hiero to an eloquent indictment of tyranny which surpasses in scope everything said in the first section: the tyrant is cut off from such good things as peace, the pleasant aspects of war, friendship, confidence, fatherland, and the company of good men; he is hated and conspired against by his nearest relatives and friends; he cannot enjoy the greatness of his own fatherland; he lives in perpetual fear for his life; he is compelled to commit grave crimes against gods and men; those who kill him, far from being punished, are greatly honored. Simonides has succeeded in increasing Hiero's tenseness far beyond the limits which it had reached during the discussion of the bodily pleasures. This shows itself particularly in those passages where the tyrant speaks of subjects already mentioned in the first section.[31] And this increase of tension is due, not only to the declaration with which the poet had opened the second round, but, above all, to the ambiguous silence with which he listens to Hiero's tirade. Is he overawed by Hiero's indictment of tyranny? Does he doubt Hiero's sincerity? Or is he just bored by Hiero's speech because his chief concern is with "food," with the pleasures of the body, the discussion of which had interested him sufficiently to make him talk? Hiero cannot know.

The meaning of Simonides' silence is partly revealed by its im-

mediate consequence. It leads to the consequence that the topics
introduced by Hiero are hardly as much as mentioned, and certainly
not discussed by Simonides in the first two sections of the dialogue.
His silence thus brings out in full relief the contrast between the
topics introduced in the first two sections by Hiero on the one hand
and by Simonides on the other. Simonides introduces the pleasures of
the body as well as wealth and power; Hiero introduces the loftier
things. Simonides, who has to convince Hiero of his competence to
give sound advice to tyrants, must guard by all means against appearing in Hiero's eyes as a poet: he limits himself to speaking about the
more pedestrian things.[32] Hiero, who tries to dissuade Simonides
from being jealous of tyrants or from aspiring to tyranny, has to
appeal from Simonides' craving for low things to his more noble
aspirations. The lesson which Xenophon ironically conveys by this
element of the conversational setting seems to be this: a teacher of
tyrants has to appear as a hardboiled man; it does not do any harm if
he makes his pupil suspect that he cannot be impressed by considerations of a more noble character.

The poet interrupts his silence only once. The circumstances of
that interruption call for some attention. Hiero had given Simonides
more than one opportunity to say something, especially by address-
ing him by name.[33] This applies especially to his discussion of friendship. Therein one can almost see Hiero urging him toward at least
some visible reaction.[34] After all his efforts to make Simonides talk
have failed, he turns to what he considers the characteristic pleasures
of private men: drink, song, and sleep, which he, having become a
tyrant, cannot enjoy any longer because he is perpetually harassed
by fear, the spoiler of all pleasures.[35] Simonides remains silent. Hiero
makes a last attempt, this one more successful. Reminding himself of
the fact that Simonides had been most vocal while food was being
discussed, he replaces "strong drink and sleep" by "food and sleep."[36]
Referring to the poet's possible experience of fear in battle, he asserts
that tyrants can enjoy food and sleep as little as, or less than, soldiers
who have the enemy's phalanx close in front of them. Simonides
replies that his military experience proves to him the possibility of
combining "living dangerously" with a healthy appetite and a sound
sleep.[37] Saying this, he tacitly denies more strongly than by his statement at the beginning of the second section the reassuring implications of his previous emphasis on the pleasures of the body.[38]

We must now step back and look again at the picture as a whole. Taken as a whole, the second section consists of Hiero's sweeping indictment of tyranny, to which Simonides listens in silence. The meaning of this silence is finally revealed by what happens in the third section (ch. 7). The third section, the shortest section of the *Hiero*, contains, or immediately prepares for, the peripeteia. It culminates in Hiero's declaration that the tyrant can hardly do better than to hang himself. By making this declaration, Hiero abdicates the leadership in the conversation in favor of Simonides, who keeps it throughout the fourth and last section (ch. 8–11).[39] We contend that this crucial event—Hiero's breakdown or the change from Hiero's leadership to Simonides' leadership—is consciously and decisively prepared by Simonides' remaining silent in the second section.

The third section opens again with a surprising move of Simonides.[40] He grants to Hiero that tyranny is as toilsome and as dangerous as the latter had asserted; yet, he says, those toils and dangers are reasonably borne because they lead to the pleasure deriving from honors, and no other human pleasure comes nearer to divinity than this kind of pleasure: tyrants are honored more than any other men. In the parallel at the beginning of the second section Simonides had spoken only of what "*many* of those who are *reputed* to be (real) men" desire, and had merely implied that what they desire is power and wealth. Now he openly declares that the desire for honor is characteristic of real men as such, i.e., as distinguished from ordinary "human beings."[41] There seems to be no longer any doubt that Simonides, who is admittedly a real man, longs for tyrannical power.

Hiero's immediate reply reveals that he is more alarmed than ever before. He had mentioned before the facts that the tyrant is in perpetual danger of being assassinated and that tyrants commit acts of injustice. But never before had he mentioned these two facts within one and the same sentence. Still less had he explicitly established a connection between them. Only now, while trying to prove that the tyrant does not derive any pleasure from the honors shown to him, does he declare that the tyrant spends night and day like one condemned by all men to die for his injustice.[42] One might think for a moment that this increase in the vehemence of Hiero's indictment of tyranny is due to the subject matter so unexpectedly introduced by Simonides: Hiero might seem to suffer most of all from the fact that the tyrant is deprived of genuine honor. But if this is the case,

ON TYRANNY

why does he not protest against Simonides' later remark that Hiero had depreciated tyranny most because it frustrated the tyrant's homosexual desires? Why did he not bring up the subject of "honor" himself instead of waiting until Simonides did it? Why did he not find fault with Simonides' misleading initial enumeration of pleasures? Last but not least, why did the earlier discussion of a similar subject—praise[43]—fail to make any noticeable impression on his mood? It is not so much the intrinsic significance of Simonides' statement on honor as its conversational significance which accounts for its conspicuous and indeed decisive effect.

At the beginning of his statement on honor, Simonides alludes to Hiero's description of the toils and dangers which attend the life of a tyrant. But Hiero had described not merely those toils and dangers, but also the moral depravity to which the tyrant is condemned: he is compelled to live "by contriving something bad and base"; he is compelled to commit the crime of robbing temples and men; he cannot be a true patriot; he desires to enslave his fellow citizens; only the consideration that a tyrant must have living subjects who walk around seems to prevent him from killing or imprisoning all his subjects. After Hiero has finished his long speech, Simonides declares that in spite of everything that the tyrant has said, tyranny is highly desirable because it leads to supreme honor. As regards the toils and dangers pointed out by Hiero, Simonides pauses to allude to them; as regards the moral flaws deplored by Hiero, he simply ignores them. That is to say, the poet is not at all impressed by the immorality, or the injustice, characteristic of the tyrannical life; certainly its inevitable immorality would not prevent him for a moment from aspiring to tyranny for the sake of honor. No wonder then that Hiero collapses shortly afterward: what overwhelms him is not Simonides' statement on honor itself, but the poet's making it in this particular context. Because it is made in that context, and merely because it is made in that context, does it make Hiero realize to what lengths a man of Simonides' exceptional "wisdom" could go in "contriving something" and in particular in "contriving something bad and base." It is by thus silently, i.e., most astutely, revealing a complete lack of scruple that the poet both overwhelms Hiero and convinces him of his competence to give sound advice to a tyrant.[44]

The lesson which Xenophon conveys by making Simonides listen silently to Hiero's long speech, as well as by his answer to that speech, can now be stated as follows. Even a perfectly just man who wants to give advice to a tyrant has to present himself to his pupil as an utterly unscrupulous man. The greatest man who ever imitated the *Hiero* was Machiavelli. I should not be surprised if a sufficiently attentive study of Machiavelli's work would lead to the conclusion that it is precisely Machiavelli's perfect understanding of Xenophon's chief pedagogic lesson which accounts for the most shocking sentences occurring in the *Prince*. But if Machiavelli understood Xenophon's lesson, he certainly did not apply it in the spirit of its originator. For, according to Xenophon, the teacher of tyrants has to appear as an utterly unscrupulous man, not by protesting that he does not fear hell nor devil, nor by expressing immoral principles, but by simply failing to take notice of the moral principles. He has to reveal his alleged or real freedom from morality, not by speech but by silence. For by doing so—by disregarding morality "by deed" rather than by attacking it "by speech"—he reveals at the same time his understanding of political things. Xenophon, or his Simonides, is more "politic" than Machiavelli; he refuses to separate "moderation" (prudence) from "wisdom" (insight).

By replying to Hiero's long speech in the manner described, Simonides compels him to use still stronger language against tyranny than he had done before. Now Hiero declares that a tyrant, as distinguished from a man who is a benefactor of his fellows and therefore genuinely honored, lives like one condemned by all men to die for his injustice. Arrived at this point, Simonides could have replied in the most natural manner that, this being the case, the tyrant ought to rule as beneficently as possible. He could have begun at once to teach Hiero how to rule well as a tyrant. But he apparently felt that he needed some further information for sizing Hiero up, or that Hiero needed a further shock before he would be prepared to listen. Therefore he asks Hiero why, if tyranny is really such a great evil for the tyrant, neither he nor any other tyrant ever yet gave up his position voluntarily. Hiero answers that no tyrant can abdicate because he cannot make amends for the robbing, imprisoning, and killing of his subjects; (just as it does not profit him to live as a tyrant, it does not profit him to live again as a private man); if it profits any man (to cease living), to hang himself, it profits the tyrant most of all.[45] This answer puts the finishing touch to the preparation for Simonides' instruction. Simonides' final attack had amounted to a veiled suggestion addressed to the tyrant to return to private life. That suggestion is the necessary conclusion which a reasonable man would draw from Hiero's comparison between tyrannical and private life. Hiero defends himself against that suggestion by revealing what might seem to be some rudimentary sense of justice: he cannot return to private life because he cannot make amends for the many acts of injustice which he has committed. This defense is manifestly hypocritical: if tyranny is what he has asserted it to be, he prefers heaping new crimes on the untold number of crimes which he has already committed rather than stop his criminal career and suffer the consequences of his former misdeeds. His real motive for not abdicating seems then to be fear of punishment. But could he not escape punishment by simply fleeing? This is indeed the crucial implication of Hiero's last word against tyranny: as if there never had been a tyrant who, after having been expelled from his city, lived quietly thereafter in exile, and although he himself had said on a former occasion[46] that while making a journey abroad, the tyrant might easily be deposed, Hiero refuses to consider the possibility of escape from his city. He thus reveals himself as a man who is unable to live as a stranger.[47] It is this citizen spirit of his—the fact that he cannot help being absolutely attached to his city—to which the wandering poet silently appeals when teaching him how to be a good ruler.

Hiero has finally been rendered incapable of any further move. He has been reduced to a condition in which he has to fetter himself by a sincere or insincere assertion, or in which he has to use the language of a man who is despondent. He uses entirely different language in the two fairly brief utterances which he makes in the fourth or last section. Whereas his indictment of tyranny in the first part of the *Hiero* had presented the tyrant as the companion of the unjust and had culminated in the description of the tyrant as injustice incarnate, he describes him in the last part of the dialogue— i.e., a few minutes later—as a man who punishes the unjust,[48] as a defender of justice. This quick change of language, or of attitude, is most astonishing. As we have seen, the vehemence of Hiero's indictment had been increasing from section to section because Simonides had not been deterred from praising tyranny by the shortcomings of tyranny pointed out by Hiero. Now, Hiero had spoken against tyranny in the third section more violently than ever before, and in the fourth section Simonides continues praising tyranny.[49] Hence one should expect that Hiero will continue still increasing the vehemence of his indictment of tyranny. Yet he takes the opposite course. What has happened? Why does Simonides' praise of tyranny in the fourth section, and especially in the early part of that section (8. 1–7), fail to arouse Hiero's violent reaction? We suggest the following answer: Simonides' praise of tyranny in the fourth section—as distinguished from his praise of tyranny in the preceding sections—is not considered by Hiero an expression of the poet's jealousy of tyrants. More precisely, Simonides' immediate reaction to Hiero's statement that a tyrant can hardly do better than to hang himself, or the use which Simonides makes of his newly acquired leadership, convinces Hiero that the poet is not concerned with "contriving something" of an undesirable character. The action by which Simonides breaks down the walls of Hiero's distrust, is the peripeteia of the dialogue.

The difficult position into which Hiero has been forced is not without its advantages. Hiero had been on the defensive because he did not know what Simonides might be contriving. By his defeat, by his declaration of bankruptcy, he succeeds in stopping Simonides to the extent that he forces him to show his hand. He presents himself as a man who knows that neither of the two ways of life—the tyrannical and the private life—profits him, but who does not know whether it would profit him to cease living by hanging himself ("*if* it profits any man . . .").[50] Simonides could have taken up in a fairly natural manner the question implicitly raised by Hiero as to whether suicide is an advisable course of action, and in particular whether there are not other forms of death preferable to, or easier than, hanging.[51] In other words, the poet could conceivably have tried to persuade the tyrant to commit suicide, or to commit suicide in the easiest manner. To exaggerate grossly for purposes of clarification: the victory of the wise man over the tyrant, achieved solely by means of speech prudently interspersed with silence, is so complete that the wise man could kill the tyrant without lifting a finger, employing only speech, only persuasion. But he does nothing of the kind: he who has the power of persuasion, he who can do what he likes with any interlocutor, prefers to make use of the obedience of a living man rather than to kill him.[52] After having made Hiero realize fully that a wise man has the power of going to any length in contriving anything, Simonides gives him to understand that the wise man would not make use of this power. Simonides' refraining from acting like a man who wants to do away with a tyrant, or to deprive him of his power, is the decisive reason for the change in Hiero's attitude.

But silence is not enough: Simonides has to say something. What he says is determined by his intention to advise Hiero, and by the impossibility of advising a man who is despondent. It is immaterial in this respect that Hiero's complaints about his situation are of questionable sincerity; for Simonides is not in a position openly to question their sincerity. He has then to comfort Hiero while advising him or prior to advising him. Accordingly, his teaching of the tyrannical art is presented in the following form: Tyranny is most desirable ("comfort") if you will only do such and such things ("advice"). The comfort element of Simonides' teaching—the praise of (beneficent) tyranny—is due to the conversational situation and cannot be presumed to be an integral part of Xenophon's teaching concerning tyranny until it has been proved to be so. On the other hand, Simonides' advice can be presumed from the outset to be identical with Xenophon's suggestions about the improvement of tyrannical rule as a radically faulty political order.

It would not have been impossible for Simonides to refute Hiero by showing that the latter's account of tyranny is exaggerated, i.e., by discussing Hiero's indictment of tyranny point by point. But such a detailed discussion would merely have led to the conclusion that tyranny is not quite as bad as Hiero had asserted. That dreary result would not have sufficed for restoring Hiero's courage or for counteracting the crushing effect of his final verdict on tyranny. Or, to disregard for one moment the conversational setting, an exact examination of Hiero's arguments would have destroyed completely the edifying effect of the indictment of tyranny in the first part of the *Hiero*. Xenophon had then to burden his Simonides with the task of drawing a picture of tyranny which would be at least as bright as the one drawn by Hiero had been dark. The abundant use of the *modus potentialis* in Simonides' speech as well as the silence of the *Hiero* and indeed of the whole *Corpus Xenophonteum* about happy tyrants who actually existed anywhere in Greece make it certain that Simonides' praise of tyranny in the second part of the *Hiero* was considered by Xenophon even more rhetorical than Hiero's indictment of tyranny in the first part.

Hiero had tried to show that tyrannical life is inferior to private life from the point of view of pleasure. In the existing situation, Simonides cannot appeal directly from the pleasant to the noble, for Hiero had just declared in the most emphatic manner that, as a matter of fact, a tyrant is a man who has committed an untold number of crimes. Simonides is therefore compelled to show (what in the first part he had hardly more than asserted) that tyrannical life is superior to private life from the point of view of pleasure. Being compelled to accept the tyrant's end, he must show that Hiero used the wrong means. In other words, he must trace Hiero's being out of heart with tyranny not to a wrong intention but to an error of judgment, to an erroneous belief.[53]

Simonides discovers the specific error which he ascribes to Hiero by reflecting on the latter's reply to the poet's statement concerning honor. Hiero had compared the honors enjoyed by tyrants with their sexual pleasures: just as services rendered by those who do not love in turn, or who act under compulsion, are no favors, services rendered by those who fear, are no honors. The *tertium comparationis* between the pleasures of sex and those of honor is that both must be granted by people who are prompted by love (φιλία) and not by fear. Now Hiero is worried most by his being deprived of the genuine pleasures of sex. But Simonides might offend him by emphasizing this fact and thus asserting that Hiero is more concerned with sex than with honor and hence perhaps not a "real man." He elegantly avoids this embarrassment by escaping into something more general, viz., into that which is common to "honor" and "sex."[54] For whether Hiero is chiefly concerned with the one or the other, he is in both cases in need of love (φιλία). And in both cases his misery is due to his belief that being a tyrant and being loved are mutually exclusive.[55] This is then the diagnosis of Hiero's illness from which Simonides starts: Hiero is out of heart with tyranny because, desiring to be loved by human beings, he believes that tyrannical rule prevents him from being so loved.[56] Simonides does not limit himself to rejecting this belief. He asserts that tyrants are more likely to gain affection than private men. For whatever might have to be said against tyranny, the tyrant is certainly a ruler, hence a man of high standing among his fellows, and "we" naturally admire men of high social standing. Above all, the prestige attending ruling positions adds an unbought grace to any act of kindness performed by rulers in general and hence by tyrants in particular.[57] It is by means of this assertion that Simonides surreptitiously suggests his cure for Hiero's illness, a cure discovered, just as the illness itself was, by reflecting on Hiero's comparison of "honor" and "sex." Hiero had granted as a matter of course that in order to receive favors, to be loved in return, one must first love: the misery of the tyrant consists in the very fact that he loves and is not loved in turn.[58] Simonides tacitly applies what Hiero had granted as regards sexual love to love in general: he who wants to be loved must love first; he who wants to be loved by his subjects in order to be genuinely honored by them must love them first; to gain favors he must first show favors. He does not state this lesson in so many words, but he transmits it implicitly by comparing the effects of a tyrant's acts of kindness with the effects of a private man's acts of kindness. He thus shifts the emphasis almost insensibly from the pleasant feelings primarily desired to the noble or praiseworthy actions which directly or indirectly bring about those pleasant feelings. He tacitly advises the tyrant to think not of his own pleasures but of the pleasures of others; not of his being served and receiving gifts, but of his doing services and making gifts.[59] That is to say, he tacitly gives the tyrant exactly the same advice which Socrates explicitly gives his companions, nay, which Virtue herself explicitly gives to Heracles.[60]

Simonides' virtuous advice does not spoil the effect of his previous indifference to moral principles because the virtuous character of his advice is sufficiently qualified by the context in which it is given. Socrates and Virtue shout their advice from the housetops to men who are of normal decency, and even potential paragons of virtue. Simonides, on the other hand, suggests substantially the same advice in the most subdued language to a tyrant who has just confessed having committed an untold number of crimes. It is true, Simonides' language becomes considerably less restrained toward the end of the conversation. But it is also true that throughout the conversation he presents the pleasant effects of a tyrant's kind actions as wholly independent of the manner in which the tyrant had come to power and of any of his previous misdeeds. Simonides' alleged or real freedom from scruple is preserved in, and operates in, his very recommendation of virtue.[61]

Hiero answers "straightway," "at once." This is the only occasion on which either of the two interlocutors says something "straightway."[62] It is Simonides' reaction to Hiero's statement that the tyrant can hardly do better than to hang himself, which induces the tyrant to answer "at once," i.e., to proceed without that slowness, or circumspection, which characterizes all other utterances of the two men. Dropping his habitual reserve, Hiero gives a sincere, not exaggerated account of the difficulties confronting the tyrant. He no longer denies that tyrants have greater power than private men to do things by means of which men gain affection; he merely denies that they are for this reason more likely to be loved than private men, because they are also compelled to do very many things by which men incur hatred. Thus, e.g., they have to exact money and to punish the unjust; and, above all, they are in need of mercenaries.[63] Simonides does not say that one should not take care of all these matters.[64] But, he believes, there are ways of taking care of things which lead to hatred and other ways which lead to gratification: a ruler should himself do the gratifying things (such as the awarding of prizes) while entrusting to others the hateful things (such as the inflicting of punishment). The implication of this advice as well as of all other advice given to Hiero by Simonides is, of course, that Hiero needs such advice, or that he is actually doing the opposite of what Simonides is advising him to do, i.e., that he is at present a most imperfect ruler. Imitating in his speech by anticipation the hoped-for behavior of his pupil Hiero, or rather giving him by his own action an example of the behavior proper to a tyrant, Simonides soon drops all explicit mention of the hateful things inseparable from tyranny, if not from government as such, while he praises the enormous usefulness of offering prizes: the hateful aspects of tyranny are not indeed annihilated, but banished from sight.[65] Simonides' praise of beneficent tyranny thus serves the purpose not merely of comforting Hiero (who is certainly much less in need of comfort than his utterances might induce the unwary reader to believe), but above all of teaching him in what light the tyrant should appear to his subjects: far from being a naïve expression of a naïve belief in virtuous tyrants, it is rather a prudently presented lesson in political prudence.[66] Simonides goes so far as to avoid in this context the very term "tyrant."[67] On the other hand, he now uses the terms "noble" as well as "good" and "useful" much more frequently than ever before, while speaking considerably less of the "pleasant." With a view to the difficulty of appealing directly from the pleasant to the noble, however, he stresses for the time being the "good" (with its "utilitarian" implications) considerably more than the "noble" or "fair."[68] Furthermore, he shows that striving for honor is perfectly compatible with being the subject of a tyrant, thus blotting out completely the odious implications of his previous statement about honor. He shows, too, that honoring subjects by means of prizes is an excellent bargain.[69] And what is most important, he strongly (but by implication) advises against disarming the citizens when he suggests that prizes be offered them for certain achievements of a military nature.[70]

Only after all these steps have been taken does there appear some agreement between Hiero and Simonides on the subject of tyranny. Only now is Hiero prepared not only to listen to Simonides' advice but to address to him a question, his only question, concerning the proper conduct of tyrannical government. The formulation of the question shows that he has learned something: he does not speak any longer of "tyrant," but of "ruler." The purport of the question is established by these facts: First, that Simonides had not said anything about the mercenaries whom Hiero had described in his preceding statement as an oppressive burden on the citizens;[71] and second, that Simonides' speech might seem to imply a suggestion that the mercenaries be replaced by citizens. Accordingly, Hiero's question consists of two parts. First, he asks Simonides to advise him how he could avoid incurring hatred on account of his employing mercenaries. Then he asks him whether he means that a ruler who has gained affection is no longer in need of a bodyguard.[72] Simonides answers emphatically that a bodyguard is indispensable:[73] the improvement of tyrannical government should not go to the extreme of undermining the very pillar of tyrannical rule. Thus Simonides' answer to Hiero's only question is tantamount to strong counsel against the abdication which he had tentatively suggested earlier. Besides, Hiero's question as to whether a bodyguard might not be dispensed with might have been prompted by his desire to save the enormous expenses involved. With a view to this possibility, Simonides' statement implies the answer that such expenses are indeed inevitable, but that the proper use of the mercenaries will dispose the subjects to pay the cost of them most cheerfully.[74] Yet, Simonides says, adding a word of advice for which he had not been asked, while the ample use of prizes and the proper use of the mercenaries will help greatly in the solution of the tyrant's financial problems, a tyrant ought not to hesitate to spend his own money for the common good.[75] Nay, a tyrant's interests are better served if he spends money for public affairs rather than for his own affairs. In this context Simonides gives the more specific advice—the giving of which may have been the only purpose of Simonides' starting a conversation with Hiero—that a tyrant should not compete with private men in chariot races and the like, but rather should take care that the greatest number of competitors should come from his city.[76] He should compete with other leaders of cities for victory in the noblest and grandest contest—viz., in making his city as happy as possible. By winning that contest, Simonides promises him, he will gain the love of all his subjects, the regard of many cities, the admiration of all men, and many other good things; by surpassing his friends in acts of kindness he will be possessed of the noblest and most blessed possession among men: he will not be envied while being happy.[77] With this outlook the dialogue ends. Any answer of the tyrant to the poet's almost boundless promise would have been an anticlimax, and, what would have been worse, it would have prevented the reader from reasonably enjoying the polite silence in which a Greek tyrant, old in crime and martial glory, could listen to a siren-song of virtue.[78]

c. The use of characteristic terms

One may say that "the gist of Xenophon's counsel to despots is that a despot should endeavour to rule like a good king."[1] It is therefore all the more striking that he avoids consistently the very term "king." By avoiding the term "king" in a work destined to teach the art of a tyrant, he complies with the rule of tact which requires that one should not embarrass people by mentioning things from the lack of which they can be presumed to suffer: a tyrant must be presumed to suffer from the lack of a valid title to his position. Xenophon's procedure may have been the model for the apparently opposite but fundamentally identical device of Machiavelli, who in his *Prince* avoids the term "tiranno": individuals who are called "tiranni" in the *Discourses* and elsewhere are called "principi" in the *Prince*.[2] We may also note the absence of the terms *demos* and *politeia*[3] from the *Hiero*.

As for Simonides in particular, he never uses the term "law." He

mentions justice only once, making it clear that he is speaking of
that justice only which is required of subjects rather than rulers:
justice in business dealings.[4] He never speaks of truth or of falsehood
or of deceiving. While laughing is never mentioned by Simonides or
by Hiero, Simonides speaks once of καταγελᾶν. This is not insignificant because in the only remark of that kind which occurs in the
Hiero, Xenophon notes that Simonides made a certain statement—it
concerns Hiero's love affairs—"laughingly"; Hiero is always serious.[5]
Simonides, who never mentions courage (ἀνδρεία),[6] once mentions
moderation (σωφροσύνη) which is never mentioned by Hiero. On the
other hand, Hiero uses the terms μέτριος, κόσμιος, and ἀκρατής which
are never used by Simonides.[7]

　　Some consideration should also be given the distribution of characteristic terms between the two main parts of the dialogue, namely,
the indictment of tyranny on the one hand, the suggestions concerning the improvement of tyrannical rule on the other. Terms which
are avoided in the second part are: law, free (freedom), nature,
courage, misery. On the other hand, moderation is mentioned only
in the second part. "Tyrant" (and derivatives) occurs relatively
much more frequently in the first part (83 times) than in the second
part (7 times); on the other hand, "ruling" (and derivatives) occurs
much more frequently in the much shorter second part (12 times)
than in the much more extensive first part (4 times): Simonides
wants to induce Hiero to think of his position in terms of "ruling"
rather than in terms of "tyranny"; for it is not good for any man
to think of his activity in odious terms. How well Simonides succeeds is shown by the fact that in his last remark[8] Hiero speaks
of "ruler" and no longer of "tyrant." Terms designating pleasure
and pain occur relatively much more frequently in the first part
(93 times) than in the second part (6 times). On the other hand,
"noble" ("fair") and "base" ("ugly") occur relatively much more
frequently in the second part (15 times) than in the first part (9
times). The reason is obvious: Simonides wants to educate Hiero to
take his bearings by the fair rather than by the pleasant. Χάρις (and
derivatives) occurs relatively much more frequently in the second
part (9 times) than in the first part (4 times). Ἀνάγκη (and derivatives) occurs relatively more frequently in the second part (9 times)
than in the first part (16 times).

IV

THE TEACHING CONCERNING
TYRANNY

SINCE TYRANNY is essentially a faulty political order, the teaching concerning tyranny necessarily consists of two parts. The first part has to make manifest the specific shortcomings of tyranny ("pathology"), and the second part has to show how these shortcomings can be mitigated ("therapeutics"). The bipartition of the *Hiero* reflects the bipartition of the "tyrannical" teaching itself. Now, Xenophon chose to present that teaching in the form of a dialogue, and he had therefore to choose a particular conversational setting. However sound, and even compelling, his reasons may have been, they certainly lead to the result that he has not given us his "tyrannical" teaching in its pure, scientific form, in the form of a treatise. The reader has to add to and to subtract from Hiero's and Simonides' speeches in order to lay hold of Xenophon's teaching. That addition and subtraction is not left to the reader's arbitrary decision. It is guided by the author's indications, some of which have been discussed in the preceding chapters. Nevertheless, a certain ambiguity remains, an ambiguity ultimately due not to the unsolved riddles implied in many individual passages of the *Hiero* but to the fact that a perfectly lucid and unambiguous connection between content and form, between a general teaching and a contingent event (e.g., a conversation between two individuals) is impossible.

Considering the primarily practical character of the "tyrannical" teaching as a political teaching, it is necessary that one interlocutor, the pupil, should be a tyrant. It is equally necessary that he should be an actual tyrant, not a potential tyrant. If the pupil were only a potential tyrant, the teacher would have to show him how to become a tyrant, and in so doing he would have to teach him injustice, whereas in the case of an actual tyrant the teacher has the much less odious task of showing him a way toward lesser injustice. Seeing that a tyrant (Periander of Corinth) was said to have instituted most of the common devices for preserving tyranny,[1] one might think that the natural teacher of the tyrannical art would be a great tyrant; but preservation of tyranny and correction of tyranny are two different things. Xenophon evidently felt that only a wise man could teach what he considered the tyrannical art, i.e., the art of ruling well as a tyrant, and that a tyrant would not be wise. This leads to the consequence that the wise man who teaches the tyrannical art cannot have learned that art from a tyrant as Socrates, who teaches the economic art, has learned it from an economist. In other words, the wise teacher of the tyrannical art has to teach it by himself, without any assistance, or he has to discover it by himself.[2] Now, the wise man might transmit to his pupil the whole "tyrannical" teaching, i.e., both the indictment of tyranny and the correction of tyranny; but Xenophon apparently thought that a tyrant's indictment of tyranny would be more impressive for the average reader.[3] Finally, the tyrant might start the conversation by complaining to a wise man about a tyrant's sad lot, in order to elicit his advice. This, however, would presuppose that the tyrant would have a wise friend whom he trusts, and that he would consider himself in need of advice.[4] To sum up, the more one considers alternatives to the conversational setting chosen by Xenophon, the more one becomes convinced that his choice was sound.

Yet this choice, however sound and even necessary, leads to the result that Xenophon's indictment of tyranny is presented by a man who is not wise and who has a selfish interest in disparaging tyranny, whereas his praise of tyranny is presented by a wise man who argues in favor of tyranny without an apparent selfish interest. Besides, since the indictment of tyranny precedes the praise of tyranny, the indictment is presented on the basis of insufficient evidence—for Hiero does not take into account the facts or possibilities set forth by Simonides in the latter part of the *Hiero*—whereas the praise of tyranny seems to be voiced *en pleine connaissance de cause*. That is to say, Xenophon could not help being led to giving a greater weight, at least apparently, to the praise of tyranny than to the indictment of tyranny. The question arises whether this is merely the inevitable result of considerations such as those sketched before, or whether it is directly intended.

One might think for a moment that the ambiguity under consideration was caused merely by Xenophon's decision to treat at all in a dialogue the question of the improvement of tyrannical rule: every ambiguity would have been avoided if he had limited himself to indicting tyranny. A comparison of his conversational treatment of tyranny with Plato's, however, shows that this suggestion does not go to the root of the matter. Plato refrained from teaching the tyrannical art and he entrusted his indictment of tyranny to Socrates. The price which he had to pay for this choice was that he had to entrust his praise of tyranny to men who were not wise (Polos, Callicles, and Thrasymachus) and who therefore were openly praising the very injustice of tyranny. To avoid the latter inconvenience, Xenophon had to pay the price of burdening a wise man with the task of praising tyranny. An effective conversational treatment of tyranny which is free from inconveniences is impossible. For there are only two possibilities apart from those chosen by Xenophon and Plato: the praise of tyranny by the wise might be succeeded by the indictment of tyranny by the unwise, and the indictment of tyranny by the wise might be succeeded by the praise of tyranny by the unwise; these alternatives are ruled out by the consideration that the wise man ought to have the last word.

It is more appropriate to say that the bearing of Xenophon's praise of tyranny is sufficiently limited, not only by the conversational setting, but above all by the fact that his wise man who praises tyranny makes sufficiently clear the essential shortcomings of tyranny. He describes tyranny at its best, but he lets it be understood that tyranny even at its best suffers from serious defects. This implied criticism of tyranny is much more convincing than Hiero's passionate indictment which serves a selfish purpose and which would be literally true only of the very worst kind of tyranny. To see the broad outline of Simonides' criticism of tyranny at its best, one has only to consider the result of his suggested correction of tyranny in the light of Xenophon's, or Socrates', definition of tyranny. Tyranny is defined in contradistinction to kingship: kingship is such rule as is exercised over willing subjects and is in accordance with the laws of the cities; tyranny is such rule as is exercised over unwilling subjects and accords, not with laws, but with the will of the ruler.[5] This definition covers the common form of tyranny, but not tyranny at its best. Tyranny at its best, tyranny as corrected according to Simonides' suggestions, is no longer rule over unwilling subjects. It is most certainly rule over willing subjects.[6] But it remains rule "not according to laws," i.e., it is absolute government. Simonides, who extols tyranny at its best, refrains from using the very term "law."[7] Tyranny is essentially rule without laws, or, more precisely, monarchic rule without laws.

Before considering the shortcomings of tyranny thus understood, we may dwell for a moment on its positive qualities. As regards the tyrant himself, Simonides asserts without hesitation that he may be perfectly happy. Furthermore, he leaves no doubt that the tyrant may be virtuous, and in fact of outstanding virtue. The correction of tyranny consists in nothing else than the transformation of the unjust or vicious tyrant who is more or less unhappy into a virtuous tyrant who is happy.[8] As for the tyrant's subjects, or his city, Simonides makes it clear that it may be very happy. The tyrant and his subjects may be united by the bonds of mutual kindness. The subjects of the virtuous tyrant are treated, not like little children, but like comrades or companions.[9] They are not deprived by him of honors.[10] They are not disarmed; their military spirit is encouraged.[11] Nor are the mercenaries, without whom tyranny is impossible, undesirable from the point of view of the city: they enable the city to wage war vigorously.[12] When Simonides recommends that the tyrant should make a most ample use of prizes and that he should promote agriculture and commerce, if agriculture to a higher degree than commerce, he simply seems to approve of policies which Xenophon considered to befit a well-ordered commonwealth. He thus creates the impression that according to Xenophon tyrannical government can live up to the highest political standards.[13]

Simonides' praise of beneficent tyranny, which at first sight seems to be boundless and rhetorically vague, proves on closer examination to be most carefully worded and to remain within very precise limits. Just as Simonides avoids in it the term "law," he avoids in it the term "freedom." The practical consequence of the absence of laws, he gives us to understand, is the absence of freedom: no laws, no liberty. All specific suggestions made by Simonides flow from this implied axiom, or reveal their political meaning in its light. For instance, when recommending to the tyrant that he consider the citizens as companions or comrades, he does not mean that the tyrant should treat the citizens as his equals, or even as freemen. For slaves may be companions as well as freemen. Furthermore, Simonides advises the tyrant that he consider the citizens as companions, and his friends as his own children:[14] if his very friends are then in every respect his subordinates, the citizens will be his subordinates in a still more far-reaching sense. The advice just referred to shows in addition that Simonides does not go so far in his praise of beneficent tyranny as to call it "paternal" rule.[15] It is true, the subjects of the beneficent tyrant are not disarmed; but in time of peace at least they do not protect themselves against the slaves and evildoers as the citizens of free commonwealths do; they are protected by the tyrant's bodyguard.[16] They are literally at the mercy of the tyrant and his mercenaries, and they can only wish or pray that the tyrant will become, or remain, beneficent. The true character of tyranny even at its best is clearly indicated by Simonides' "Machiavellian" suggestion that the tyrant should do the gratifying things (such as the awarding of prizes) himself, while entrusting to others the punitive actions.[17] It is hardly necessary to say that the tyrant's refraining from openly taking responsibility for punitive action does not bespeak a particular mildness of his rule: Non-tyrannical rulers take that responsibility without any concealment[18] because their authority, deriving from law, is secure. Similarly, the extraordinarily ample use of prizes, especially for the promotion of agriculture, seems to serve the "tyrannical" purpose of keeping the subjects busy with their private concerns rather than with public affairs.[19] At the same time it compensates for the lack of the natural incentives to increase one's wealth, a lack due to the precarious character of property rights under a tyrant. The best tyrant would consider his fatherland his estate. This may be preferable to his impoverishing his fatherland in order to increase his private estate; yet it certainly implies that the best tyrant would consider his fatherland his private property which he would naturally administer

according to his own discretion. Thus no subject of a tyrant could
have any property rights against the tyrant. The subjects would
pay as much as he deems necessary in the form of gifts or voluntary
contributions.[20] Nor can the tyrant be said to honor the citizens
because he awards prizes or distinctions to some of them; he may be
able and willing to enrich his subjects: he cannot accord to them
the "equality of honor" which is irreconcilable with tyrannical rule
and from the lack of which they may be presumed always to suffer.[21]

These shortcomings of tyranny at its best are not, however,
necessarily decisive. How Simonides, and Xenophon, judged of the
value of tyranny at its best depends on what they thought of the
importance of freedom. As for Simonides, he seems to esteem nothing as highly as honor or praise; and of praise he says that it will
be the more pleasant the freer are those who bestow it.[22] This leads
to the consequence that the demands of honor or praise cannot be
satisfied by tyranny however perfect. The tyrant will not enjoy
honor of the highest kind because his subjects lack freedom, and on
the other hand the tyrant's subjects will not enjoy full honor for
the reason mentioned before. As for Xenophon himself, we have to
start from the facts that freedom was considered the aim of democracy, as particularly distinguished from aristocracy, the aim of
which was said to be virtue;[23] and that Xenophon was not a
democrat. Xenophon's view is reflected in Hiero's implicit assertion
that the wise are not concerned with freedom.[24] To establish Xenophon's attitude toward tyranny at its best as characterized by
Simonides, we have to consider the relation of tyranny at its best,
not to freedom, but to virtue. Only if virtue were impossible without freedom, would the demand for freedom be absolutely justified
from Xenophon's point of view.

The term "virtue" occurs five times in the *Hiero*. In only two
out of the five cases is it applied to human beings.[25] Only once is
it applied to the tyrant. Never is it applied to the tyrant's
subjects. Simonides advises the tyrant to be proud of "the
happiness of his city" rather than of "the virtue of his chariot
horses": he does not mention the virtue of the city as a possible
goal of tyrannical rule. It is safe to say that a city ruled by
a tyrant is not supposed by him to "practice gentlemanliness as a
matter of public concern."[26] But, as has been proved by Socrates'
life, there are virtuous men in cities which do not "practice gentle-

manliness as a matter of public concern." It is therefore an open
question whether and how far virtue is possible under a tyrant. The
beneficent tyrant would award prizes for "prowess in war" and for
"justice in contractual relations":[27] he would not be concerned with
fostering prowess simply and justice simply. This confirms Hiero's
assertion that the brave and the just are not desirable as subjects of
a tyrant.[28] Only a qualified, or reduced, form of courage and
justice befits the subjects of a tyrant. For prowess simply is closely
akin to freedom, or love of freedom,[29] and justice simply is obedience to laws. The justice befitting the subjects of a tyrant is the
least political form of justice, or that form of justice which is most
remote from public-spiritedness: the justice to be observed in contractual, private relations.[30]

But how can a virtuous man—and Simonides' beneficent tyrant
would seem to be a virtuous man—rest satisfied with the necessity
of preventing his subjects from reaching the summit of virtue? Let
us then reconsider the facts mentioned in the preceding paragraph.
As regards the fact that Simonides ascribes to the tyrant's subjects
a qualified form of prowess only, and fails to ascribe courage to
them, we have to remember that in Xenophon's two lists of the
virtues of Socrates, courage does not occur.[31] As regards Simonides'
failure to ascribe to the tyrant's subjects justice simply, we have to
remember that justice can be understood as a part of moderation
and that, according to an explicit statement of Simonides, the
tyrant's subjects may very well possess moderation.[32] As regards
Simonides' failure to ascribe to the tyrant's subjects virtue as such,
we have to remember that virtue is not necessarily a generic term,
but may indicate a specific virtue distinguished from justice in
particular.[33] However this may be, the question of what Simonides
thought about the possibility of virtue under tyrannical rule seems
to be definitely settled by an explicit statement of his according to
which "gentlemen" may live, and live happily, under a beneficent
tyrant.[34] In order not to misinterpret Simonides' ascribing to the
tyrant's subjects only qualified forms of courage and justice, we
have to compare it with Xenophon's failure, in his *Lacedaemoniorum
respublica,* to ascribe justice in any sense to the Spartans themselves.
The utmost one is entitled to say is that the virtue possible under
a tyrant will have a specific color, a color different from that of
republican virtue. It may tentatively be suggested that the place

occupied within republican virtue by courage is occupied within the virtue befitting the subjects of the excellent tyrant by moderation which is produced by fear.[35] But one has no right to assume that the virtue befitting the subjects of a good tyrant is meant to be inferior in dignity to republican virtue. How little Xenophon believed that virtue is impossible without freedom is shown most strikingly by his admiration for the younger Cyrus whom he does not hesitate to describe as a "slave."[36]

If gentlemen can live happily under a beneficent tyrant, tyranny as corrected according to Simonides' suggestions might seem to live up to Xenophon's highest political standard. To see at once that this is the case, one merely has to measure Simonides' excellent tyrant by the criterion set forth in Xenophon's, or Socrates', definition of the good ruler. The virtue of the good ruler consists in making happy those he rules. The aim of the good ruler can be achieved by means of laws—this was done, according to Xenophon, in the most remarkable manner in Lycurgus' city—or by rule without laws, i.e., by tyranny: the beneficent tyrant as described by Simonides makes his city happy.[37] It is certainly most significant that, as regards the happiness achieved by means of laws, Xenophon can adduce an actual example (Sparta), whereas as regards the happiness achieved by tyranny, he offers no other evidence than the promise of a poet. In other words, it is of very great importance that, according to Xenophon, the aim of the good ruler is much more likely to be achieved by means of laws than by means of absolute rule. This does not do away, however, with the admission that, as a matter of principle, rule of laws is not essential for good government.

Xenophon does not make this admission in so many words. He presents Simonides as describing tyranny at its best and as declaring that the tyrant can make his city happy. Considering the situation in which Simonides expounds his views of tyranny, the objection is justified that what he says serves the purpose of comforting a somewhat disturbed tyrant or at any rate is said *ad hominem* and ought not to be taken as expressing directly Xenophon's own views. We have therefore to consider whether the thesis that tyranny can live up to the highest political standard is defensible on the basis of Xenophon's, or Socrates', political philosophy.

To begin with, it must appear most paradoxical that Xenophon should have had any liking whatsoever for tyranny however good.

Tyranny at its best is still rule without laws and, according to Socrates' definition, justice is identical with legality or obedience to laws.[38] Thus tyranny in any form seems to be irreconcilable with the requirement of justice. On the other hand, tyranny would become morally possible if the identification of "just" and "legal" were not absolutely correct, or if "everything according to law were (only) *somehow* ($\pi\omega\varsigma$) just."[39] The laws which determine what is legal are the rules of conduct upon which the citizens have agreed.[40] "The citizens" may be "the multitude" or "the few"; "the few" may be the rich or the virtuous. That is to say, the laws, and hence what is legal, depend on the political order of the community for which they are given. Could Xenophon or his Socrates have believed that the difference between laws depending on a faulty political order and laws depending on a good political order is wholly irrelevant as far as justice is concerned? Could they have believed that rules prescribed by a monarch, i.e., not by "the citizens," cannot be laws?[41] Besides, is it wholly irrelevant for justice whether what the laws prescribe is reasonable or unreasonable, good or bad? Finally, is it wholly irrelevant for justice whether the laws enacted by the legislator (the many, the few, the monarch) are forcibly imposed on, or voluntarily agreed to by, the other members of the community? Questions such as these are not raised by Xenophon, or his Socrates, but only by Xenophon's young and rash Alcibiades who, however, was a pupil of Socrates at the time when he raised those questions; only Alcibiades, and not Socrates, is presented by Xenophon as raising the Socratic question, "What is law?"[42] Socrates' doubt of the unqualified identification of justice and legality is intimated, however, by the facts that, on the one hand, he considers an enactment of the "legislator" Critias and his fellows a "law" which, he says, he is prepared to obey; and that, on the other hand, he actually disobeys it because it is "against the laws."[43] But apart from the consideration that the identification of "just" and "legal" would make impossible the evidently necessary distinction between just and unjust laws, there are elements of justice which necessarily transcend the dimension of the legal. Ingratitude, e.g., while not being illegal, is unjust.[44] The justice in business dealings—Aristotle's commutative justice proper—which is possible under a tyrant, is for this very reason not essentially dependent on law. Xenophon is thus led to suggest another definition, a more adequate definition, of justice. According to it, the just man is a man who does not hurt anyone, but helps everyone who has dealings with him. To be just, in other words, simply means to be beneficent.[45] If justice is then essentially translegal, rule without laws may very well be just: beneficent absolute rule is just. Absolute rule of a man who knows how to rule, who is a born ruler, is actually superior to the rule of laws, in so far as the good ruler is "a seeing law,"[46] and laws do not "see," or legal justice is blind. Whereas a good ruler is necessarily beneficent, laws are not necessarily beneficent. To say nothing of laws which are actually bad and harmful, even good laws suffer from the fact that they cannot "see." Now, tyranny is absolute monarchic rule. Hence the rule of an excellent tyrant is superior to, or more just than, rule of laws. Xenophon's realization of the problem of law, his understanding of the essence of law, his having raised and answered the Socratic question, "What is law?" enables and compels him to grant that tyranny may live up to the highest political standard. His giving, in the *Hiero*, a greater weight to the praise of tyranny than to the indictment of tyranny is then more than an accidental consequence of his decision to present the teaching concerning tyranny in the form of a dialogue.

Yet Simonides goes much beyond praising beneficent tyranny: he praises in the strongest terms the hoped-for beneficent rule of a tyrant who previously had committed a considerable number of crimes. By implication he admits that the praiseworthy character of tyranny at its best is not impaired by the unjust manner in which the tyrant originally acquired his power or in which he ruled prior to his conversion. Xenophon would have been prevented from fully agreeing with his Simonides regarding tyranny if he had been a legitimist or constitutionalist. Xenophon's Socrates makes it clear that there is only one sufficient title to rule: only knowledge, and not force and fraud or election, or, we may add, inheritance makes a man a king or ruler. If this is the case, "constitutional" rule, rule derived from elections in particular, is not essentially more legitimate than tyrannical rule, rule derived from force or fraud. Tyrannical rule as well as "constitutional" rule will be legitimate to the extent to which the tyrant or the "constitutional" rulers will listen to the counsels of him who "speaks well" because he "thinks well." At any rate, the rule of a tyrant who, after having come to power by means of force and fraud, or after having committed any number of crimes, listens to the suggestions of reasonable men, is essentially more legitimate than the rule of elected magistrates who refuse to listen to such suggestions, i.e., than the rule of elected magistrates as such. Xenophon's Socrates is so little committed to the cause of "constitutionalism" that he can describe the sensible men who advise the tyrant as the tyrant's "allies." That is to say, he conceives of the relation of the wise to the tyrant in almost exactly the same way as does Simonides.[47]

While Xenophon seems to have believed that beneficent tyranny or the rule of a tyrant who listens to the counsels of the wise is, as a matter of principle, preferable to the rule of laws or to the rule of elected magistrates as such, he seems to have thought that tyranny at its best could hardly, if ever, be realized. This is shown most clearly by the absence of any reference to beneficent and happy tyrants who actually existed, not only from the *Hiero,* but from the *Corpus Xenophonteum* as a whole. It is true, in the *Education of Cyrus* he occasionally refers to a tyrant who was apparently happy;[48] he does not say, however, that he was beneficent or virtuous. Above all, the monarch in question was not a Greek: the chances of tyranny at its best seem to be particularly small among Greeks.[49] The reason why Xenophon was so skeptical regarding the prospects of tyranny at its best is indicated by a feature common to the two thematic treatments of tyranny at its best which occur in his works. In the *Hiero* as well as in the *Memorabilia,* the tyrant is presented as a ruler who needs guidance by another man in order to become a good ruler: even the best tyrant is, as such, an imperfect, an inefficient ruler.[50] Being a tyrant, being called a tyrant and not a king, means having been unable to transform tyranny into kingship, or to transform a title which is generally considered defective into a title which is generally considered valid.[51] The ensuing lack of unquestioned authority leads to the consequence that tyrannical government is essentially more oppressive and hence less stable than nontyrannical government. Thus no tyrant can dispense with a bodyguard which is more loyal to him than to the city and which enables him to maintain his power against the wishes of the city.[52] Reasons such as these explain why Xenophon, or his Socrates, preferred, for all practical purposes, at least as far as Greeks were concerned, the rule of laws to tyranny, and why they identified, for all practical purposes, the just with the legal.

The "tyrannical" teaching—the teaching which expounds the view that a case can be made for beneficent tyranny, and even for a beneficent tyranny which was originally established by force or fraud—has then a purely theoretical meaning. It is not more than a most forceful expression of the problem of law and legitimacy. When Socrates was charged with teaching his pupils to be "tyrannical," this doubtless was due to the popular misunderstanding of a theoretical thesis as a practical proposal. Yet the theoretical thesis by itself necessarily prevented its holders from being unqualifiedly loyal to Athenian democracy, e.g., for it prevented them from believing that democracy is simply the best political order. It prevented them from being "good citizens" (in the precise sense of the term)[53] under a democracy. Xenophon does not even attempt to defend Socrates against the charge that he led the young to look down with contempt on the political order established in Athens.[54] It goes without saying that the theoretical thesis in question might have become embarrassing for its holder in any city not ruled by a tyrant, i.e., in almost every city. Socrates' and Xenophon's acceptance of the "tyrannical" teaching would then explain why they became suspect to their fellow citizens, and, therefore, to a considerable extent, why Socrates was condemned to death and Xenophon was condemned to exile.

It is one thing to accept the theoretical thesis concerning tyranny; it is another thing to expound it publicly. Every written exposition is to a smaller or larger degree a public exposition. The *Hiero* does not expound the "tyrannical" teaching. But it enables, and even compels, its reader to disentangle that teaching from the writings in which Xenophon speaks in his own name or presents the views of Socrates. Only if read in the light of the question posed by the *Hiero* do the relevant passages of Xenophon's other writings reveal their full meaning. The *Hiero* reveals, however, if only indirectly, the conditions under which the "tyrannical" teaching may be expounded. If the city is essentially the community kept together and ruled by law, the "tyrannical" teaching cannot exist for the citizen as citizen. The ultimate reason why the very tyrant Hiero strongly indicts tyranny is precisely that he is at bottom a citizen.[55] Accordingly, Xenophon entrusted the only explicit praise of tyranny which he ever wrote to a "stranger," a man who does not have citizen responsibilities and who, in addition, voices the praise of tyranny not publicly but in a strictly private conversation with a tyrant, and for a purpose which supplies him with an almost perfect excuse. Socrates did not consider it good that the wise man should be simply a stranger;[56] Socrates was a citizen-philosopher. He could not, therefore, with propriety be presented as praising tyranny under any circumstances. There is no fundamental difference in this respect between Xenophon and Plato. Plato entrusted his discussion of the problematic character of the "rule of laws" to a stranger: Plato's Socrates is as silent about this grave, not to say awe-inspiring, subject as is Xenophon's Socrates.[57] Simonides fulfills in the *Corpus Xenophonteum* a function comparable to that fulfilled in the *Corpus Platonicum* by the stranger from Elea.

□ □ □

V

THE TWO WAYS OF LIFE

THE PRIMARY SUBJECT of the conversation described in the *Hiero* is not the improvement of tyrannical government, but the difference between tyrannical and private life with regard to human enjoyments and pains. The question concerning that difference is identical, in the context, with the question as to whether tyrannical life is more choiceworthy than private life or *vice versa*. Insofar as "tyrant" is eventually replaced by "ruler," and the life of the ruler is the political life in the strict sense,[1] the question discussed in the *Hiero* concerns the relative desirability of the life of the ruler, or of political life, on the one hand, and of private life on the other. But however the question discussed in the dialogue may be formulated, it is in any case only a special form of the fundamental Socratic question of how man ought to live, or of what way of life is the most choiceworthy.[2]

In the *Hiero,* the difference between the tyrannical and the private life is discussed in a conversation between a tyrant and a private man. This means that the same subject is presented in two different manners. It is presented most obviously by the explicit and thematic statements of the two characters. Yet none of the two characters can be presumed to have stated exactly what Xenophon thought about the subject. In addition, the two characters cannot be presumed to have stated exactly what they themselves thought about it: Hiero is afraid of Simonides, and Simonides is guided by a pedagogic intention. Xenophon presents his view more directly, although less obviously, by the action of the dialogue, by what the characters silently do and unintentionally or occasionally reveal, or by the actual contrast as conceived by him between the tyrant Hiero and the private man Simonides. Insofar as Hiero reveals himself as a citizen in the most radical sense and Simonides proves to be a stranger in the most radical sense, the dialogue presents the contrast between the citizen and the stranger. At any rate, Simonides is not a "private man" simply,[3] and he is not an ordinary representative of private life. However silent he may be about his own way of life, he reveals himself by his being or by deed as a wise man. If one considers the conversational setting, the dialogue reveals itself as an attempt to contrast the tyrannical life, or the life of the ruler, not simply with private life but with the life of the wise man.[4] Or, more specifically, it is an attempt to contrast an educated tyrant, a tyrant who admires, or wishes to admire, the wise, with a wise man who stoops to converse with tyrants.[5] Ultimately, the dialogue serves the purpose of contrasting *the* two ways of life: the political life and the life devoted to wisdom.[6]

One might object that according to Xenophon there is no contrast between the wise man and the ruler: the ruler in the strict sense is he who knows how to rule, who possesses the most noble kind of knowledge, who is able to teach what is best; and such knowledge is identical with wisdom.[7] Even if this objection were not exposed to any doubts, there would still remain the difference between the wise man or ruler who wishes to rule or does actually rule, and the wise man or ruler (e.g., Socrates and the poet Simonides) who does not wish to rule and does not engage in politics, but leads a life of privacy and leisure.[8]

The ambiguity that characterizes the *Hiero* is illustrated by nothing more strikingly than by the fact that the primary question discussed in the work does not receive a final and explicit answer. To discover the final answer that is implicitly given, we have to start from the explicit, if provisional, answers. In discussing both the explicit or provisional and the implicit or final answers, we have to distinguish between the answers of the two characters; for we have no right to assume that Hiero and Simonides are in agreement.

Hiero's explicit answer is to the effect that private life is absolutely preferable to tyrannical life.[9] But he cannot deny Simonides' contention that tyrants have greater power than private men to do things by means of which men gain love, and he spontaneously praises being loved more highly than anything else. It is true, he retorts that tyrants are also more likely to incur hatred than private men; but Simonides succeeds in silencing this objection by implicitly distinguishing between the good or prudent and the bad or foolish tyrant. In his last utterance, Hiero grants that a ruler or tyrant may gain the affection of his subjects.[10] If one accepts Hiero's premise that love, i.e., being loved, is the most choiceworthy thing, one is led by Simonides' argument to the conclusion that the life of a beneficent tyrant is preferable in the most important respect to private life. As the conclusion follows from Hiero's premise and is eventually not contested by him, we may regard it as his final answer.

Since Hiero is less wise, or competent, than Simonides, his answer is much less important than the poet's. Simonides asserts first that tyrannical life is superior to private life in every respect. He is soon compelled, or able, to admit that tyrannical life is not superior to private life in every respect. But he seems to maintain that tyrannical life is superior to private life in the most important respect: he praises nothing so highly as honor, and he asserts that tyrants are honored above other men.[11] With a view to his subsequent distinction between the good and the bad tyrant, we may state his final thesis as follows: the life of the beneficent tyrant is superior to private life in the most important respect. Simonides and Hiero seem to reach the same conclusion by starting from different premises.

On closer examination, it appears, however, that Simonides' praise of the tyrannical life is ambiguous. In order to lay hold of his view, we have to distinguish in the first place between what he explicitly says and what Hiero believes him to say.[12] Secondly, we have to distinguish between what Simonides says in the first part of the *Hiero* in which he hides his wisdom, and what he says in the second part to which he contributes so much more than to the first part, and in which he speaks no longer as a somewhat diffident pupil but with the confidence of a teacher. We have to attach particular weight to the fact that Simonides' most emphatic statement regarding the superiority of tyrannical life occurs in the first section in which he hides his wisdom to a higher degree than in any subsequent section.[13]

Simonides states to begin with that tyrants experience many more pleasures of all kinds and many fewer pains of all kinds than private men. He grants soon afterward that in a number of minor respects, if not in all minor respects, private life is preferable to tyrannical life. The question arises whether he thus simply retracts or merely qualifies the general statement made at the beginning: Does he believe that tyrannical life is superior to private life in the most important respect? He never answers this question explicitly. When comparing tyrannical and private life with regard to things more important than bodily pleasures, he uses much more reserved language than he did in his initial and general assertion. In particular, when speaking about honor, he says, after having enumerated the various ways in which people honor tyrants: "for these are of course the kinds of things that subjects do for the tyrants and to *anyone else* whom they happen to honor at the moment." By this he seems to say that the most outstanding honor is not a preserve of tyrants. On the other hand, he says almost immediately thereafter that "you (*sc.* the tyrants) are honored above (all) other men." What he says in the first part of the dialogue might well appear to be ambiguous or inconclusive to the detached reader of the *Hiero* as distinguished from the rather disturbed interlocutor Hiero.[14] In the second part he nowhere explicitly says that tyrannical life is superior to private life in regard to the greatest pleasure. He does assert that the life of tyrants is superior to private life in regard to love. But he never says anywhere in the dialogue that love, or friendship, is the most pleasant thing.[15]

To arrive at a more exact formulation of the difficulty, we start again from the crucial fact that Simonides praises nothing as highly as honor. His contribution to the first part culminates in the assertion that the characteristic difference between the species "real man" (ἀνήρ) and the other kinds of living beings, ordinary human beings of course included, consists in the desire for honor which is characteristic of the former, and in the suggestion that the most outstanding honors are reserved for rulers, if not for tyrants in particular. It is true, he declares in the same context that no human pleasure seems to be superior to the pleasure deriving from honor, and he thus seems to grant that other human pleasures might equal

it.[16] On the other hand, he nowhere explicitly excludes the possibility
that pleasure is not the sole or ultimate criterion. We have already
observed that in the second part of the dialogue the emphasis tacitly
shifts from the pleasant to the good and the noble.[17] This change
reaches its climax in Simonides' final statement (11.7–15). At its
beginning he indicates clearly that the noblest and grandest contest
among human beings, and hence the victory in it, is reserved for
rulers: victory in that contest consists in rendering very happy the
city of which one is the chief. He thus leads one to expect that no
human being other than a ruler can reach the summit of happiness:
can anything rival victory in the noblest and grandest contest?
This question is answered in the concluding sentence, according to
which Hiero, by becoming the benefactor of his city, would be
possessed of the most noble and the most blessed possession to be
met with among human beings: he would be happy without being
envied. Simonides does not say that the most noble and most blessed
possession accessible to human beings is victory in the most noble
and most grand contest among them. He does not even say that one
cannot become happy without being envied but by making the city
which one rules most happy. In the circumstances he had the
strongest reasons for praising the beneficent ruler as emphatically,
as explicitly as possible. By refraining from explicitly identifying
"making one's city most happy" with "the most noble and most
blessed possession," he seems to suggest that there are possibilities
of bliss outside of, or beyond, the political life. The very phrasing
of the last sentence seems to suggest it. The farmers and artisans who
do their work well, are content with their lot and enjoy the simple
pleasures of life, are at least as likely to be happy without being
envied as rich and powerful rulers however beneficent.[18] What is
true of the common people is equally true of other types of men,
and in particular of that type which seems to be most important in
the conversational situation: those who come to display before the
tyrant the wise or beautiful or good things which they possess, who
share in the amenities of court life and are rewarded with royal
munificence.[19] The highest goal which the greatest ruler could reach
only after having made the most extraordinary exertions, seems to
be within easy reach of every private man.

This interpretation is open to a very strong objection. We shall
not insist on the facts that "being happy" in Simonides' final sentence

("while being happy, you will not be envied") might very well mean "being powerful and wealthy" [20] and that tyrants are superior to private men in regard to power and wealth as not even Hiero can deny. For Simonides might have understood by happiness continuous joy or contentment.[21] Suffice it to say that precisely on account of the essential ambiguity of "being happy" the purport of Simonides' final sentence depends decisively on its second part, viz., the expression "you will not be envied." What this expression means for the decision of the crucial issue becomes clear if we remind ourselves of the following facts: that the purpose of the *Hiero* is to contrast the ruler, not simply with private men in general, but with the wise; that *the* representative of wisdom is Socrates; and that Socrates was exposed, and fell victim, to the envy of his fellow citizens. If the beneficent ruler can be "happy" without being envied, whereas even Socrates' "happiness" was accompanied by envy,[22] the political life, the life of the ruler or of the tyrant, would seem to be unambiguously superior to the life of the wise man. It would seem then that Simonides' praise of tyranny, in spite of his ironical overstatements and his pedagogic intention, is at bottom serious. True happiness—this seems to be Xenophon's thought—is possible only on the basis of excellence or superiority, and there are ultimately only two kinds of excellence—the excellence of the ruler and that of the wise man. All superior men are exposed to envy on account of their excellence. But the ruler, as distinguished from the wise man, is able to do penance for his superiority by becoming the servant of all his subjects: the hardworking and beneficent ruler, and not the retiring wise man, can put envy at rest.[23]

This must be taken with a grain of salt. It goes without saying that the prospect by means of which Simonides attempts to educate Hiero is incapable of fulfillment. Xenophon knew too well that if there are any forms of superiority which do not expose their possessors to envy, political power, however beneficent, would not be one of them. Or, to put it somewhat differently, if it is true that he who wants to receive kindness must first show kindness, it is not certain that his kindness will not be requited with ingratitude.[24] The thought that a superior man who does not successfully hide his superiority would not be exposed to envy is clearly a delusion. It forms the fitting climax of the illusory image of the tyrant who is happy because he is virtuous. Its aptness consists precisely in this: that it makes intelligible the whole illusory image as the momentary illusion of a wise man, i.e., as something more than a noble lie invented for the benefit of an unwise pupil. Being wise, he is most happy and exposed to envy. His bliss would seem to be complete if he could escape envy. If it were true that only experience could fully reveal the character of tyrannical life—it is this assumption on which the explicit argument of the *Hiero* is largely based—the wise man could not be absolutely certain whether the beneficent tyrant would not be beyond the reach of envy. He could indulge the hope that by becoming a beneficent tyrant, i.e., by actually exercising that tyrannical or royal art which flows from wisdom (if it is not identical with wisdom), he would escape envy while retaining his superiority. Simonides' climactic assertion that by acting on his advice Hiero would become happy without being envied intimates the only reason why a wise man could be imagined for a moment to wish to be a ruler or to envy the man who rules well. It thus reveals the truth underlying Hiero's fear of the wise: that fear proves to be based on a misunderstanding of a momentary velleity of the wise. It reveals at the same time the constant preoccupation of Hiero himself: his misunderstanding is the natural outcome of the fact that he himself is greatly tormented by other people's envy of his happiness. It reveals finally the reason why Simonides could not possibly be envious of Hiero. For the irony of Simonides' last sentence consists, above all, in this: that, if *per impossibile* the perfect ruler would escape from envy, his very escape from envy would expose him to envy; by ceasing to be envied by the multitude, he would begin to be envied by the wise. He would be envied for not being envied. Simonides could become dangerous to Hiero only if Hiero followed his advice. Hiero's final silence is a fitting answer to all the implications of Simonides' final statement.

At any rate, the wise are not envious, and the fact that they are envied does not impair their happiness or bliss.[25] Even if they would grant that the life of the ruler is in a certain respect superior to the life of the wise man, they would wonder whether the price which has to be paid for that superiority is worthwhile. The ruler cannot escape envy but by leading a life of perpetual business, care and trouble.[26] The ruler whose specific function is "doing" or "well-doing" has to serve all his subjects, Socrates, on the other hand, whose specific function is "speaking" or discussing, does not engage in discussion except with those with whom he likes to converse. The wise man alone is free.[27]

To sum up, Simonides' final statement does not imply the view that political life is preferable to private life. This conclusion is confirmed by the carefully chosen expression which he uses for describing the character of happiness unmarred by envy. He calls it "the most noble and most blessed possession to be met with among human beings." He does not call it the greatest good. The most noble and most blessed possession for human beings is choiceworthy, but there are other things which are equally or more choiceworthy. It may even be doubted whether it is simply the most choiceworthy "possession." Euthydemus, answering a question of Socrates, says that freedom is a most noble and most magnificent possession for real men and for cities. The older Cyrus says in a speech addressed to the Persian nobility that the most noble and most "political" possession consists in deriving the greatest pleasure from praise. Xenophon himself says to Seuthes that for a real man and in particular for a ruler, no possession is more noble or more splendid than virtue and justice and gentility. Antisthenes calls leisure the most delicate or luxurious possession.[28] Socrates, on the other hand, says that a good friend is the best, or the most all-productive, possession and that no possession is more pleasant for a free human being than agriculture.[29] Xenophon's Simonides agrees with Xenophon's Socrates and in fact with Xenophon himself by failing to describe "happiness unmarred by envy" as the most pleasant possession for human beings or as the most noble possession for real men or simply as the best possession.[30] We need not discuss here how Xenophon conceived of the exact relation between "possession" and "good." It is safe to assume that he used "possession" mostly in its less strict sense according to which a possession is a good only conditionally, i.e., only if the possessor knows how to use it or to use it well.[31] If this is the case, even the possession which is simply best would not be identical with the greatest good. While people in general are apt to identify the best possession with the greatest good, Socrates makes a clear distinction between the two things. According to him, the greatest good is wisdom, whereas education is the greatest good for human beings,[32] and the best possession is a good friend. Education cannot be the greatest good simply, because gods do not need education. Education, i.e., the most excellent education, which is education to wisdom, is the greatest good for human beings, i.e., for human beings as such, for men in so far as they do not transcend humanity by approaching divinity: God alone is simply wise.[33] The wise man or the philosopher who partakes of the highest good will be blessed although he does not possess "the most noble and most blessed possession to be met with among human beings."

The *Hiero* is silent about the status of wisdom. Although most explicit about various kinds of pleasure. it is silent about the specific pleasures of the wise, such as, for example, friendly discussion.[34] It is silent about the way of life of the wise. This silence cannot be explained by the fact that the thematic subject of the dialogue is the comparison of the life of the ruler, not with the life of the wise man, but with private life in general. For the thematic subject of the parallel dialogue, the *Oeconomicus*, is the economist, or the management of the household, and yet its central chapter contains a most striking confrontation of the life of the economist (who is a ruler) with the Socratic way of life. The *Hiero* is reserved about the nature of wisdom because the purpose of the dialogue, or of Simonides, requires that "wisdom" be kept in its ordinary ambiguity. If we consider, however, how profoundly Socrates or Xenophon agree with Simonides regarding tyranny, we may be inclined to impute to Xenophon's Simonides the Socratic view that is nowhere contradicted by Xenophon, according to which wisdom is the highest good. Certainly, what Simonides says in his final statement in praise of the life of the ruler accords perfectly with the Socratic view.

In the *Hiero*, Xenophon indicates his view of wisdom by incidental remarks entrusted to Simonides and by the action of the dialogue. Simonides mentions two ways of "taking care" of things which lead to gratification: teaching the things that are best (or teaching what things are best), on the one hand; and praising and honoring him who executes what is best in the finest manner, on the other. When applying this general remark to rulers in particular, he does not mention teaching at all; he silently limits the ruler's way of taking care which leads to gratification, to praising and honoring, or more specifically to the offering and distributing of prizes. The specific function of the ruler appears to be strictly subordinate to that of the wise man. In the best case imaginable, the ruler would be the one who, by means of honoring, to say nothing of punishing, would put into practice the teaching or the prescriptions of the wise man.[35] The wise man is the ruler of rulers. Similarly, the ruler is supposed merely to encourage the discovery of, or the looking out for, "something good"; he is not supposed to engage in these intellectual activities himself.[36] It deserves mention that the passage in which Simonides adumbrates his view of the relation of wisdom and rule is one of the two chapters in which the very term tyrant is avoided: Simonides describes by the remarks in question not merely the tyrant, but the ruler in general.[37]

The superiority of the wise man to the ruler is brought to light by the action of the dialogue. The tyrannical life, or the life of the ruler, is chosen by Hiero not only prior to the conversation, but again within the conversation itself: he rejects Simonides' veiled suggestion to return to private life. And Hiero proves to be less wise than Simonides, who rejects the political life in favor of the wise man's private life.[38] At the beginning of the conversation, Simonides suggests that not he, but Hiero, has a better knowledge of the two ways of life or their difference. This suggestion does not lack a certain plausibility as long as one understands by the two ways of life the tyrannical life and private life in general; it proves to be simply ironical if it is considered in the light of the setting, i.e., if it is applied to the difference between the life of the ruler and the life of the wise man. For Hiero proves to be ignorant of the life of the wise man and its goal, whereas Simonides knows, not only his own way of life, but the political life as well, as is shown by his ability to teach the art of ruling well. Only Simonides, and not Hiero, is competent to make a choice between the two ways of life.[39] At the beginning, Simonides bows to Hiero's leadership; he even permits Hiero to defeat him. But in the moment of his victory Hiero becomes aware of the fact that far from really defeating Simonides, he has merely prepared his own downfall. The wise man sits leisurely upon the very goal toward which the ruler is blindly and furiously working his way and which he will never reach. At the end, Simonides' leadership is firmly established: the wise man defeats the ruler. This most obvious aspect of the action is a peculiarity of the *Hiero*. In most of Xenophon's dialogues, no change of leadership takes place: Socrates is the leader from the beginning to the end. In Xenophon's Socratic dialogue *par excellence*, the *Oeconomicus*, a change of leadership does occur; but it is a change from the leadership of the wise man (Socrates) to the leadership of the ruler (the economist Ischomachus). Whereas in the *Oeconomicus* the wise man surrenders to the ruler, in the *Hiero* the ruler surrenders to the wise man. The *Hiero*, and not the *Oeconomicus*, reveals by its action the true relation of rule and wisdom. In addition, the *Hiero* is that work of Xenophon which draws our attention most forcefully to the problem of that relation. It can be said to do this for several reasons. In the first place, because its primary subject is the difference between private life and the life of a certain type of ruler. In the second place, because it does contrast a wise man and a ruler more explicitly than any other Xenophontic writing. And finally, the *Hiero*'s most obvious practical aim (the improvement of tyranny) is hardly capable of fulfillment, which precludes the possibility that the obvious practical aim of the work coincides with its final purpose. Here again we may note a profound agreement between Xenophon and Plato. The precise relation between the philosopher and the political man (i.e., their fundamental difference) is the thematic premise, not of the *Republic* and the *Gorgias* in which Socrates as citizen-philosopher is the leading character, but of the *Politicus* in which a stranger occupies the central position.

From what has been said it may be inferred that Simonides' emphatic praise of honor cannot possibly mean that he preferred honor as such to all other things. After all, his statement on honor belongs to that part of the dialogue in which he hides his wisdom almost completely. Besides, its bearing is sufficiently qualified by the sentences with which it opens and ends.[40] One might even think to begin with that his praise of honor can be explained completely by his pedagogic intention. His intention is to show Hiero, who reveals a remarkable indifference to virtue, a way to virtuous rule by appealing, not to virtue or the noble, but to the pleasant; and the pleasure deriving from honor seems to be the natural substitute for the pleasure deriving from virtue. Yet Simonides appeals in his teaching primarily not to Hiero's desire for honor, but to his desire for love. It could not be otherwise since Hiero had bestowed spontaneously the highest praise not on honor, but on love. We may take it then that by extolling honor Simonides reveals his own preferences rather than those of his pupil[41]: Simonides, and not Hiero, prefers the pleasure deriving from honor to the other pleasures explicitly mentioned by him. We may even say that of all desires which are natural, i.e., which "grow" in human beings independently of any education or teaching,[42] he considered the desire for honor the highest because it is the foundation of the desire for any excellence, be it the excellence of the ruler or that of the wise man.[43]

Whereas Simonides is concerned with honor, he is not concerned with love. Hiero has to demonstrate to him not only that as regards love tyrants are worse off than private men, but even that love is a great good and that private men are particularly loved by their children, parents, brothers, wives, and companions. In discussing love, Hiero feels utterly unable to appeal to the poet's experience or previous knowledge as he did when discussing the pleasures of the table and even of sex. He urges him to acquire the rudiments of knowledge regarding love immediately or in the future without being in any way certain that Simonides would wish to acquire them.[44]

Just as desire for honor is characteristic of Simonides, desire for love is characteristic of Hiero.[45] In so far as Hiero represents the ruler and Simonides represents the wise man, the difference between love and honor as interpreted in the *Hiero* will throw some light on Xenophon's view of the difference between the ruler and the wise man. What Xenophon has primarily in mind is not simply the difference between love and honor in general: Hiero desires to be loved by "human beings," i.e., not merely by real men, but by everyone regardless of his qualities, and Simonides is concerned with admiration or praise, not by everybody, but by "those who are free in the highest degree."[46] The desire which Xenophon or his Simonides ascribes to Hiero, or the ruler, is fundamentally the same as the erotic desire for the common people which Plato's Socrates ascribes to Callicles.[47] Only because the ruler has the desire to be loved by "human beings" as such is he able to become the willing servant and benefactor of all his subjects and hence to become a good ruler. The wise man, on the other hand, has no such desire; he is satisfied with the admiration, the praise, the approval of a small minority.[48] It would seem, then, that the characteristic difference between the ruler and the wise man manifests itself in the objects of their passionate interest and not in the character of their passion itself.[49] Yet it is no accident that Simonides is primarily concerned with being praised by the competent minority, and not with being loved by them, whereas Hiero is primarily concerned with being loved by human beings in the mass, and not with being admired by them. The characteristic difference between the ruler and the wise man may therefore be presumed to manifest itself somehow in the difference between love and admiration.

The meaning of this difference is indicated by Simonides in his praise of the beneficent ruler. The beneficent ruler will be loved by

his subjects, he will be passionately desired by human beings, he will
have earned the affectionate regard of many cities, whereas he will
be praised by all human beings and will be admirable in the eyes of
all. Everyone present, but not everyone absent, will be his ally, just
as not everyone will be afraid that something might happen to him
and not everyone will desire to serve him. Precisely by making his
city happy, he will antagonize and hurt her enemies who cannot be
expected to love him and to extol his victory. But even the enemies
will have to admit that he is a great man: they will admire him and
praise his virtue.[50] The beneficent ruler will be praised and admired
by all men, whereas he will not be loved by all men: the range of
love is more limited than that of admiration or praise. Each man
loves what is somehow his own, his private possession; admiration
or praise is concerned with the excellent regardless of whether it is
one's own or not. Love as distinguished from admiration requires
proximity. The range of love is limited not only in regard to space,
but likewise—although Xenophon's Simonides in his delicacy refrains
from even alluding to it—in regard to time. A man may be admired
many generations after his death whereas he will cease to be loved
once those who knew him well are dead.[51] Desire for "inextinguish-
able fame,"[52] as distinguished from desire for love, enables a man to
liberate himself from the shackles of the Here and Now. The beneficent ruler is praised and admired by all men, whereas he is loved
mainly by his subjects: the limits of love coincide normally with the
borders of the political community, whereas admiration of human
excellence knows no boundaries.[53] The beneficent ruler is loved by
those whom he benefits or serves on account of his benefits or
services,[54] whereas he is admired even by those to whom he has done
the greatest harm and certainly by many whom he did not serve or
benefit at all: admiration seems to be less mercenary than love. Those
who admire the beneficent ruler while loving him do not necessarily
make a distinction between their benefactor and the man of excellence; but those who admire him without loving him—e.g., the
enemy cities—rise above the vulgar error of mistaking one's benefactor for the man of excellence.[55] Admiration is as much superior to
love as the man of excellence is to one's benefactor as such. To
express this somewhat differently, love has no criterion of its rele-
vance outside itself, but admiration has. If admiration does not presuppose services rendered by the admired to the admirer, one is led
to wonder whether it presupposes any services, or any prospect of

services, by the admired at all. This question is answered explicitly in the affirmative by Hiero, and tacitly in the negative by Simonides.[56] Hiero is right as regards the ruler: the ruler does not gain the admiration of all men but by rendering services to his subjects. Simonides is right as regards the wise man: the wise man is admired, not on account of any services which he renders to others, but simply because he is what he is. The wise man need not be a benefactor at all in order to be admired as a man of excellence.[57] More precisely: the specific function of the ruler is to be beneficent; he is essentially a benefactor; the specific function of the wise man is to understand; he is a benefactor only accidentally. The wise man is as self-sufficient as is humanly possible; the admiration which he gains is essentially a tribute to his perfection, and not a reward for any services.[58] The desire for praise and admiration as distinguished and divorced from the desire for love is the natural foundation for the predominance of the desire for one's own perfection.[59] This is what Xenophon subtly indicates by presenting Simonides as chiefly interested in the pleasures of eating, whereas Hiero appears to be chiefly interested in the pleasures of sex: for the enjoyment of food, as distinguished from sexual enjoyments, one does not need other human beings.[60]

The specific function of the wise man is not bound up with an individual political community: the wise man may live as a stranger. The specific function of the ruler on the other hand consists in rendering happy the individual political community of which he is the chief. The city is essentially the potential enemy of other cities. Hence one cannot define the function of the ruler without thinking of war, enemies, and allies: the city and her ruler need allies, whereas the wise man does not.[61] To the specific functions correspond specific natural inclinations. The born ruler, as distinguished from him who is born to become wise, must have strong warlike inclinations. Hiero mentions the opinion according to which peace is a great good and war a great evil. He does not simply adopt it, however, for he feels too keenly that war affords great pleasures. When enumerating the very great pleasures which private citizens enjoy in war, he assigns the central place to the pleasure which they derive from killing their enemies. He notes with regret that the tyrant cannot have this great pleasure or at least cannot openly show it and boast of the deed. Simonides does not reveal any delight in war or killing. The most he says in favor of war is that Hiero had greatly exaggerated the detrimental effect on appetite and sleep of that fear which fills men's minds before a battle.[62] Not victory in war as such, but the happiness of one's city, is described by him as the goal of the noblest and grandest contest.[63] Hiero's statement about peace and war[64] doubtless serves the purpose of drawing our attention to the particularly close connection between tyranny and war.[65] But a comparison of this passage with what Xenophon tells us about the inclinations of the king Cyrus makes it clear that he considered a streak of cruelty an essential element of the great ruler in general.[66] The difference between the tyrant and the nontyrannical ruler is ultimately not a simple opposition, but rather that in the case of the tyrant certain elements of the character of the ruler are more strongly developed or less easily hidden than in the case of the nontyrannical ruler. Nor is it necessarily true that the pleasure which the ruler takes in hurting enemies is surpassed by his desire to be loved by friends. To say nothing of the fact that what Hiero enjoys most in his sexual relations are the quarrels with the beloved one, he apparently prefers "taking from enemies against their will" to all other pleasures.[67] According to him, the tyrant is compelled to free the slaves, but desirous to enslave the free:[68] if he could afford to indulge his desires, everyone would be his slave. Simonides had limited himself to stating that tyrants are most capable of hurting their enemies and helping their friends. When reproducing this statement, Hiero puts a considerably greater weight on "hurting the enemies" than on "helping the friends"; and when discussing it, he implies that Simonides has an interest of his own in helping his friends but none in hurting his enemies: he can easily see Simonides helping his friends; he cannot see him as well hurting his enemies.[69] Since the wise man does not need human beings in the way in which, and to the extent to which, the ruler does, his attitude toward them is free, not passionate, and hence not susceptible of turning into malevolence or hatred. In other words, the wise man alone is capable of justice in the highest sense. When Hiero distinguishes between the wise and the just man, he implies that the just man is the good ruler. Accordingly, he must be presumed to understand by justice political justice, the justice which manifests itself in helping friends and hurting enemies. When Socrates assumes that the wise man is just, he understands by justice transpolitical justice, the justice which is irreconcilable with hurting anyone. The highest form of justice is the preserve of those who have the greatest self-sufficiency which is humanly possible.[70]

◰ ◰ ◰

VI

PLEASURE AND VIRTUE

THE *Hiero* ALMOST leads up to the suggestion that tyranny may be
perfectly just. It starts from the opinion that tyranny is radically
unjust. The tyrant is supposed to reject the just and noble, or virtue,
in favor of the pleasant; or, since virtue is human goodness, he is
supposed to reject the good in favor of the pleasant. This opinion is
based on the general premise that the good and the pleasant are
fundamentally different from each other in such a way that the right
choice has to be guided by considerations of the good, and not by
considerations of the pleasant.[1]

The thesis that tyranny is radically unjust forms the climax of
Hiero's indictment of tyranny. That indictment is exaggerated;
Hiero simply reproduces without full conviction the gentleman's
image of the tyrant.[2] But the very fact that he is capable of using
that image for a selfish purpose proves that his thesis is not altogether
wrong. Xenophon has taken some pains to make it clear that while
Hiero is not as unjust as he declares the tyrant to be, he is remark-
ably indifferent to virtue. He does not think of mentioning virtue
among the greatest goods or the most choice-worthy possessions. At
best, he considers virtuous men, i.e., the virtue of others, to be useful.
But even the virtue of others is not regarded by him as an object of
delight: he does not seek, and never sought, his companions among
the virtuous men. Not he, but Simonides, points out the insignifi-
cance of bodily pleasures.[3] Only after having been driven into a
corner by Simonides does he praise the virtue of the benefactor of

human beings with a view to the fact that such virtue is productive of the highest honor and of unimpaired happiness.[4]

In attempting to educate a man of this kind, Simonides has no choice but to appeal to his desire for pleasure. In order to advise Hiero to rule as a virtuous tyrant, he has to show him that the tyrant cannot obtain pleasure, and in particular that kind of pleasure with which Hiero is chiefly concerned, viz., the pleasure deriving from being loved, but by being as virtuous as possible. What he shows Hiero is a way not so much to virtue as to pleasure. Strictly speaking, he does not advise him to become virtuous. He advises him to do the gratifying things himself while entrusting to others the things for which men incur hatred; to encourage certain virtues and pursuits among his subjects by offering prizes; to keep his bodyguard, yet to use it for the benefit of his subjects; and, generally speaking, to be as beneficent to his fellow citizens as possible. Now, the benefactor of his fellow citizens is not necessarily a man of excellence or a virtuous man. Simonides does not advise Hiero to practise any of the things which distinguish the virtuous man from the mere benefactor.

A comparison of the *Hiero* with Isocrates' work on the tyrannical art (*To Nicocles*) makes perfectly clear how amazingly little of moral admonition proper there is in the *Hiero*. Simonides speaks only once of the virtue of the tyrant, and he never mentions any of the special virtues (moderation, courage, justice, wisdom, and so on) when speaking of the tyrant. Isocrates, on the other hand, does not tire of admonishing Nicocles to cultivate his mind, to practise virtue, wisdom, piety, truthfulness, meekness, self-control, moderation, urbanity, and dignity; he advises him to love peace and to prefer a noble death to a base life, as well as to take care of just legislation and adjudication; he calls a good counsellor the most useful and most "tyrannical" possession.[5]

If Simonides can be said to recommend virtue at all, he recommends it, not as an end, but as a means. He recommends just and noble actions to the tyrant as means to pleasure. In order to do this, Simonides, or Xenophon, had to have at his disposal a hedonistic justification of virtue. Moreover, Simonides prepares his teaching by starting a discussion of whether tyrannical life is superior to private life from the point of view of pleasure. In discussing this subject, Hiero and Simonides are compelled to examine a number of valuable

things from the point of view of pleasure. The *Hiero* could only
have been written by a man who had at his disposal a comprehensive
hedonistic interpretation of human life.

Expression of essential parts of that hedonistic interpretation has
been entrusted to Simonides who in one of his poems had said: "For
what life of mortals, or what tyranny, is desirable without pleasure.
Without her not even the lasting life of gods is to be envied."[6] It is
difficult to say how Simonides conceived of the relation between
pleasure and virtue except that he cannot have considered desirable
a virtuous life which is devoid of pleasure. From the verses which he
addressed to Scopas, it appears that he considered virtue essentially
dependent on a man's fate: no one is protected against coming into
situations in which he is compelled to do base things.[7] He gave the
advice to be playful throughout, and not to be entirely serious about
anything. Play is pleasant, and virtue, or gentlemanliness, is the
serious thing *par excellence*.[8] If a sophist is a man who uses his
wisdom for the sake of gain and who employs arts of deception,
Simonides was a sophist.[9] The way in which he is presented in the
Hiero does not contradict what we are told about the historical
Simonides. Xenophon's Simonides is an "economist"; he rejects the
gentleman's view of what is most desirable in favor of the view of
the "real man"; he would be capable of going to any length in "contriving something"; and he is free from the responsibility of the
citizen.[10] While he speaks of the noblest and grandest contest and
of the noblest and most blessed possession, he does not speak of the
noblest and grandest, or most splendid possession ("virtue and
justice and gentility"): he reserves his highest praise, not for virtue,
but for happiness unmarred by envy, and, above all, for honor.[11] The
amazingly amoral nature of the tyrannical teaching embodied in the
second part of the *Hiero* as well as the hedonistic consideration of
human things that is given in the first part accord perfectly with
Simonides' character.

Xenophon's Simonides not only has a definite leaning toward
hedonism; he even has at his disposal a philosophic justification for
his views about the importance of pleasure. What he says in his
initial statement about the various kinds of pleasure and pain reveals
a definite theoretical interest in the subject. He divides all pleasures
into three classes: pleasures of the body, pleasures of the soul, and
pleasures common to body and soul. He subdivides the pleasures of

the body into those related to a special organ (eyes, ears, nose, sexual organs) and those related to the whole body. His failure to subdivide the pleasures of the soul may not be due merely to his wish to stress the pleasures of the body in order to present himself as a lover of those pleasures; it may have to be traced also to the theoretical reasons that there are no parts of the soul in the sense in which there are parts of the body and that the pleasures common to men and brutes are more fundamental and therefore, from a certain theoretical point of view, more important than those characteristic of human beings.[12] He makes it clear that all pleasures and pains presuppose some kind of knowledge, an act of distinction or judgment, a perception of the senses or of thought.[13] He distinguishes the knowledge presupposed by every pleasure and pain from the knowledge or perception of our pleasure or pain. He does not consider it unimportant to indicate that whereas we feel our own pleasures and pains, we merely observe those of others. He possibly alludes to a distinction between the δι' οὗ and the ᾧ with regard to pleasures and perceptions.[14] When mentioning the pleasure deriving from sleep, he does not limit himself to pointing out that sleep is unambiguously pleasant; he raises in addition the theoretical question of how and by what and when we enjoy sleep; since he feels that he cannot answer this question, he explains why it is so particularly difficult to answer it.

If we understand by hedonism the thesis that the pleasant is identical with the good, Xenophon's Simonides is not a hedonist. Before he ever mentions the pleasant, he mentions the good: he mentions at the very outset "better" knowledge, by which, of course, he does not mean "more pleasant" knowledge.[15] In his enumeration of the various kinds of pleasure he makes it clear that he considers the pleasant and the good fundamentally different from each other: the good and the bad things are sometimes pleasant and sometimes painful. He does not explicitly say how he conceives of the precise relation between the pleasant and the good.[16] To establish his view on the subject, we have to pay proper attention to the nonhedonistic principle of preference which he recognizes when he speaks with emphasis of "(ordinary) human beings" and of "(real) men." First, regarding "human beings," he seems to make a distinction between such pleasures as are in accordance with human nature and such pleasures as are against human nature:[17] the preferable or good pleasures are those which agree with human nature. Simonides' nonhedonistic principle of preference would then be "what agrees with human nature." Now, ordinary human beings may enjoy as much pleasure as real men; yet real men are to be esteemed more highly than ordinary human beings.[18] Hence, we may define Simonides' nonhedonistic principle of preference more precisely by identifying it with "what agrees with the nature of real men." Seeing that he praises nothing as highly as honor, and honor is most pleasant to real men as distinguished from ordinary human beings, we may say that the ultimate and complete principle of preference to which Simonides refers in the *Hiero* is the pleasure which agrees with the nature of real men. What he praises most highly is pleasant indeed, but pleasure alone does not define it sufficiently; it is pleasant on a certain level, and that level is determined, not by pleasure, but by the hierarchy of beings.[19] He is then a hedonist only in so far as he rejects the view that considerations of pleasure are irrelevant for right choice: the right goal towards which one has to aim, or with reference to which one has to judge, must be something which is intrinsically pleasant. This view seems to have been held by the historical Simonides as is shown by his verses on pleasure quoted above. We may ascribe the same view to Xenophon's Hiero, who admits the distinction between the good and the pleasant and who characterizes friendship, than which he praises nothing more highly, as both very good and very pleasant.[20]

This qualified hedonism guides Simonides and Hiero in their examination of a number of valuable things. That examination leads to the conclusion suggested by Hiero that friendship has a higher value than city or fatherland or patriotism.[21] Friendship, i.e., being loved and cared for by the small number of human beings whom one knows intimately (one's nearest relatives and companions) is not only "a very great good"; it is also "very pleasant." It is a very great good because it is intrinsically pleasant. Trust, i.e., one's trusting others, is "a great good." It is not a very great good, because it is not so much intrinsically pleasant as the *conditio sine qua non* of intrinsically pleasant relations. A man whom one trusts is not yet a friend: a servant or a bodyguard must be trustworthy, but there is no reason why they ought to be one's friends. While trust is not intrinsically pleasant, it stands in a fairly close relation to pleasure: when discussing trust, Hiero mentions pleasure three times. On the other hand, in the passage immediately following in which he dis-

cusses "fatherlands," he does not mention pleasure at all.[22] Not only
are "fatherlands" not intrinsically pleasant; they do not even stand in
a close relation to pleasure. "Fatherlands are worth very much"
because the citizens afford each other protection without pay against
violent death and thus enable each citizen to live in safety. That for
which the fatherland is "worth very much" is life in safety; safety,
or freedom from fear, the spoiler of all pleasures, is the *conditio sine
qua non* of every pleasure however insignificant; but to live in safety
and to live pleasantly are clearly two different things. More precisely,
the fatherland is not, as is trust, the specific condition of the great
pleasures deriving from friendship: "strangers," men like Simonides,
may enjoy friendship.[23] Friendship and trust are good for human
beings as such, but the cities are good primarily, not to say exclusively, for the citizens and the rulers; they are certainly less good for
strangers, and still less for slaves.[24] The fatherland, or the city, is
good for the citizens because it liberates them from fear. This does
not mean that it abolishes fear; it rather replaces one kind of fear
(the fear of enemies, evil-doers, and slaves) by another (the fear of
the laws or of the law-enforcing authorities).[25] The city, as distinguished from friendship and trust, is not possible without compulsion; and compulsion, constraint, or necessity (ἀνάγκη) is essentially
unpleasant.[26] Friendship, i.e., being loved, is pleasant, while being
patriotic is necessary.[27] While friendship, as praised by Hiero, is not
only pleasant but also good, its goodness is not moral goodness or
nobility: Hiero praises him who has friends regardless of whether
the friends are morally good or not.[28] In so far as friendship is being
loved, preferring friendship to fatherland is tantamount to preferring
oneself to others: when speaking about friendship, Hiero is silent
about the mutuality to which he explicitly refers when discussing
trust and fatherland. It is tantamount to preferring one's pleasure to
one's duties to others.

The thesis that friendship is a greater good than the fatherland is
suggested by Hiero who has a strong motive for asserting that
private life is superior to the life of the ruler which is the political
life *par excellence*. But that thesis is more than a weapon convenient
for Hiero's purpose. Simonides, who could have been induced by
his pedagogic intention rather to prefer fatherland to friendship,
tacitly adopts Hiero's thesis by advising the tyrant to consider his
fatherland as his estate, his fellow citizens as his comrades, his

friends as his children, and his sons as the same thing as his life or soul.[29] He is even less capable than Hiero of assigning to the fatherland the most exalted place among the objects of human attachment. He adopts Hiero's thesis not only "by speech," but "by deed" as well: he lives as a stranger; he chooses to live as a stranger. Contrary to Hiero, he never praises the fatherland or the city. When he urges Hiero to think of the common good, and of the happiness of the city, he emphasizes the fact that this advice is addressed to a tyrant or ruler. Not Simonides, but Hiero, is concerned with being loved by "human beings" in the mass and therefore has to be a lover of the city in order to reach his goal. Simonides desires nothing as much as praise by the small number of competent judges: he can be satisfied with a small group of friends.[30] It is hardly necessary to repeat that his spontaneous praise of honor is concerned exclusively with the benefit of him who is honored or praised and is silent about the benefits to be rendered to others or the duties to others.

The view that a nonpolitical good such as friendship is more valuable than the city was not the view of the citizen as such.[31] It remains to be considered whether it was acceptable to citizen philosophers. Socrates agrees with Hiero as regards the fact that "the fatherlands are worth very much" because they afford safety, or protection against injury, to the citizens.[32] Xenophon seems to indicate by the plan of the *Memorabilia* that Socrates attached a greater importance to the self than to the city.[33] This is in accordance with Xenophon's distinction between the man of excellence and the benefactor of his fellow citizens. Xenophon himself was induced to accompany Cyrus, an old enemy of Athens, on his expedition against his brother by the promise of Proxenus, an old guest-friend of his, that he would make him a friend of Cyrus if he would come. Proxenus, a pupil of Gorgias, of a man who had no fixed domicile in any city,[34] explicitly stated that he himself considered Cyrus worth more to him than his fatherland. Xenophon does not say in so many words that he might conceivably come to consider Cyrus' friendship preferable to his fatherland; but he certainly was not shocked by Proxenus' statement and he certainly acted as if he were capable of sharing Proxenus' sentiment. Socrates had some misgivings regarding Xenophon's becoming a friend of Cyrus and he advised him therefore to consult Apollo about the journey; but Xenophon was so anxious to join

Cyrus or to leave his fatherland that he decided at once to accept
Proxenus' invitation. Even after everything had gone wrong with
Cyrus' expedition, Xenophon was not anxious to return to his
fatherland, although he was not yet exiled. If his comrades had
not passionately protested, he would have founded a city "in some
barbarian place"; not Xenophon, but his opponents, felt that one
ought not to esteem anything more highly than Greece.[35] Later on,
he did not hesitate to accompany Agesilaus on his campaign against
Athens and her allies which culminated in the battle of Coronea.[36]

Lest we be carried away by blind indignation,[37] we shall try
to understand what we might call Xenophon's theoretical and
practical depreciation of the fatherland or the city[38] in the light
of his political teaching in general and of the teaching of the *Hiero*
in particular. If wisdom or virtue is the highest good, the fatherland or the city cannot be the highest good. If virtue is the highest
good, not the fatherland as such, but only the virtuous community
or the best political order can command a good man's undivided
loyalty. If he has to choose between a fatherland which is corrupt
and a foreign city which is well ordered, he may be justified in
preferring that foreign city to his fatherland. Precisely because he
is a good man, he will not be a good citizen in a bad polity.[39] Just
as in choosing horses one looks for the best, and not for those which
are born in the country, the wise general will fill the ranks of his
army not merely with his fellow citizens but with every available
man who can be expected to be virtuous.[40] In the spirit of this
maxim Xenophon himself devoted his most extensive work to an
idealizing description of the achievements of the "barbarian" Cyrus.

The reason why the city as such cannot lay claim to man's
ultimate attachment is implied in Xenophon's "tyrannical" teaching. We have stated that according to that teaching beneficent
tyranny is theoretically superior and practically inferior to rule of
laws and legitimate government. In doing so, we might seem to
have imputed to Xenophon the misologist view that a political
teaching may be "morally and politically false . . . in proportion
as (it is) metaphysically true." But a pupil of Socrates must be
presumed to have believed rather that nothing which is practically
false can be theoretically true.[41] If Xenophon did then not seriously
hold the view that beneficent tyranny is superior to rule of laws
and legitimate government, why did he suggest it at all? The

"tyrannical" teaching, we shall answer, serves the purpose, not of solving the problem of the best political order, but of bringing to light the nature of political things. The "theoretical" thesis which favors beneficent tyranny is indispensable in order to make clear a crucial implication of the practically and hence theoretically true thesis which favors rule of law and legitimate government. The "theoretical" thesis is a most striking expression of the problem, or of the problematic character, of law and legitimacy: legal justice is a justice which is imperfect and more or less blind, and legitimate government is not necessarily "good government" and almost certainly will not be government by the wise. Law and legitimacy are problematic from the highest point of view, namely, from that of wisdom. In so far as the city is the community kept together, nay, constituted, by law, the city cannot so much as aspire to that highest moral and intellectual level attainable by certain individuals. Hence the best city is morally and intellectually on a lower plane than the best individual.[42] The city as such exists on a lower plane than the individual as such. "Individualism" thus understood is at the bottom of Xenophon's "cosmopolitanism."

The emphasis on pleasure which characterizes the argument of the *Hiero* leads to a certain depreciation of virtue. For there is nothing in the dialogue to suggest that Simonides considered virtue intrinsically pleasant. The beneficence or virtue of the good tyrant procures for him the most noble and most blessed possession: it is not itself that possession. Simonides replaces the praise of virtue by a praise of honor. As appears from the context, this does not mean that only virtue can lead to honor. But even if it meant this much, his praise of honor would imply that not virtue, but the reward or result of virtue, is intrinsically pleasant.[43]

Xenophon might seem to have revealed his, or his Socrates', attitude toward hedonism, however understood, in a conversation between Socrates and Aristippus which he has recorded or invented. That conversation is chiefly concerned with the unequivocal connection between love of pleasure and the rejection of the life of a ruler: the pleasure-loving Aristippus goes so far as to prefer explicitly the life of a stranger to political life in any sense. Socrates concludes the conversation by reciting a summary of Prodicus' writing on Hercules in which the pursuit of pleasure is almost identified with vice.[44] This is appropriate only if Aristippus' view is taken to imply a remarkable depreciation of virtue. It is not impossible that the historical Aristippus has served to some extent as a model for Xenophon's Simonides. To say nothing of his hedonistic teaching, he was the first of the Socratics to take pay for his teaching and he could adjust himself to places, times, and men so well that he was particularly popular with the Syracusan tyrant Dionysius.[45]

Be this as it may, the conversation referred to between Socrates and Aristippus tells us very little about Xenophon's attitude toward hedonism. After all, Socrates and Aristippus discuss almost exclusively the pleasures of the body; they barely mention the pleasures deriving from honor or praise. Besides, it would be rash to exclude the possibility that Xenophon's account of that conversation is to a certain extent ironical. That possibility is suggested by the disproportionately ample use which Socrates explicitly makes of an epideictic writing of the sophist Prodicus as an instrument of moral education.[46] Let us not forget the fact that in the only conversation between Socrates and Xenophon which is recorded in the latter's Socratic writings, Xenophon presents himself as a lover of certain sensual pleasures and as being rebuked by Socrates in much more severe terms than Aristippus ever was. This is not surprising, of course, since Xenophon is more explicit than Aristippus in praising the pursuit of sensual pleasure.[47] To point, therefore, to facts which are perhaps less ambiguous, Xenophon no more than his Simonides contends that virtue is the most blessed possession; he indicates that virtue is dependent on external goods and, far from being an end in itself, ought to be in the service of the acquisition of pleasure, wealth, and honors.[48]

At first glance, it is not altogether wrong to ascribe the same view even to Socrates. A distinguished historian did ascribe it, not only to Xenophon's Socrates, but to Plato's as well. "D'une part, son bon sens et sa grande sagesse pratique lui font sentir qu'il doit y avoir un principe d'action supérieur à l'agréable ou au plaisir immédiat; d'autre part, quand il s'efforce de déterminer ce principe lui-même, il ne parvient pas à le distinguer de l'utile, et l'utile lui-même ne diffère pas essentiellement de l'agréable." Yet one cannot leave it at that; one has to acknowledge that Socrates' teaching is characterized by a fundamental contradiction: "Socrate recommande de pratiquer les diverses vertus à cause des avantages matériels qu'elles sont susceptibles de nous procurer; mais ces avantages il n'en jouit jamais." [49] Could Socrates, who insisted so strongly on the indispensable harmony between deed and speech completely have failed to account "by speech" for what he was revealing "by deed"? To solve the contradiction in question, one merely has to remind oneself of the distinction which Xenophon's Socrates makes silently and Plato's Socrates makes explicitly between two kinds of virtue or gentlemanliness: between common or political virtue, whose ends are wealth and honor, and true virtue which is identical with self-sufficient wisdom.[50] The fact that Socrates sometimes creates the impression that he was oblivious of true virtue, or that he mistook common virtue for true virtue, is explained by his habit of leading his discussions, as far as possible, "through the opinions accepted by human beings." [51] Thus the question of Socrates' attitude toward hedonism is reduced to the question as to whether wisdom, the highest good, is intrinsically pleasant. If we may trust Xenophon, Socrates has disclosed his answer in his last conversation: not so much wisdom, or true virtue itself, as one's consciousness of one's progress in wisdom or virtue, affords the highest pleasure.[52] Thus Socrates ultimately leaves no doubt as to the fundamental difference between the good and the pleasant. No man can be simply wise; therefore, not wisdom, but progress toward wisdom is the highest good for man. Wisdom cannot be separated from self-knowledge; therefore, progress toward wisdom will be accompanied by awareness of that progress. And that awareness is necessarily pleasant. This whole—the progress and the awareness of it—is both the best and the most pleasant thing for man. It is in this sense that the highest good is intrinsically pleasant. Concerning the thesis that the most choiceworthy thing must be intrinsically pleasant, there is then no difference between the historical Simonides, Xenophon's Simonides, and Xenophon's Socrates, and, indeed, Plato's Socrates.[53] Nor is this all. There is even an important agreement between Xenophon's Simonides and his Socrates as regards the object of the highest pleasure. For what else is the pleasant consciousness of one's progress in wisdom or virtue but one's reasonable and deserved satisfaction with, and even admiration of,[54] oneself? The difference between Socrates and Simonides seems then to be that Socrates is not at all concerned with being admired or praised by others, whereas Simonides is concerned exclusively with it. To reduce this difference to its proper proportions, it is well to remember that Simonides' statement on praise or honor is meant to serve a pedagogical function. The *Hiero* does not supply us then with the most adequate formulation of Xenophon's view regarding the relation of pleasure and virtue. But it is the only writing of Xenophon which has the merit, and even the function, of posing the problem of that relation in its most radical form: in the form of the question as to whether the demands of virtue cannot be completely replaced by, or reduced to, the desire for pleasure, if for the highest pleasure.

◻ ◻ ◻

VII

PIETY AND LAW

AFTER ADVISING THE DEMOCRATIC RULERS of Athens how they could overcome the necessity under which they found themselves of acting unjustly, Xenophon reminds them of the limitations of his advice, and, indeed, of all human advice, by giving them the additional advice to inquire of the gods in Dodona and in Delphi whether the reforms suggested by him would be salutary to the city both now and in the future. Yet even divine approval of his suggestions would not suffice. He gives the Athenians the crowning advice, in case the gods should approve of his suggestions, that they further ask the gods to which of the gods they ought to sacrifice in order to be successful. Divine approval and divine assistance seem to be indispensable for salutary political action. These remarks must be of special interest to the interpreter of the *Hiero* on account of the place where they occur in the *Corpus Xenophonteum,* for they occur at the end of the *Ways and Means.*[1] Still, their content cannot be surprising to any reader of our author: pious sentiments are expressed, more or less forcefully, in all those of his writings in which he speaks in his own or in Socrates' name.

One of the most surprising features of the *Hiero,* i.e., of the only work of Xenophon in which he never speaks in the first person, is its complete silence about piety. Simonides never mentions piety. He does not say a word about the advisability of asking any gods whether his suggestions regarding the improvement of tyrannical rule would be salutary. Nor does he remind

Hiero of the need of divine assistance. He does not admonish him in any way to worship the gods.[2] Hiero, too, is silent about piety. In particular, when enumerating the various virtues, he was almost compelled to mention piety: he fails to do so.

It might seem that this silence is sufficiently explained by the subject matter of the work. The tyrant, and indeed any absolute ruler, may be said to usurp honors rightfully belonging to the gods alone.[3] Yet the *Hiero* deals, not so much with how tyrants usually live, as with how tyranny can best be preserved or rather improved. If we may believe Aristotle, piety is rather more necessary for preserving and improving tyrannical government than it is for the preservation and improvement of any other political order. We might be inclined to credit Xenophon with the same view, since he indicates that the regime of Cyrus became the more pious in proportion as it became more absolute.[4] But Cyrus is not a tyrant strictly speaking. According to Xenophon, tyranny is in any case rule without laws, and according to his Socrates, piety is knowledge of the laws concerning the gods:[5] where there are no laws, there cannot be piety. However, the identification of piety with knowledge of the laws concerning the gods is not Xenophon's last word on the subject. In his final characterization of Socrates he says that Socrates was so pious that he would do nothing without the consent of the gods. When he describes how Socrates made his companions pious, he shows how he led them to a recognition of divine providence by making them consider the purposeful character of the universe and its parts.[6] It seems, then, that just as he admits a translegal justice, although his Socrates identifies justice with legality, so he admits a piety which emerges out of the contemplation of nature and which has no necessary relation to law; a piety, that is, whose possibility is virtually denied by the definition suggested by his Socrates. We shall conclude that the silence of the *Hiero* about piety cannot be fully explained by the subject matter of the work. For a full explanation one would have to consider the conversational situation, the fact that the *Hiero* is a dialogue between an educated tyrant and a wise man who is not a citizen-philosopher.

While the *Hiero* is silent about piety, it is not silent about the gods. But the silence about piety is reflected in what it says, or does not say, about the gods. In the sentence with which he concludes his statement about friendship, Hiero uses an expression which is reminiscent of an expression used in a similar context by Ischomachus in the *Oeconomicus*. Hiero speaks of those who are born by nature, and at the same time compelled by law, to love. Whereas Hiero speaks of a cooperation of nature and law, Ischomachus speaks of a cooperation of the god (or the gods) and law.[7] Hiero replaces "the god" or "the gods" by "nature." Xenophon's Simonides never corrects him. He seems to be the same Simonides who is said repeatedly to have postponed and finally abandoned the attempt to answer the question which Hiero had posed him, What is God?[8] It is true, both Hiero and Simonides mention "the gods," but there is no apparent connection between what they say about "nature" and what they say about "the gods."[9] It is possible that what they mean by "the gods" is chance rather than "nature" or the origin of the natural order.[10]

The practical bearing of the difference between Ischomachus' and Hiero's statements appears from the different ways in which they describe the cooperation of gods or nature and law in the parallel passages cited. Ischomachus says that a certain order which has been established by the gods is at the same time praised by the law. Hiero says that men are prompted by nature to a certain action or feeling, to which they are at the same time compelled by the law. Ischomachus, who traces the natural order to the gods, describes the specific work of the law as praising; Hiero who does not take that step, describes it as compelling. One's manner of understanding and evaluating the man-made law depends then on one's manner of understanding the order which is not man-made and which is only confirmed by the law. If the natural order is traced to the gods, the compulsory character of the law recedes into the background. Conversely, the law as such is less likely to appear as an immediate source of pleasure if one does not go beyond the natural order itself. The law assumes a higher dignity if the universe is of divine origin. The notion linking "praise" and "gods" is gentlemanliness. Praise as distinguished from compulsion suffices for the guidance of gentlemen, and the gods delight at gentlemanliness.[11] As we have seen, Hiero's and Simonides' gentlemanliness is not altogether beyond doubt. Ischomachus, on the other hand, who traces the natural order to the gods and who describes in the cited passage the work of the law as praising, is the gentleman *par excellence*. What the attitude of the citizen-philosopher Socrates was can be ascertained only by a comprehensive and detailed analysis of Xenophon's Socratic writings.

◨ ◨ ◨

NOTES

Introduction

1. Compare *Social Research*, v. 13, 1946, pp. 123–124.—Hobbes, *Leviathan*, "A Review and Conclusion" (ed. by A. R. Waller, p. 523): ". . . the name of Tyranny, signifieth nothing more, nor lesse, than the name of Sovereignty, be it in one, or many men, saving that they that use the former word, are understood to be angry with them they call Tyrants. . . ."—Montesquieu, *De l'Esprit des Lois*, XI 9: "L'embarras d'Aristote paraît visiblement quand il traite de la monarchie. Il en établit cinq espèces: il ne les distingue pas par la forme de la constitution, mais par des choses d'accident, comme les vertus ou les vices des princes. . . ."

2. *Principe*, ch. 15, beginning; *Discorsi* I, beginning.

3. The most important reference to the *Cyropaedia* occurs in the *Principe*. It occurs a few lines before the passage in which Machiavelli expresses his intention to break with the whole tradition (ch. 14, toward the end). The *Cyropaedia* is clearly referred to in the *Discorsi* at least four times. If I am not mistaken, Machiavelli mentions Xenophon in the *Principe* and in the *Discorsi* more frequently than he does Plato, Aristotle, and Cicero taken together.

4. *Discorsi* II 2.

5. Classical political science took its bearings by man's perfection or by how men ought to live, and it culminated in the description of the best political order. Such an order was meant to be one whose realization was possible without a miraculous or nonmiraculous change in human nature, but its realization was not considered probable, because it was thought to depend on chance. Machiavelli attacks this view both by demanding that one should take one's bearings, not by how men ought to live but by how they actually live, and by suggesting that chance

could or should be controlled. It is this attack which laid the foundation for all specifically modern political thought. The concern with a guarantee for the realization of the "ideal" led to both a lowering of the standards of political life and to the emergence of "philosophy of history": even the modern opponents of Machiavelli could not restore the sober view of the classics regarding the relation of "ideal" and "reality."

I. The Problem

1. *Hiero* 1.8–10; 2.3–6; 3.3–6; 8.1–7; 11.7–15.

2. *Memorabilia* II 1.21; *Cyropaedia* VIII 2.12. Compare Aristotle, *Politics* 1325a34 ff. and Euripides, *Phoenissae* 524–5.

3. *Memorabilia* I 2.56.

4. *Hiero* 1.1; 2.5.

5. *Hiero* 8.1. Compare *Memorabilia* IV 2.23–24 with *ibid.* 16–17.

6. *Hiero* 1.14–15; 7.2. Compare Plato, *Seventh Letter* 332d6–7 and Isocrates, *To Nicocles* 3–4.

II. The Title and the Form

1. How necessary it is to consider carefully the titles of Xenophon's writings is shown most clearly by the difficulties presented by the titles of the *Anabasis*, of the *Cyropaedia* and, though less obviously, of the *Memorabilia*. Regarding the title of the *Hiero*, see also IV note 50, below.

2. There is only one more writing of Xenophon which would seem to serve the purpose of teaching a skill, the π. ἱππικῆς; we cannot discuss here the question why it is not entitled Ἱππικός. The purpose of the *Cyropaedia* is theoretical rather than practical, as appears from the first chapter of the work.

3. Compare *Cyropaedia* I 3.18 with Plato, *Theages* 124e11–125e7 and *Amatores* 138b15 ff.

4. *De vectigalibus* 1.1. Compare *Memorabilia* IV 4.11–12 and *Symposium* 4. 1–2.

5. *Hiero* 4.9–11; 7.10, 12; 8.10; 10.8; 11.1.

6. *Memorabilia* I 2.9–11; III 9.10; IV 6.12 (compare IV 4). *Oeconomicus* 21.12. *Resp. Lac.* 10.7; 15.7–8. *Agesilaus* 7.2. *Hellenica* VI 4.33–35; VII 1.46 (compare V 4.1; VII 3.7–8). The opening sentence of the *Cyropaedia* implies that tyranny is the least stable regime. (See Aristotle, *Politics* 1315b10 ff.)

7. *Hiero* 4.5. *Hellenica* V 4.9, 13; VI 4.32. Compare *Hiero* 7.10 with *Hellenica* VII 3.7. See also Isocrates, *Nicocles* 24.

8. Plato, *Republic* 393c11.

9. *Memorabilia* III 4.7–12; 6.14; IV 2.11.

10. *Oeconomicus* 1.23; 4.2–19; 5.13–16; 6.5–10; 8.4–8; 9.13–15; 13.4–5; 14.3–10; 20. 6–9; 21.2–12. The derogatory remark on tyrants at the end of

the work is a fitting conclusion for a writing devoted to the royal art as such. Since Plato shares the "Socratic" view according to which the political art is not essentially different from the economic art, one may also say that it can only be due to secondary considerations that his *Politicus* is not entitled *Oeconomicus*.

11. *Memorabilia* IV 6.12.

12. *Apologia Socratis* 34.

13. *Memorabilia* I 2.31 ff.; III 7.5–6.

14. Plato, *Hipparchus* 228b–c (cf. 229b). Aristotle, *Resp. Athen.* 18.1.

15. Plato, *Second Letter* 310e5 ff.

16. *Memorabilia* I 5.6.

17. Aristophanes, *Pax* 698–9. Aristotle, *Rhetoric* 1391a8–11; 1405b24–28. See also Plato, *Hipparchus* 228c. Lessing called Simonides the Greek Voltaire.

18. *Oeconomicus* 6.4; 2.2, 12 ff. Compare *Memorabilia* IV 7.1 with *ibid.* III 1.1 ff. Compare *Anabasis* VI 1.23 with *ibid.* I 10.12.

19. *Hiero* 9.7–11; 11.4, 13–14, Compare *Oeconomicus* 1.15.

20. *Hiero* 1.2, 10; 2.6.

21. Note the almost complete absence of proper names from the *Hiero*. The only proper name that occurs in the work (apart, of course, from the names of Hiero, Simonides, Zeus, and the Greeks) is that of Daïlochus, Hiero's favorite. I George Grote, *Plato and the other companions of Socrates* (London, 1888, v. I, 222), makes the following just remark: "When we read the recommendations addressed by Simonides, teaching Hiero how he might render himself popular, we perceive at once that they are alike well intentioned and ineffectual. Xenophon could neither find any real Grecian despot corresponding to this portion . . . nor could he invent one with any show of plausibility." Grote continues, however, as follows: "He was forced to resort to other countries and other habits different from those of Greece. To this necessity probably we owe the Cyropaedia." For the moment, it suffices to remark that, according to Xenophon, Cyrus is not a tyrant but a king. Grote's error is due to the identification of "tyrant" with "despot."

22. Simonides barely alludes to the mortality of Hiero or of tyrants in general (*Hiero* 10.4): Hiero, being a tyrant, must be supposed to live in perpetual fear of assassination. Compare especially *Hiero* 11.7, end, with *Agesilaus* 9.7 end. Compare also *Hiero* 7.2 and 7.7 ff. as well as 8.3 ff. (the ways of honoring people) with *Hellenica* VI 1.6 (honoring by solemnity of burial). Cf. *Hiero* 11.7, 15 with Plato, *Republic* 465d2–e2.

III. The Setting

a. The characters and their intentions

1. *Hiero* 1.12; 2.8. Compare Plato, *Republic* 579b3–c3.

2. Aristotle, *Rhetoric* 1391a8–11.

3. *Hiero* 1.13; 6.13; 11.10.

4. *Memorabilia* I 2.33. *Oeconomicus* 7.2. *Cyropaedia* I 4.13; III 1.14; VIII 4.9.

5. *Hiero* 1.1–2.

6. Aristotle, *Politics* 1311a4–5. Compare the thesis of Callicles in Plato's *Gorgias*.

7. Observe the repeated εἰκός in *Hiero* 1.1–2. The meaning of this indication is revealed by what happens during the conversation. In order to know better than Simonides how the two ways of life differ in regard to pleasures and pains, Hiero would have to possess actual knowledge of both ways of life; i.e., Hiero must not have forgotten the pleasures and pains characteristic of private life; yet Hiero suggests that he does not remember them sufficiently (1.3). Furthermore, knowledge of the difference in question is acquired by means of calculation or reasoning (1.11, 3), and the calculation required presupposes knowledge of the different value, or of the different degree of importance, of the various kinds of pleasure and pain; yet Hiero has to learn from Simonides that some kinds of pleasure are of minor importance as compared with others (2.1; 7.3–4). Besides, in order to know better than Simonides the difference in question, Hiero would have to possess at least as great a power of calculating or reasoning as Simonides; yet Simonides shows that Hiero's alleged knowledge of the difference (a knowledge which he had not acquired but with the assistance of Simonides) is based on the fatal disregard of a most relevant factor (8.1–7). The thesis that a man who has experienced both ways of life knows the manner of their difference better than he who has experienced only one of them is then true only if important qualifications are added; in itself, it is the result of an enthymeme and merely plausible.

8. *Hiero* 1.8, 14, 16. Simonides says that tyrants are universally admired or envied (1.9), and he implies that the same is of course not true of private men as such. His somewhat more reserved statements in 2.1–2 and 7.1–4 about specific kinds of pleasure must be understood, to begin with, in the light of his general statement about all kinds of pleasure in 1.8. The statement that Simonides makes in 2.1–2 is understood by Hiero in the light of Simonides' general statement, as appears from 2.3–5; 4.6; and 6.12. (Compare also 8.7 with 3.3.) For the interpretation of Simonides' initial question, consider Isocrates, *To Nicocles* 4–5.

9. *Hiero* 2.3–5. One should also not forget the fact that the author of the *Hiero* never was a tyrant. Compare Plato, *Republic* 577a–b and *Gorgias* 470d5–e11.

10. *Memorabilia* I 3.2; IV 8.6; 5.9–10. Compare *Anabasis* VI 1.17–21.

11. *Memorabilia* IV 6.1, 7; III 3.11; I 2.14.

12. *Hiero* 1.21, 31.

13. Compare *Hiero* 11.5–6 and *Agesilaus* 9.6–7 with Pindar, *Ol.* I and *Pyth.* I–III.

14. *Hiero* 1.14. The same rule of conduct was observed by Socrates. Compare the manner in which he behaved when talking to the "legislators" Critias and Charicles, with his open blame of the Thirty which he pronounced "somewhere," i.e., not in the presence of the tyrants, and which had to be "reported" to Critias and Charicles (*Memorabilia* I 2.32–38; observe the repetition of ἀπαγγελθέντος). In Plato's *Protagoras* (345e–346b8) Socrates excuses Simonides for having praised tyrants under compulsion.

15. *Hiero* 1.9–10, 16–17; 2.3–5.

16. *Hiero* 1.10; 8.1.

17. *Hiero* 2.3–5.

18. While all men consider tyrants enviable, while the multitude is deceived by the outward splendor of tyrants, the multitude does not wish to be ruled by tyrants but rather by the just. Compare *Hiero* 2.3–5 with *ibid.* 5.1 and 4.5. Compare Plato, *Republic* 344b5–c1.

19. Compare the end of the *Oeconomicus* with *ibid.* 6.12 ff. See also *Memorabilia* II 6.22 ff.

20. *Hiero* 5.1; 1.1.

21. *Hiero* 6.5. Aristotle, *Politics* 1314a10–13.

22. *Hiero* 4.2. See note 14 above.

23. *Hiero* 5.1–2.

24. Hiero mentions "contriving something bad and base" in 4.10, i.e., almost immediately before the crucial passage. Compare also 1.22–23.

25. *Memorabilia* I 2.31; IV 2.33. *Symposium* 6.6. *Apologia Socratis* 20–21. *Cyropaedia* III 1.39. Compare Plato, *Apol. Socr.* 23d4–7 and 28a6–b1, as well as *Seventh Letter* 344c1–3.

26. *Memorabilia* I 6.12–13.

27. Compare *Oeconomicus* 6.12 ff. and 11.1 ff with *Memorabilia* I 1.16 and IV 6.7. Compare Plato, *Republic* 489e3–490a3. The distinction between the two meanings of "gentleman" corresponds to the Platonic distinction between common or political virtue and genuine virtue.

28. *Cyropaedia* I 1.1. *Memorabilia* I 2.56; 6.11–12. Compare *Memorabilia* IV 2.33 with *Symposium* 3.4. See Plato, *Seventh Letter* 333b3 ff. and 334a1–3 as well as *Gorgias* 468e6–9 and 469c3 (cf. 492d2–3); also *Republic* 493a6 ff.

29. *Memorabilia* I 2.31 ff.; IV 4.3. *Symposium* 4.13. Compare Plato, *Apol. Socr.* 20e8–21a3 and 32c4–d8 as well as *Gorgias* 480e6 ff.; also *Protagoras* 329e2–330a2. Cf. note 14 above.

30. *Hellenica* IV 4.6. Compare *Symposium* 3.4.

31. Whereas Hiero asserts that the tyrant is unjust, he does not say that he is foolish. Whereas he asserts that the entourage of the tyrant consists of the unjust, the intemperate, and the servile, he does not say

that it consists of fools. Consider the lack of correspondence between the virtues mentioned in *Hiero* 5.1. and the vices mentioned in 5.2. Moreover, by proving that he is wiser than the wise Simonides, Hiero proves that the tyrant may be wise indeed.

32. According to Xenophon's Socrates, he who possesses the specific knowledge required for ruling well is *eo ipso* a ruler (*Memorabilia* III 9.10; 1.4). Hence he who possesses the tyrannical art is *eo ipso* a tyrant. From Xenophon's point of view, Hiero's distrust of Simonides is an ironic reflection of the Socratic truth. It is ironic for the following reason: From Xenophon's point of view, the wise teacher of the royal art, or of the tyrannical art, is not a potential ruler in the ordinary sense of the term, because he who knows how to rule does not necessarily wish to rule. Even Hiero grants by implication that the just do not wish to rule, or that they wish merely to mind their own business (cf. *Hiero* 5.1 with *Memorabilia* I 2.48 and II 9.1). If the wise man is necessarily just, the wise teacher of the tyrannical art will not wish to be a tyrant. But it is precisely the necessary connection between wisdom and justice which is questioned by Hiero's distinction between the wise and the just.

33. *Hiero* 2.3–5 (compare the wording with that used *ibid.* 1.9 and in *Cyropaedia* IV 2.28). It should be emphasized that in this important passage Hiero does not speak explicitly of wisdom. (His only explicit remark on wisdom occurs in the central passage, in 5.1). Furthermore, Hiero silently qualifies what he says about happiness in 2.3–5 in a later passage (7.9–10) where he admits that bliss requires outward or visible signs.

34. *Hiero* 2.6; 1.10.

35. Hiero states at the beginning that Simonides is a wise *man* (ἀνήρ); but as Simonides explains in 7.3–4, [real] men (ἄνδρες) as distinguished from [ordinary] human beings (ἄνθρωποι) are swayed by ambition and hence apt to aspire to tyrannical power. (The ἀνδρός at the end of 1.1 corresponds to the ἀνθρώποις at the end of 1.2. Cf. also 7.9, beginning.) Shortly after the beginning, Hiero remarks that Simonides is "at present still a private man" (1.3), thus implying that he might well become a tyrant. Accordingly, Hiero speaks only once of "you [private men]," whereas Simonides speaks fairly frequently of "you [tyrants]": Hiero hesitates to consider Simonides as merely a private man (6.10. The "you" in 2.5 refers to the reputedly wise men as distinguished from the multitude. Simonides speaks of "you tyrants" in the following passages: 1.14, 16, 24, 26; 2.2; 7.2, 4; 8.7). For the distinction between "real men" and "ordinary human beings," compare also *Anabasis* I 7.4; *Cyropaedia* IV 2.25; V 5.33; Plato, *Republic* 550a1; *Protagoras* 316c5–317b5.

36. *Hiero* 1.9; 6.12. ζηλόω, the term used by Simonides and later on by Hiero, designates jealousy, the noble counterpart of envy rather than envy proper (cf. Aristotle, *Rhetoric* II 11). That the tyrant is exposed

to envy in the strict sense of the term appears from Hiero's remark in 7.10 and from Simonides' emphatic promise at the end of the dialogue: the tyrant who has become the benefactor of his subjects will be happy without being envied. Cf. also 11.6, where it is implied that a tyrant like Hiero is envied (cf. note 13 above). In *Hiero* 1.9, Simonides avoids speaking of "envy" because the term might suggest that all men bear ill-will to the tyrant, and this implication would spoil completely the effect of his statement. Hiero's statement in 6.12, which refers not only to 1.9 but to 2.2 as well, amounts to a correction of what Simonides had said in the former passage; Hiero suggests that not all men, but only men like Simonides, are jealous of the tyrant's wealth and power. As for Simonides' distinction (in 1.9) between "all men" who are jealous of tyrants and the "many" who desire to be tyrants, it has to be under- stood as follows: many who consider a thing an enviable possession do not seriously desire it, because they are convinced of their inability to acquire it. Compare Aristotle, *Politics* 1311a29–31 and 1313a17–23.

37. By using the tyrant's fear as a means for his betterment, Simonides acts in accordance with a pedagogic principle of Xenophon; see *Hip- parchicus* 1.8; *Memorabilia* III 5.5–6; *Cyropaedia* III 1.23–24.

38. Compare *Hiero* 1.14 with 1.16. Note the emphatic character of Simonides' assent to Hiero's reply (1.16, beginning). Compare also 2.2 with 11.2–5.

39. Compare *Hiero* 4.5 with *Hellenica* VI 4.32 and VII 3.4–6.

40 Compare *Hiero* 6.14 with *Hellenica* VII 3.12.

41. Compare *Hiero* 6.1–3 with *Cyropaedia* I 3.10, 18.

42. Compare *Hiero* 8.6 with *ibid*. 2.1. The statement is not contradicted by Hiero; it is prepared, and thus to a certain extent confirmed, by what Hiero says in 1.27 (Νῦν δή) and 1.29. In 7.5, Hiero indicates that agree- ment had been reached between him and Simonides on the subject of sex.

43. *Hiero* 2.12–18.

44. By showing this, Hiero elaborates what we may call the gentle- man's image of the tyrant. Xenophon pays a great compliment to Hiero's education by entrusting to him the only elaborate presentation of the gentleman's view of tyranny which he ever wrote. Compare p. 30 above on the relation between the *Hiero* and the *Agesilaus*. The relation of Hiero's indictment of tyranny to the true account of tyranny can be compared to the relation of the Athenian story about the family of Pisistratus to Thucydides' "exact" account. One may also compare it to the relation of the *Agesilaus* to the corresponding sections of the *Hellenica*.

45. *Memorabilia* IV 4.10. *Agesilaus* 1.6. As for the purpose of the *Hellenica*, compare IV 8.1 and V 1.4 with II 3.56 as well as with *Symposium* 1.1 and *Cyropaedia* VIII 7.24.

46. *Memorabilia* I 2.58–61. While Xenophon denies the charge that

Socrates had interpreted the verses in question in a particularly obnoxious manner, he does not deny the fact that Socrates frequently quoted the verses. Why Socrates liked them, or how he interpreted them, is indicated *ibid*. IV 6.13–15: Socrates used two types of dialectics, one which leads to the truth and another which, by never leaving the dimension of generally accepted opinions, leads to (political) agreement. For the interpretation of the passage, compare *Symposium* 4.59–60 with *ibid*. 4.56–58.

47. *Symposium* 3.6. Compare Plato, *Republic* 378d6–8 and a1–6.

48. To summarize our argument, we shall say that if Hiero is supposed to state the truth or even merely to be completely frank, the whole *Hiero* becomes unintelligible. If one accepts either supposition, one will be compelled to agree with the following criticism by Ernst Richter ("Xenophon-Studien," *Fleckeisen's Jahrbücher für classische Philologie*, 19. Supplementband, 1893, 149): "Einem solchen Manne, der sich so freimüthig über sich selbst äussert, und diese lobenswerten Gesinnungen hegt, möchte man kaum die Schreckensthaten zutrauen, die er als von der Tyrannenherrschaft unzertrennlich hinstellt. Hat er aber wirklich soviel Menschen getötet und übt er täglich noch soviel Übelthaten aus, ist für ihn wirklich das Beste der Strick—und er musste es ja wissen—, so kommen die Ermahnungen des Simonides im zweiten Teil ganz gewiss zu spät. . . . Simonides gibt Ratschläge, wie sie nur bei einem Fürsten vom Schlage des Kyros oder Agesilaos angebracht sind, nie aber bei einem Tyrannen, wie ihn Hieron beschreibt, der schon gar nicht mehr weiss, wie er sich vor seinen Todfeinden schützen kann." Not to repeat what we have said in the text, the quick transition from Hiero's indictment of the tyrant's injustice (7.7–13) to his remark that the tyrants punish the unjust (8.9) is unintelligible but for the fact that his account is exaggerated. If one supposes then that Hiero exaggerates, one has to wonder why he exaggerates. Now, Hiero himself makes the following assertions: that the tyrants trust no one; that they fear the wise; that Simonides is a real man; and that Simonides admires, or is jealous of, the tyrants' power. These assertions of Hiero supply us with the only authentic clue to the riddle of the dialogue. Some of the assertions referred to are without doubt as much suspect of being exaggerated as almost all other assertions of Hiero. But this very fact implies that they contain an element of truth, or that they are true if taken with a grain of salt.

b. The action of the dialogue

1. *Hiero* 1.3. As for the duration of Hiero's reign, see Aristotle, *Politics* 1315b35 ff. and Diodorus Siculus XI 38. Hiero shows later on (*Hiero* 6.1–2) that he recalls very well certain pleasures of private men of which he had not been reminded by Simonides.

2. *Hiero* 1.4–5. The "we" in "we all know" in 1.4 refers of course to private men and tyrants alike. Compare 1.29 and 10.4.

3. *Hiero* 1.4–6. To begin with, i.e., before Simonides has aroused his opposition, Hiero does not find any difference between tyrants and private men in regard to sleep (1.7). Later on, in an entirely different conversational situation, Hiero takes up "the pleasures of private men of which the tyrant is deprived"; in that context, while elaborating the gentleman's image of the tyrant (with which Simonides must be presumed to have been familiar from the outset), Hiero speaks in the strongest terms of the difference between tyrants and private men in regard to the enjoyment of sleep (6.3,7–10).

4. Twelve out of fifteen classes of pleasant or painful things are unambiguously of a bodily nature. The three remaining classes are (1) the good things, (2) the bad things, and (3) sleep. As for the good and the bad things, Simonides says that they please or pain us sometimes through the working of the soul alone and sometimes through that of the soul and the body together. As regards sleep, he leaves open the question by means of what kind of organ or faculty we enjoy it.

5. Compare *Hiero* 2.1 and 7.3 with *Memorabilia* II 1.

6. *Hiero* 1.19. Compare Isocrates, *To Nicocles* 4.

7. Compare *Hiero* 4.8–9 with *Memorabilia* IV 2.37–38.

8. *Hiero* 1.7–10. Hiero's oath in 1.10 is the first oath occurring in the dialogue. Hiero uses the emphatic form μὰ τὸν Δία.

9. See in *Hiero* 1.10 the explicit reference to the order of Simonides' enumeration.

10. The proof is based on λογισμός, i.e., on a comparison of data that are supplied by experience or observation. Compare *Hiero* 1.11 (λογιζόμενος εὐρίσκω) with the reference to ἐμπειρία in 1.10. Compare *Memorabilia* IV 3.11 and *Hellenica* VII 4.2.

11. The passage consists of five parts: (1) "sights" (Hiero contributes 163 words, Simonides is silent); (2) "sounds" (Hiero 36 words, Simonides 68 words); (3) "food" (Hiero 230 words, Simonides 76 words); (4) "odors" (Hiero is silent, Simonides 32 words); (5) "sex" (Hiero 411 words, Simonides 42 words). Hiero is most vocal concerning "sex"; Simonides is most vocal concerning "food."

12. Compare III a, note 42, and III b, notes 11 and 19. As for the connection between sexual love and tyranny, cf. Plato, *Republic* 573e6–7, 574e2 and 575a1–2.

13. *Hiero* 1.31–33.

14. Compare *Hiero* 1.16 with the parallels in 1.14, 24, 26.

15. Simonides' first oath (μὰ τὸν Δία) occurs in the passage dealing with sounds, i.e., with praise (1.16).

16. Rudolf Hirzel, *Der Dialog*, I, Leipzig, 1895, 171, notes "die geringe

Lebendigkeit des Gesprächs, die vorherrschende Neigung zu längeren Vorträgen": all the more striking is the character of the discussion of "food."

17. Simonides grants this by implication in *Hiero* 1.26.

18. Mr. Marchant (Xenophon, *Scripta Minora, Loeb's Classical Library*, XV–XVI) says: "There is no attempt at characterization in the persons of the dialogue. . . . The remark of the poet at c.1.22 is singularly inappropriate to a man who had a liking for good living." In the passage referred to, Simonides declares that "acid, pungent, astringent and kindred things" are "very unnatural for human beings": he says nothing at all against "sweet and kindred things." The view that bitter, acid, etc., things are "against nature," was shared by Plato (*Timaeus* 65c–66c), by Aristotle (*Eth. Nic.* 1153a5–6; cf. *De anima* 422b 10–14) and, it seems, by Alcmæon (cf. Aristotle, *Metaphysics* 986a22–34). Moreover, Simonides says that acid, pungent, etc., things are unnatural for "human beings"; but "human beings" may have to be understood in contradistinction to "real men" (cf. III a, note 35 above). At any rate, the fare censured by Simonides is recommended as a fare for soldiers by Cyrus in a speech addressed to "real men" (*Cyropaedia* VI 2.31). (Compare also *Symposium* 4.9.) Above all, Marchant who describes the *Hiero* as "a naïve little work, not unattractive," somewhat naïvely overlooks the fact that Simonides' utterances serve primarily the purpose, not of characterizing Simonides, but of influencing Hiero; they characterize the poet in a more subtle way than the one which alone is considered by Marchant: the fact that Simonides indicates, or fails to indicate, his likes or dislikes according to the requirements of his pedagogic intentions, characterizes him as wise.

19. *Hiero* 1.26. "Sex" is the only motive of which Simonides ever explicitly says that it could be the only motive for desiring tyrannical power. Compare note 12 above.

20. *Hiero* 7.5–6.

21. *Hiero* 8.6.

22. Note the increased emphasis on "(real) men" in *Hiero* 2.1. In the parallel passage of the first section (1.9), Simonides had spoken of "most able (real) men." Compare the corresponding change of emphasis in Hiero's replies (see the following note).

23. Compare *Hiero* 1.16–17 with 2.1, where Simonides declares that the bodily pleasures appear to him to be very minor things and that, as he observes, many of those who are reputed to be real men do not attach any great value to those pleasures. Hiero's general statement in 2.3–5, which is so much stronger than his corresponding statement in the first section (1.10), amounts to a tacit rejection of Simonides' claim: Hiero states that the view expressed by Simonides in 2.1–2, far from being non-vulgar, is *the* vulgar view.

24. *Hiero* 2.1–2. Simonides does not explicitly speak of "wealth and power." "Wealth and power" had been mentioned by Hiero in 1.27. (Compare Aristotle, *Politics* 1311a8–12.) On the basis of Simonides' initial enumeration (1.4–6), one would expect that the second section (ch. 2–6) would deal with the three kinds of pleasure that had not been discussed in the first section, *viz.* the objects perceived by the whole body, the good and bad things, and sleep. Only good and bad things and, to a lesser degree, sleep are clearly discernible as subjects of the second section. As for good and bad things, see the following passages: 2.6–7; 3.1, 3, 5; 4.1; 5.2, 4. (Compare also 2.2 with *Anabasis* III 1.19–20.) As for sleep, see 6.3–9. As for objects perceived by the whole body, compare 1.5 and 2.2 with *Memorabilia* III 8.8–9 and 10.13. Sleep (the last item of the initial enumeration) is not yet mentioned in the retrospective summary at the beginning of the second section, whereas it is mentioned in the parallel at the beginning of the third section (cf. 2.1 with 7.3); in this manner Xenophon indicates that the discussion of the subjects mentioned in the initial enumeration is completed at the end of the second section: the third section deals with an entirely new subject.

25. Simonides merely intimates it, for he does not say in so many words that "they aspire to greater things, to power and wealth." Taken by itself, the statement with which Simonides opens the second section is much less far-reaching than the statements with which he had opened the discussion of the first section (1.8–9, 16). But one has to understand the later statement in the light of the earlier ones, if one wants to understand the conversational situation. Compare III a, note 8 above.

26. Simonides fails to mention above all the field or farm which occupies the central position among the objects desired by private men (*Hiero* 4.7) and whose cultivation is praised by Socrates as a particularly pleasant possession (*Oeconomicus* 5.11). Compare also *Hiero* 11.1–4 with *ibid.* 4.7 and *Memorabilia* III 11.4. Simonides pushes into the background the pleasures of private men who limit themselves to minding their own business instead of being swayed by political ambition (see *Memorabilia* I 2.48 and II 9.1). Farming is a skill of peace (*Oeconomicus* 4.12 and 1.17). Simonides also fails to mention dogs (compare *Hiero* 2.2 with *Agesilaus* 9.6). Compare *De vectigalibus* 4.8.

27. Whereas we find in the first section an explicit reference to the order of Simonides' enumeration (1.10), no such reference occurs in the second section. In the second section Hiero refers only once explicitly to the statement with which Simonides had opened the section, i.e., to 2.1–2; he does this, however, only after (and in fact almost immediately after) Simonides has made his only contribution to the discussion of the second section (6.12–13). An obvious, although implicit, reference to 2.2 occurs in 4.6–7. (Cf. especially the θᾶττον ... ... κατεργάζεσθαι in 4.7 with the

ταχυ κατεργάζεσθε in 2.2). The αὐτίκα in 2.7 (peace–war) refers to the last item mentioned in 2.2 (enemies–friends). These references merely underline the deviation of Hiero's speech from Simonides' enumeration. Simonides' silence is emphasized by Xenophon's repeated mention of the fact that Simonides has been listening to Hiero's speeches, i.e., that Simonides had not spoken (see 6.9; 7.1, 11). There is no mention of Hiero's listening to Simonides' statements.

28. See note 25 above.

29. As for Simonides, see pp. 32–33 above. Hiero's concern with wealth is indicated by the fact that, deviating from Simonides, he explicitly mentions the receiving of gifts among the signs of honor (compare 7.7–9 with 7.2). To comply with Hiero's desire, Simonides promises him later on (11.12) gifts among other things. Compare Aristotle, *Politics* 1311a8 ff. and note 74 below. Consider also the emphatic use of "possession" in Simonides' final promise. Simonides' silence about love of gain as distinguished from love of honor (compare *Hiero* 7.1–4 with *Oeconomicus* 14.9–10) is remarkable. It appears from *Hiero* 9.11 and 11.12–13 that the same measures which would render the tyrant honored, would render him rich as well.

30. Friendship as discussed by Hiero in ch. 3 is something different from "helping friends" which is mentioned by Simonides in 2.2. The latter topic is discussed by Hiero in 6.12–13.

31. Compare 2.8 with 1.11–12; 3.7–9 with 1.38; 3.8 and 4.1–2 with 1.27–29; 4.2 with 1.17–25. In the cited passages of ch. 1, as distinguished from the parallels in ch. 2 ff., no mention of "killing of tyrants" occurs. Compare also the insistence on the moral depravity of the tyrant, or on his injustice, in the second section (5.1–2 and 4.11) with the only mention of "injustice" in the first section (1.12): in the first section only the "injustice" *suffered* by tyrants is mentioned. As regards 1.36, see note 41 below.

32. Marchant (*loc. cit.*, XVI) remarks that Xenophon "makes no attempt anywhere to represent the courtier poet; had he done so he must have made Simonides bring in the subject of verse panegyrics on princes at c. I.14." It is hard to judge this suggested improvement on the *Hiero* since Marchant does not tell us how far the remark on verse panegyrics on princes would have been more conducive than what Xenophon's Simonides actually says toward the achievement of Simonides' aim. Besides, compare *Hiero* 9.4 with 9.2. We read in Macaulay's essay on Frederick the Great: "Nothing can be conceived more whimsical than the conferences which took place between the first literary man and the first practical man of the age, whom a strange weakness had induced to exchange their parts. The great poet would talk of nothing but treaties and guarantees, and the great king of nothing but metaphors and rhymes."

33. *Hiero* 3.6; 4.6; 5.1.

34. Note the frequent use of the second person singular in ch. 3, and the ascent from the κατaθέασαι in 3.1 to the εἰ βούλει εἰδέναι, ἐπίσκεψάι in 3.6 and finally to the εἰ τοίνυν ἐθέλεις κατανοεῖν in 3.8.

35. *Hiero* 6.1–6.

36. Compare *Hiero* 6.7 with *ibid.* 6.3.

37. *Hiero* 6.7–9. The importance of Simonides' remark is underlined by the following three features of Hiero's reply: First, that reply opens with the only oath that occurs in the second section. Second, that reply, being one of the three passages of the *Hiero* in which laws are mentioned (3.9; 4.4; 6.10), is the only passage in the dialogue in which it is clearly intimated that tyrannical government is government without laws, i.e., it is the only passage in Xenophon's only work on tyranny in which the essential character of tyranny comes, more or less, to light. Third, Hiero's reply is the only passage of the *Hiero* in which Hiero speaks of "you (private men)" (see III a, note 35 above). Compare also III b, note 27 above.

38. The character of Simonides' only contribution to the discussion of the second section can also be described as follows: While he was silent when friendship was being discussed, he talks in a context in which war is mentioned; he is more vocal regarding war than regarding friendship. See note 26 above.

39. The situation is illustrated by the following figures: In the first section (1.10–38) Simonides contributes about 218 words out of about 1058; in the second section (2.3–6.16) he contributes 28 words out of about 2,000; in the third section (ch. 7) he contributes 220 words out of 522; in the fourth section (ch. 8–11) he contributes about 1,475 words out of about 1,600.—K. Lincke, "Xenophon's Hiero und Demetrios von Phaleron," *Philologus*, v. 58, 1899, 226, correctly describes the "Sinnesänderung" of Hiero as "die Peripetie des Dialogs."

40. Compare note 24 above. The initial enumeration had dealt explicitly with the pleasures of "human beings" (see III a, note 35 above), but honor, the subject of the third section, is the aim, not of "human beings," but of "real men." One has no right to assume that the subject of the third section is the pleasures or pains of the soul, and the subject of the second section is the pleasures or pains common to body and soul. In the first place, the pleasures or pains of the soul precede in the initial enumeration the pleasures or pains common to body and soul; besides, ἐπινοεῖν, which is mentioned in the enumeration that opens the second section (2.2), is certainly an activity of the soul alone; finally, the relation of honor to praise as well as the examples adduced by Simonides show clearly that the pleasure connected with honor is not meant to be a pleasure of the soul alone (compare 7.2–3 with 1.14). When Simonides

says that no human pleasure comes nearer to the divine than the pleasure concerning honors, he does not imply that that pleasure is a pleasure of the soul alone, for, apart from other considerations, it is an open question whether Simonides, or Xenophon, considered the deity an incorporeal being. As for Xenophon's view on this subject, compare *Memorabilia* I 4.17 and context (for the interpretation consider Cicero, *De natura deorum* I 12.30–31 and III 10.26–27) as well as *ibid.* IV 3.13–14. Compare *Cynegeticus* 12.19 ff.

41. Compare *Hiero* 7.1–4 with *ibid.* 2.1–2. See III a, note 8, and III b, note 22 above. The "many" (in the expression "for many of those who are reputed to be real men") is emphasized by the insertion of "he said" after "for many" (2.1), and the purpose of this emphasis is to draw our attention to the still limited character of the thesis that opens the second section. This is not the only case in which Xenophon employs this simple device for directing the reader's attention. The "he said" after "we seem" in 1.5 draws our attention to the fact that Simonides uses here for the first time the first person when speaking of private men. The two re-dundant "he said"'s in 1.7–8 emphasize the "he answered" which pre-cedes the first of these two "he said"'s, thus making it clear that Simonides' preceding enumeration of pleasures has the character of a question addressed to Hiero, or that Simonides is testing Hiero. The second "he said" in 1.31 draws our attention to the preceding σύ, i.e., to the fact that Hiero's assertion concerning tyrants in general is now ap-plied by Simonides to Hiero in particular. The "he said" in 1.36 draws our attention to the fact that the tyrant Hiero hates to behave like a brigand. The redundant "he said" in 7.1 draws our attention to the fact that the following praise of honor is based on εἰκότα. The "he said" in 7.13 emphasizes the preceding ἴσθι, i.e., the fact that Hiero does not use in this context the normally used εὖ ἴσθι, for he is now describing in the strongest possible terms how bad tyranny is.

42. *Hiero* 7.5–10.

43. Compare *Hiero* 7.3 with *ibid.* 1.14–15.

44. In the third section, Simonides completely abandons the vulgar opinion not in favor of the gentleman's opinion but of the opinion of the real man. The aim of the real man is distinguished from that of the gentleman by the fact that honor as striven for by the former does not essentially presuppose a just life. Compare *Hiero* 7.3 with *Oeconomicus* 14.9.

45. *Hiero* 7.11–13. I have put in brackets the thoughts which Hiero does not express. As for Simonides' question, compare *Anabasis* VII 7.28.

46. *Hiero* 1.12. As for the tyrant's fear of punishment, see *ibid.* 5.2.

47. Regarding strangers, see *Hiero* 1.28; 5.3; 6.5.

48. Compare *Hiero* 8.9 with *ibid.* 7.7 and 5.2.

49. Simonides continues asserting that tyrannical life is superior to private life; compare *Hiero* 8.1–7 with *ibid.* 1.8 ff.; 2.1–2; 7.1 ff.

50. *Hiero* 7.12–13.

51. When comparing *Hiero* 7.13 with *Apologia Socratis* 7 and 32, one is led to wonder why Hiero is contemplating such an unpleasant form of death as hanging: does he belong to those who never gave thought to the question of the easiest way of dying? Or does he thus reveal that he never seriously considered committing suicide? Compare also *Anabasis* II 6.29.

52. *Memorabilia* I 2.10–11, 14.

53. "You are out of heart with tyranny because you believe. . . ." (*Hiero* 8.1).

54. Compare also the transition from "tyranny" to the more general "rule" in *Hiero* 8.1 ff. Regarding the relation of "tyranny" and "rule," see *Memorabilia* IV 6.12; Plato, *Republic* 338d7–11; Aristotle, *Politics* 1276a2–4.

55. *Hiero* 7.5–6, 9; compare *ibid.* 1.37–38 and 3.8–9.

56. *Hiero* 8.1.

57. *Hiero* 8.1–7. Compare note 54 above.

58. Compare *Hiero* 1.36–38.

59. In this context (8.3), there occur allusions to the topics discussed in 1.10 ff: ἰδών (sights), ἐπαινεσάντων (sounds), θύσας (food). The purpose of this is to indicate the fact that Simonides is now discussing the subject matter of the first part from the opposite point of view.

60. *Memorabilia* II 1.27–28; 3.10–14; 6.10–16. Compare *Anabasis* I 9. 20 ff.

61. If Simonides had acted differently, he would have appeared as a just man, and Hiero would fear him. Whereas Hiero's fear of the just is definite, his fear of the wise is indeterminate (see pp. 41–45 above); it may prove to be unfounded in a given case. This is what actually happens in the *Hiero*: Simonides convinces Hiero that the wise can be friends of tyrants. One cannot help being struck by the contrast between Simonides' "censure" of the tyrant Hiero and the prophet Nathan's accusation of the Lord's anointed King David (II Samuel 12).

62. *Hiero* 8.8. The equally unique πάλιν (εἶπεν) in 9.1 draws our attention to the εὐθύς in 8.8.

63. *Hiero* 8.8–10. Compare *ibid.* 6.12–13.

64. *Hiero* 9.1. Observe the negative formulation of Simonides' assent to a statement dealing with unpleasant aspects of tyrannical rule.

65. Simonides' speech consists of two parts. In the fairly short first part (9.1–4), he states the general principle. In the more extensive second part (9.5–11), he makes specific proposals regarding its application by the tyrant. In the second part punishment and the like are no longer mentioned. The unpleasant aspects of tyranny, or of government in general,

are also barely alluded to in the subsequent chapters. Probably the most charming expression of the poet's dignified silence about these disturbing things occurs in 10.8. There, Simonides refrains from mentioning the possibility that the tyrant's mercenaries, these angels of mercy, might actually punish the evildoers: he merely mentions how they should behave toward the innocent, toward those who intend to do evil and toward the injured. Compare the preceding note. Compare also the statement of the Athenian stranger in Plato's *Laws* 711b4–c2 with the subsequent statement of Clinias.

66. As for bewitching tricks to be used by absolute rulers, see *Cyropaedia* VIII 1.40–42; 2.26; 3.1. These less reserved remarks are those of a historian or a spectator rather than of an adviser. Compare Aristotle, *Politics* 1314a40: the tyrant ought to *play* the king.

67. Ch. 9 and ch. 10 are the only parts of the *Hiero* in which "tyrant" and derivatives are avoided.

68. Compare especially *Hiero* 9.10 with *ibid.* 11.10.

69. *Hiero* 9.7, 11.

70. *Hiero* 9.6. Compare Aristotle, *Politics* 1315a31–40.

71. *Hiero* 8.10.

72. *Hiero* 10.1.

73. *Hiero* 10.2. Compare Aristotle, *Politics* 1314a33 ff.

74. Compare *Hiero* 4.9, 11 with 4.3 ("without pay") and 10.8.

75. Compare *Hiero* 11.1 with 9.7–11 and 10.8.

76. *Hiero* 11.1–6. Compare p. 38 above. One is tempted to suggest that the *Hiero* represents Xenophon's interpretation of the contest between Simonides and Pindar.

77. *Hiero* 11.7–15. Compare Plato, *Republic* 465d2–e2.

78. K. Lincke (*loc. cit.*, 244), however, feels "dass Hiero eines Besseren belehrt worden wäre, muss der Leser sich hinzudenken, obgleich es . . . besser wäre, wenn man die Zustimmung ausgesprochen sähe." The Platonic parallel to Hiero's silence at the end of the *Hiero* is Callicles' silence at the end of the *Gorgias* and Thrasymachus' silence in books II-X of the *Republic*.

c. The use of characteristic terms

1. Marchant, *loc. cit.*, XVI.

2. For instance, Nabis is called "principe" in *Principe* IX and "tiranno" in *Discorsi* I 40, and Pandolfo Petruzzi is called "principe" in *Principe* XX and XXII, and "tiranno" in *Discorsi* III 6. Compare also the transition from "tyrant" to "ruler" in the second part of the *Hiero*.

3. Compare *Hellenica* VI 3.8, end.

4. *Hiero* 9.6.

5. *Hiero* 11.6; 1.31. Compare *Apologia Socratis* 28, a remark which Socrates made "laughingly."

6. Compare the absence of courage (or manliness) from the lists of Socrates' virtues: *Memorabilia* IV 8.11 (cf. IV 4.1 ff.) and *Apologia Socratis* 14, 16. Compare *Symposium* 9.1 with *Hiero* 7.3. But consider also II, note 22 above.

7. Compare *Hiero* 9.8 on the one hand with 1.8, 19 and 5.1–2 on the other.

8. *Hiero* 10.1.

IV. The Teaching Concerning Tyranny

1. Aristotle, *Politics* 1313a33–38.

2. This explanation does not contradict the one suggested on pp. 32–33 above, for the difference between a wise man who does not care to discover, or to teach, the tyrannical art and a wise man who does remains important and requires an explanation.

3. *Hiero* 1.9–10; 2.3, 5.

4. Compare *Hiero* 5.2 with the situations in *Cyropaedia* VII 2.10 on the one hand, and *ibid.* VII 5.47 on the other.

5. *Memorabilia* IV 6.12. Compare *Cyropaedia* I 3.18 and 1.1; *Hellenica* VII 1.46; *Agesilaus* 1.4; *De vectigalibus* 3.11; Aristotle, *Politics* 1295a15–18.

6. *Hiero* 11.12. Compare *Hellenica* V 1.3–4.

7. Compare pp. 65–66 and III b, note 37 above. In *Hiero* 7.2 Simonides says that *all* subjects of tyrants execute *every* command of the tyrant. Compare his additional remark that all rise from their seats in honor of the tyrant with *Resp. Lac.* 15.6: no ephors limit the tyrant's power. According to Rousseau (*Contrat social* III 10), the *Hiero* confirms his thesis that the Greeks understood by a tyrant not, as Aristotle in particular did, a bad monarch but a usurper of royal authority regardless of the quality of his rule. According to the *Hiero,* the tyrant is necessarily "lawless" not merely because of the manner in which he acquired his position, but above all because of the manner in which he rules: he follows his own will, which may be good or bad, and not any law. Xenophon's "tyrant" is identical with Rousseau's "despot" (*Contrat social* III 10 end). Compare Montesquieu, *De l'esprit des lois* XI 9 and XIV 13 note.

8. *Hiero* 11.8, 15. Compare *ibid.* 8.9 with 7.10–12, 7 and 11.1. Compare also 1.11–14 with the parallel in the *Memorabilia* (II 1.31). Regarding the fact that the tyrant may be just, compare Plato, *Phaedrus* 248e3–5.

9. *Hiero* 11.5, 7, 14–15.

10. *Hiero* 8.3 and 9.2–10.

11. *Hiero* 9.6 and 11.3, 12. Compare *Hellenica* II 3.41; also Aristotle, *Politics* 1315a32–40 and Machiavelli, *Principe* XX.

12. *Hiero* 10.6. Compare *Hellenica* IV 4.14.

13. As regards prizes, compare especially *Hiero* 9.11 with *Hipparchicus*

1.26. Ernst Richter (*loc. cit.*, 107) goes so far as to say that "die Forderungen des zweiten (Teils des *Hiero*) genau die des Sokrates (sind)."

14. *Hiero* 11.14; compare *ibid.* 6.3 and 3.8.

15. Compare *Cyropaedia* VIII 1.1 and 8.1.

16. Compare *Hiero* 10.4 with *ibid.* 4.3.

17. *Hiero* 9.1 ff. Compare Machiavelli, *Principe* XIX and XXI, toward the end as well as Aristotle, *Politics* 1315a4–8. See also Montesquieu, *De l'esprit des lois* XII 23–24. As for the reference to the division of the city into sections in Hiero 9.5–6 (cf. Machiavelli, *Principe* XXI, toward the end), one might compare Aristotle, *Politics* 1305a30–34 and Hume's "Idea of a perfect commonwealth" (toward the end).

18. *Memorabilia* III 4.8, *Oeconomicus* 4.7–8; 9.14–15; 12.19. *Resp. Lac.* 4.6 and 8.4. *Cyropaedia* V 1.13. *Anabasis* V 8.18 and II 6.19–20. Compare, however, *Cyropaedia* VIII 1.18.

19. Compare *Hiero* 9.7–8 with *Resp. Lac.* 7.1–2. Compare Aristotle, *Politics* 1305a18–22 and 1313b18–28 as well as Montesquieu, *De l'esprit des lois* XIV 9.

20. *Hiero* 11.12–14. Compare *Cyropaedia* VIII 2.15, 19; 1.17 ff.

21. Compare *Hiero* 8.10 and 11.13 with *Oeconomicus* 14.9.

22. *Hiero* 1.16.

23. Plato, *Republic* 562b9–c3; *Euthydemus* 292b4–c1. Aristotle, *Eth. Nic.* 1131a26–29 and 1161a6–9; *Politics* 1294a10–13; *Rhetoric* 1365b29 ff.

24. Compare pp. 42–43 above.

25. *Hiero* 7.9 and 11.8. Compare *ibid.* 2.2 (horses), 6.15 (horses) and 11.5 (chariots). The horse is the example used for the indirect characterization of political virtue in the *Oeconomicus* (11.3–6): a horse can possess virtue without possessing wealth; whether a human being can possess virtue without possessing wealth, remains there an open question. The political answer to the question is given in the *Cyropaedia* (I 2.15) where it is shown that aristocracy is the rule of well-bred men of independent means. Compare pp. 71–72 above about the insecurity of property rights under a tyrant.

26. *Resp. Lac.* 10.4 (cf. Aristotle, *Eth. Nic.* 1180a24 ff.). *Cyropaedia* I 2.2 ff.

27. *Hiero* 9.6.

28. *Hiero* 5.1–2.

29. Compare *Hiero* 9.6 with *ibid.* 5.3–4, *Anabasis* IV 3.4 and *Hellenica* VI 1.12. Compare *Hiero* 9.6 with the parallel in the *Cyropaedia* (I 2.12). A reduced form of prowess might seem to be characteristic of eunuchs; see *Cyropaedia* VII 5.61 ff.

30. This is the kind of justice that might exist in a nonpolitical society like Plato's first city or city of pigs (*Republic* 371e12–372a4). Compare *Oeconomicus* 14.3–4 with Aristotle, *Eth. Nic.* 1130b6, 30 ff.

31. *Memorabilia* IV 8.11. *Apol. Socr.* 14, 16.

32. Compare *Hiero* 9.8 with *Memorabilia* IV 3.1 and *Hellenica* VII 3.6. Compare Plato, *Gorgias* 507a7–c3.

33. *Anabasis* VII 7.41.

34. *Hiero* 10.3. Compare Montesquieu, *De l'esprit des lois* III 9: "Comme il faut de la vertu dans une république, et dans une monarchie de l'honneur, il faut de la crainte dans un gouvernement despotique: pour la vertu, elle n'y est pas *nécessaire*, et l'honneur y serait *dangereux*." Virtue is then not dangerous to "despotism." (The italics are mine.)

35. Compare *Hiero* 10.3 with *Cyropaedia* III 1.16 ff. and VIII 4.14 as well as with *Anabasis* VII 7.30.

36. *Anabasis* I 9.29.

37. Compare *Hiero* 11.5, 8 with *Memorabilia* III 2 and *Resp. Lac.* 1.2.

38. *Memorabilia* IV 4.12 ff. Compare *ibid.* IV 6.5–6 and *Cyropaedia* I 3.17.

39. Aristotle, *Eth. Nic.* 1129b12.

40. *Memorabilia* IV 4.13.

41. *Oeconomicus* 14.6–7.

42. *Memorabilia* I 2.39–47 and I 1.16.

43. *Memorabilia* I 2.31 ff.; IV 4.3.

44. *Agesilaus* 4.2. Compare *Cyropaedia* I 2.7.

45. Compare *Memorabilia* IV 8.11 with *ibid.* I 2.7 and *Apol. Socr.* 26. See also *Agesilaus* 11.8. Compare Plato, *Crito* 49b10 ff. (cf. Burnet *ad loc.*); *Republic* 335d11–13 and 486b10–12; *Clitopho* 410a7–b3; Aristotle, *Politics* 1255a17–18 and *Rhetoric* 1367b5–6.

46. *Cyropaedia* VIII 1.22. In *Hiero* 9.9–10 Simonides recommends honors for those who discover something useful for the city. There is a connection between this suggestion, which entails the acceptance of many and frequent changes, and the nature of tyrannical government as government not limited by laws. When Aristotle discusses the same suggestion which had been made by Hippodamus, he rejects it as dangerous to political stability and he is quite naturally led to state the principle that the "rule of law" requires as infrequent changes of laws as possible (*Politics* 1268a6–8, b 22 ff.). The rule of laws as the classics understood it can exist only in a "conservative" society. On the other hand, the speedy introduction of improvements of all kinds is obviously compatible with beneficent tyranny.

47. *Hiero* 11.10–11. *Memorabilia* III 9.10–13. Compare Aristotle, *Politics* 1313a9–10. It may be useful to compare the thesis of Xenophon with the thesis of such a convinced constitutionalist as Burke. Burke says (in his "Speech on a motion for leave to bring in a bill to repeal and alter certain acts respecting religious opinions"): ". . . it is not perhaps so much by the

assumption of unlawful powers, as by the unwise or unwarrantable use of those which are most legal, that governments oppose their true end and object, for there is such a thing as tyranny as well as usurpation."

48. *Cyropaedia* I 3.18.

49. Compare *Anabasis* III 2.13. Incidentally, the fact mentioned in the text accounts for the way in which tyranny is treated in Xenophon's emphatically Greek work, the *Hellenica*.

50. *Memorabilia* III 9.12–13. Compare Plato, *Laws* 710c5–d1. We are now in a position to state more clearly than we could at the beginning (pp. 31–32 above) the conclusion to be drawn from the title of the *Hiero*. The title expresses the view that Hiero is a man of eminence (cf. III a, note 44 above), but of questionable eminence; that the questionable character of his eminence is revealed by the fact that he is in need of a teacher of the tyrannical art; and that this is due, not only to his particular shortcomings, but to the nature of tyranny as such. The tyrant needs essentially a teacher, whereas the king (Agesilaus and Cyrus, e.g.) does not. We need not insist on the reverse side of this fact, *viz.*, that the tyrant rather than the king has any use for the wise man or the philosopher (consider the relation between Cyrus and the Armenian counterpart of Socrates in the *Cyropaedia*). If the social fabric is in order, if the regime is legitimate according to the generally accepted standards of legitimacy, the need for, and perhaps even the legitimacy of, philosophy is less evident than in the opposite case. Compare note 46 above and V, note 60 below.

51. For an example of such transformations, compare *Cyropaedia* I 3.18 with *ibid.* I 2.1.

52. *Hiero* 10.1–8. Compare Aristotle, *Politics* 1311a7–8 and 1314a34 ff.

53. Aristotle, *Politics* 1276b29–36; 1278b1–5; 1293b3–7.

54. *Memorabilia* I 2.9–11.

55. Compare pp. 57–58 above.

56. *Memorabilia* II 1.13–15.

57. Compare also the qualified praise of the good tyrant by the Athenian stranger in Plato's *Laws* (709d10 ff. and 735d). In 709d10 ff. the Athenian stranger declines responsibility for the recommendation of the use of a tyrant by emphatically ascribing that recommendation to "the legislator."

V. *The Two Ways of Life*

1. *Memorabilia* I 1.8; IV 6.14.

2. Compare *Hiero* 1.2, 7 with *Cyropaedia* II 3.11 and VIII 3.35–48; *Memorabilia* II 1 and I 2.15–16; also Plato, *Gorgias* 500c–d.

3. Consider the twofold meaning of ἰδιώτης in *Hiero* 4.6. Compare

Aristotle, *Politics* 1266a31–32. Whereas Hiero often uses "the tyrants" and "we" promiscuously, and Simonides often uses "the tyrants" and "you" promiscuously, Hiero makes only once a promiscuous use of "private men" and "you." Simonides speaks unambiguously of "we (private men)" in *Hiero* 1.5, 6 and 6.9. For other uses of the first person plural by Simonides see the following passages: 1.4, 6, 16; 8.2, 5; 9.4; 10.4; 11.2. Compare III a, note 35 and III b, notes 2 and 41 above.

4. Rudolf Hirzel, *loc. cit.*, 170 n. 3: "Am Ende klingt aus allen diesen (im Umlauf befindlichen) Erzählungen (über Gespräche zwischen Weisen und Herrschern) . . . dasselbe Thema wieder von dem *Gegensatz*, der zwischen den Mächtigen der Erde und den Weisen besteht und in deren gesamter Lebensauffassung und Anschauungsweise zu Tage tritt." (Italics mine.)

5. *Hiero* 5.1. See p. 34 and III a, note 44 above.

6. Plato, *Gorgias* 500c–d. Aristotle, *Politics* 1324a24 ff.

7. Compare *Hiero* 9.2 with *Memorabilia* III 9.5, 10–11. Compare III a, note 32 above.

8. *Memorabilia* I 2.16, 39, 47–48; 6.15; II 9.1; III 11.16.

9. *Hiero* 7.13.

10. Compare *Hiero* 8.1–10.1 with *ibid.* 3.3–5 and 11.8–12.

11. *Hiero* 7.4. Compare *ibid.* 1.8–9 with 1.14, 16, 21–22, 24, 26 and 2.1–2.

12. The difference between Simonides' explicit statements and Hiero's interpretation of them appears most clearly from a comparison of *Hiero* 2.1–2 with the following passages: 2.3–5; 4.6; 6.12.

13. See pp. 39 and 52 and III b, notes 39 and 44 above. In the second part (i.e., the fourth section) to which he contributes about three times as much as to the first part, Simonides uses expressions like "it seems to me" or "I believe" much less frequently than in the first part, while he uses in the second part three times ἐγὼ φημί which he never uses in the first part.

14. *Hiero* 7.2,4. The ambiguity of διαφερόντως in 7.4 ("above other men" or "differently from other men") is not accidental. Compare with διαφερόντως in 7.4 the πολὺ διαφέρετε in 2.2, the πολὺ διαφερόντως in 1.29 and the πολλαπλάσια in 1.8. Compare III a, note 8 and III b, notes 25 and 40 above.

15. *Hiero* 8.1–7. Compare III b, note 38 above.

16. *Hiero* 7.3–4.

17. See pp. 63–64 and 66 above. Regarding the connection between "honor" and "noble," see *Cyropaedia* VII 1.13; *Memorabilia* III 1.1; 3.13; 5.28; *Oeconomicus* 21.6; *Resp. Lac.* 4.3–4; *Hipparchicus* 2.2.

18. *Memorabilia* II 7.7–14 and III 9.14–15. *Cyropaedia* VIII 3.40 ff.

19. *Hiero* 11.10; 1.13; 6.13. Compare *Cyropaedia* VII 2.26–29.

20. In *Hiero* 11.15, the only passage in which Simonides applies

"happy" and "blessed" to individuals, he does not explain the meaning of these terms. In the two passages in which he speaks of the happiness of the city, he understands by happiness power, wealth, and renown (11.5, 7. Cf. *Resp. Lac.* 1.1–2). Accordingly, one could expect that he understands by the most noble and most blessed possession that possession of power, wealth, and renown which is not marred by envy. This expectation is, to say the least, not disproved by 11.13–15. Compare also *Cyropaedia* VIII 7.6–7; *Memorabilia* IV 2.34–35; *Oeconomicus* 4.23–5.1; *Hellenica* IV 1.36.

21. It is Hiero who on a certain occasion alludes to this meaning of "happiness" (2.3–5). Compare III a, note 33 above.

22. *Memorabilia* IV 8.11; I 6.14. Compare p. 42 and III a, note 25 above.

23. As for the danger of envy, see *Hiero* 11.6 and 7.10. As for the work and toil of the ruler, see 11.15 (ταῦτα πάντα) and 7.1–2. Compare *Memorabilia* II 1.10.

24. *De vectigalibus* 4.4; *Resp. Lac.* 15.8; *Symposium* 3.9 and 4.2–3; *Anabasis* V 7.10. Compare also *Cyropaedia* I 6.24 and p. 63 above.

25. *Memorabilia* III 9.8; *Cynegeticus* 1.17. Compare Socrates' statements in the *Memorabilia* (IV 2.33) and the *Apol. Socr.* (26) with Xenophon's own statement in the *Cynegeticus* (1.11).

26. Compare note 23 above. Compare *Memorabilia* III 11.16; *Oeconomicus* 7.1 and 11.9; *Symposium* 4.44.

27. *Memorabilia* I 2.6; 5.6; 6.5; II 6.28–29; IV 1.2. *Symposium* 8.41. Compare *Memorabilia* IV 2.2 and *Cyropaedia* I 6.46. Consider the fact that the second part of the *Hiero* is characterized by the fairly frequent occurrence, not only of χάρις but of ἀνάγκη as well (see p. 66 above).

28. *Memorabilia* IV 5.2; *Cyropaedia* I 5.12; *Anabasis* VII 7.41–42; *Symposium* 4.44.

29. *Memorabilia* II 4.5, 7; *Oeconomicus* 5.11. Compare III b, note 26 above.

30. As for the agreement between Simonides' final statement and the views expressed by Socrates and Xenophon, compare *Hiero* 11.5 with *Memorabilia* III 9.14, and *Hiero* 11.7 with *Agesilaus* 9.7.

31. Compare *Oeconomicus* 1.7 ff. with *Cyropaedia* I 3.17. Compare Isocrates, *To Demonicus* 28.

32. *Memorabilia* IV 5.6 and *Apol. Socr.* 21. Compare *Memorabilia* II 2.3; 4.2; I 2.7. As regards the depreciating remark on wisdom in *Memorabilia* IV 2.33, one has to consider the specific purpose of the whole chapter as indicated at its beginning. Ruling over willing subjects is called an almost divine good, not by Socrates but by Ischomachus (*Oeconomicus* 21.11–12).

33. *Memorabilia* I 4 and 6.10; IV 2.1 and 6.7. Regarding the distinction between education and wisdom, see also Plato, *Laws* 653a5–c4 and

659c9 ff., and Aristotle, *Politics* 1282a3–8. Compare also *Memorabilia* II 1.27, where the παιδεία of Heracles is presented as preceding his deliberate choice between virtue and vice.

34. Compare *Hiero* 3.2 (and 6.1–3) with the parallel in the *Symposium* (8.18).

35. *Hiero* 9.1–11. Simonides does not explain what the best things are. From 9.4 it appears that according to Xenophon's Simonides the things which are taught by the teachers of choruses do not belong to the best things: the instruction given by the teachers of choruses is not gratifying to the pupils, and instruction in the best things is gratifying to the pupils. Following Simonides, we shall leave it open whether the subjects mentioned in 9.6 (military discipline, horsemanship, justice in business dealings, etc.) meet the minimum requirements demanded of the best things, *viz.*, that instruction in them is gratifying to the pupils. The fact that he who executes these things well is honored by prizes, does not prove that they belong to the best things (cf. 9.4 and *Cyropaedia* III 3.53). Whether the things Simonides teaches are the best things will depend on whether the instruction that he gives to the tyrant is gratifying to the latter. The answer to this question remains as ambiguous as Hiero's silence at the end of the dialogue. Xenophon uses in the *Hiero* the terms εὖ εἰδέναι and εὖ ποιεῖν fairly frequently (note especially the "meeting" of the two terms in 6.13 and 11.15). He thus draws our attention to the question of the relation of knowing and doing. He indicates his answer by the synonymous use of βέλτιον εἰδέναι and μᾶλλον εἰδέναι in the opening passage (1.1–2; observe the density of εἰδέναι). Knowledge is intrinsically good, whereas action is not (cf. Plato, *Gorgias* 467e ff.): to know to a greater degree is to know better, whereas to do to a greater degree is not necessarily to "do" better. Κακῶς ποιεῖν is as much ποιεῖν as is εὖ ποιεῖν whereas κακῶς εἰδέναι is practically identical with not knowing at all. (See *Cyropaedia* III 3.9 and II 3.13).

36. *Hiero* 9.9–10. The opposite view is stated by Isocrates in his *To Nicocles* 17.

37. The distinction suggested by Simonides between the wise and the rulers reminds one of Socrates' distinction between his own pursuit which consists in making people capable of political action on the one hand, and political activity proper on the other (*Memorabilia* I 6.15). According to Socrates, the specific understanding required of the ruler is not identical with wisdom, strictly speaking. (Compare the explicit definition of wisdom in *Memorabilia* IV 6.7—see also *ibid.* 6.1 and I 1.16— with the explicit definition of rule in III 9.10–13 where the term "wisdom" is studiously avoided.) In accordance with this, Xenophon hesitates to speak of the wisdom of either of the two Cyruses, and when calling Agesilaus "wise," he evidently uses the term in a loose sense, not

to say in the vulgar sense (*Agesilaus* 6.4–8 and 11.9). In the *Cyropaedia*, he adumbrates the relation between the ruler and the wise man by the conversations between Cyrus on the one hand, his father (whose manner of speaking is reminiscent of that of Socrates) and Tigranes (the pupil of a sophist whose fate is reminiscent of the fate of Socrates) on the other. Compare pp. 33 and 66 above. Compare IV, note 50 above.

38. See pp. 39–40 above. Compare Plato, *Republic* 620c3–d2.

39. See p. 21 above. Compare Plato, *Republic* 581e6–582e9.

40. "Honor *seems* to be something great" and "no human pleasure *seems* to come nearer to divinity than the enjoyment connected with honors." (*Hiero* 7.1, 4). See also the ὡς ἔοικε in 7.2 and the εἰκότως δοκεῖτε in 7.4. Compare III b, note 41 above.

41. Since the preferences of a wise man are wise, we may say that Simonides reveals his wisdom in his statement on honor to a much higher degree than in his preceding utterances. The effect of that statement on Hiero would therefore ultimately be due to the fact that through it he faces Simonides' wisdom for the first time in the conversation. Without doubt, he interprets Simonides' wisdom, at least to begin with, in accordance with his own view—the vulgar view—of wisdom. Compare note 12 above.

42. ἐμφύεται . . . ἐμφύῃ (*Hiero* 7.3). Compare *Cyropaedia* I 2.1–2 and *Oeconomicus* 13.9.

43. In *Hiero* 8.5–6 (as distinguished from *ibid.* 7.1–4) Simonides does not suggest that rulers are honored more than private men. He does not say that only rulers, and not private men, are honored by the gods (cf. *Apol. Socr.* 14–18). He says that a given individual is honored more highly when being a ruler than when living as a private man; he does not exclude the possibility that that individual is in all circumstances less honored than another man who never rules. In the last part of 8.5 he replaces "ruler" by the more general "those honored above others" (cf. *Apol. Socr.* 21). The bearing of 8.6 is still more limited as appears from a comparison of the passage with 2.1 and 7.3. Love of honor may seem to be characteristic of those wise men who converse with tyrants. Plato's Socrates says of Simonides that he was desirous of honor in regard to wisdom (*Protagoras* 343b7–c3).

44. *Hiero* 3.1, 6, 8. Compare *ibid.* 1.19, 21–23, 29 and 4.8. See III b, note 34 above.

45. Compare *Hiero* 3.1–9 with *ibid.* 8.1 and 11.8 (the emphatic "you"). See also Hiero's last utterance in 10.1. Hiero's praise of honor in 7.9–10 is clearly not spontaneous but solicited by Simonides' praise of honor in 7.1–4. Hiero's praise of honor differs from Simonides' in this, that only according to the former is love a necessary element of honor. Furthermore, it should be noted that Hiero makes a distinction between pleasure

and the satisfaction of ambition (1.27). Xenophon's characterization of Hiero does not contradict the obvious fact that the tyrant is desirous of honors (cf. 4.6 as well as the emphasis on Hiero's concern with being loved with Aristotle's analysis in *Eth. Nic.* 1159a12 ff.). But Xenophon asserts by implication that the tyrant's, or the ruler's, desire for honor is inseparable from the desire for being loved by human beings. The most obvious explanation of the fact that Hiero stresses "love" and Simonides stresses "honor" would of course be this: Hiero stresses the things which the tyrant lacks, whereas Simonides stresses the things which the tyrant enjoys. Now, tyrants are commonly hated (cf. Aristotle, *Politics* 1312b19–20) but they are honored. This explanation is correct but insufficient because it does not account for Simonides' genuine concern with honor or praise and for his genuine indifference to being loved by human beings.

46. Compare *Hiero* 7.1–4 with *ibid.* 1.16 and the passages cited in the preceding note. The forms of honor other than praise and admiration partake of the characteristic features of love rather than of those of praise and admiration. The fact that Simonides speaks in the crucial passage (*Hiero* 7.1–4) of honor in general, is due to his adaptation to Hiero's concern with love. Consider also the emphasis on honor rather than on praise in ch. 9.

47. Plato, *Gorgias* 481d4–5 and 513c7–8. Compare also the characterization of the tyrant in the *Republic* (see III b, note 12 above). As regards the disagreement between Hiero and Simonides concerning the status of "human beings," compare the disagreement between the politician and the philosopher on the same subject in Plato's *Laws* (804b5–c1).

48. This explains also the different attitude of the two types to envy. See p. 87 above.

49. Compare Plato, *Gorgias* 481d4–5.

50. *Hiero* 11.8–15. Compare *Agesilaus* 6.5 and 11.15.

51. *Hiero* 7.9. Compare Plato, *Republic* 330c3–6 and *Laws* 873c2–4; Aristotle, *Politics* 1262b22–24. Compare also p. 34 and II, note 22 above. Cf. 1 Peter 1.8 and Cardinal Newman's comment: "St. Peter makes it almost a description of the Christian, that he loves whom he has not seen."

52. Simonides fr. 99 Bergk.

53. Cf. the use of φίλοι in the sense of fellow-citizens as opposed to strangers or enemies in *Hiero* 11.15, *Memorabilia* I 3.3, and *Cyropaedia* II 2.15.

54. *Hiero* 8.1–7. That this is not the last word of Xenophon on love, appears most clearly from *Oeconomicus* 20.29.

55. Compare *Hiero* 7.9 and 11.14–15 with *Hellenica* VII 3.12 (*Cyropaedia* III 3.4) and *Memorabilia* IV 8.7. The popular view is apparently

adopted in Aristotle's *Politics* 1286b11–12 (cf. 1310b33 ff.). Compare Plato, *Gorgias* 513e5 ff. and 520e7–11.

56. Compare *Hiero* 7.9 with *ibid.* 7.1–4.

57. Men of excellence in an emphatic sense are Hesiod, Epicharmus, and Prodicus (*Memorabilia* II 1.20–21). Compare also *Memorabilia* I 4.2–3 and 6.14.

58. *Memorabilia* I 2.3 and 6.10. Simonides' statement that no human pleasure seems to come nearer to the divine than the enjoyment connected with honors (*Hiero* 7.4) is ambiguous. In particular, it may refer to the belief that the very gods derive pleasure from being honored (whereas they presumably do not enjoy the other pleasures discussed in the dialogue) or it may refer to the connection between the highest ambition and godlike self-sufficiency. Compare VI note 6 below.

59. As for the connection between this kind of selfishness and wisdom, compare Plato, *Gorgias* 458a2–7 and the definition of justice in the *Republic*. Considerations which were in one respect similar to those indicated in our text seem to have induced Hegel to abandon his youthful "dialectics of love" in favor of the "dialectics of the desire for recognition." See A. Kojève, *Introduction à l'étude de Hegel*, Paris (Gallimard), 1947, 187 and 510–12, and the same author's "Hegel, Marx et le Christianisme," *Critique*, 1946, 350–52.

60. Compare Simonides' disparaging remark on a kind of pleasure which is enjoyed by others rather than by oneself in *Hiero* 1.24 (cf. III b, note 11 above). Consider also the ambiguity of "food" (*Memorabilia* III 5.10; Plato, *Protagoras* 313c5–7). As regards the connection between friendship ("love") and sex, cf. *Hiero* 1.33, 36–38 and 7.6. The explanation suggested in the text can easily be reconciled with the fact that Hiero's concern with the pleasures of sex, if taken literally, would seem to characterize him, not as a ruler in general, but as an imperfect ruler. Xenophon's most perfect ruler, the older Cyrus, is characterized by the almost complete absence of concern with such pleasures. What is true of the perfect ruler, is still more true of the wise: whereas Cyrus does not dare to look at the beautiful Panthea, Socrates visits the beautiful Theodote without any hesitation (cf *Cyropaedia* V 1.7 ff. with *Memorabilia* III 11.1; *Memorabilia* I 2.1 and 3.8–15; *Oeconomicus* 12.13–14; *Agesilaus* 5.4–5). To use the Aristotelian terms, whereas Cyrus is continent, Socrates is temperate or moderate. In other words, Cyrus' temperance is combined with inability or unwillingness to look at the beautiful or to admire it (cf. *Cyropaedia* V 1.8 and VIII 1.42), whereas Socrates' temperance is the foundation for his ability and willingness to look at the beautiful and to admire it. To return to Hiero, he reveals a strong interest in the pleasures of sight (*Hiero* 1.11–13; cf. 11.10). He is concerned not so much with the pleasures of sex in general as with those of homosexuality.

This connects him somehow with Socrates: love of men seems to bespeak a higher aspiration than love of women. (*Symposium* 8.2, 29; *Cyropaedia* II 2.28; Plato, *Symposium* 208d ff. Cf. Montesquieu, *De l'esprit des lois* VII 9 note: "Quant au vrai amour, dit Plutarque, les femmes n'y ont aucune part. Il parlait comme son siècle. Voyez Xénophon, au dialogue intitulé *Hiéron*.") Hiero is presented as a ruler who is capable of conversing with the wise and of appreciating them (cf. III a, note 44 above). Does Hiero's education explain why he is not a perfect ruler? Only the full understanding of the education of Cyrus would enable one to answer this question. Compare IV, note 50 above.

61. *Hiero* 11.7, 11–15. *Memorabilia* I 2.11.

62. *Hiero* 6.9. How little Simonides impresses Hiero, a good judge in this matter, as being warlike, is indicated by the latter's "*if* you too have experience of war" (6.7) as compared with his "I *know* well that you too have experience" regarding the pleasures of the table (1.19). Cf. also *ibid.* 1.29, 23. Consider Simonides' silence about "manliness" (p. 66 above), and compare III b, notes 18 and 38, and III c, note 6 above.

63. *Hiero* 11.7. In the parallel in the *Agesilaus* (9.7) the qualifying words "among human beings" are omitted.

64. *Hiero* 2.7–18. (Consider the conditional clauses in 2.7.) The emphasis in this passage is certainly on war. The passage consists of two parts: In the first part (2.7–11) in which Hiero shows that if peace is good and war bad, tyrants are worse off than private citizens, "peace" occurs three times and "war" (and derivations) seven times; in the second part (2.12–18) in which he shows that as regards the pleasures of war—or more specifically as regards the pleasures of wars waged against forcibly subjected people, i.e., against rebellious subjects—tyrants are worse off than private citizens, "peace" does not occur at all but "war" (and derivatives) occurs seven times.

65. Plato, *Republic* 566e6–567a9. Aristotle, *Politics* 1313b28–30 and 1305a18–22.

66. *Cyropaedia* I 4.24; VII 1.13. *Memorabilia* III 1.6. Compare Plato, *Republic* 375c1–2 and 537a6–7 with Aristotle, *Politics* 1327b38–1328a11.

67. *Hiero* 1.34–35. As regards the relation between Eros and Ares, compare Simonides fr. 43 Bergk and Aristotle, *Politics* 1269b24–32.

68. *Hiero* 6.5; compare *ibid.* 6.14.

69. *Hiero* 2.2; 6.12–14. Compare the use of the second person singular in 6.13 on the one hand, and in 6.14 on the other.

70. *Hiero* 5.1. *Apol. Socr.* 16. *Memorabilia* I 6.10. Socrates does not teach strategy whereas he does teach economics (compare *Memorabilia* III 1 and IV 7.1 with the *Oeconomicus*). Compare Plato, *Republic* 366c7–d1 and the passages indicated in IV, note 45 above.

VI. Pleasure and Virtue

1. Compare *Memorabilia* IV 8.11.

2. See pp. 45–48 and III a, note 44 above.

3. Compare *Hiero* 8.6 with *ibid.* 2.1 and 7.3. Compare *Hiero* 5.1–2 with *ibid.* 3.1–9 and 6.1–3 on the one hand, and with *Memorabilia* II 4 and I 6.14 on the other. Compare *Hiero* 1.11–14 with *Memorabilia* II 1.31: Hiero does not mention one's own virtuous actions as the most pleasant sight. Compare *Hiero* 3.2 with *Symposium* 8.18: he does not mention the common enjoyment of friends about their noble actions among the pleasures of friendship. He replaces Simonides' ἐπινοεῖν by ἐπιθυμεῖν (*Hiero* 2.2 and 4.7).

4. *Hiero* 7.9–10.

5. Aristotle's suggestions for the improvement of tyrannical government (in the fifth book of the *Politics*) are more akin in spirit to Xenophon's suggestions than to Isocrates'; they are, however, somewhat more moralistic than those made in the *Hiero*.

6. Fr. 71 Bergk. When Xenophon's Simonides says that no human pleasure seems to come nearer to the divine than the enjoyment connected with honors, he may imply that "the divine" is pure pleasure. Compare V, note 58 above.

7. Compare *Hiero* 4.10 with frs. 5, 38, 39 and 42 Bergk. Compare Plato, *Protagoras* 346b5–8. Compare also Simonides' definition of nobility as old wealth with Aristotle's view according to which it is not so much wealth as virtue that is of the essence of nobility (*Politics* 1255a32 ff., 1283a33–38, 1301b3–4).

8. *Lyra Graeca*, ed. by J. M. Edmonds, vol. 2, revised and augmented edition, 258. Compare p. 66 above. See *Hellenica* II 3.19 and *Apol. Socr.* 30.

9. *Lyra Graeca*, ed. cit., 250, 256 and 260. Compare Plato, *Protagoras* 316d3–7, 338e6 ff. and 340e9 ff.; also *Republic* 331e1–4 and context (Simonides did not say that to say the truth is of the essence of justice).

10. Compare pp. 33, 40, 52, 53f, 56–7, 78–9.

11. Compare pp. 90 ff. above.

12. This would also explain why Simonides emphasizes somewhat later the pleasures connected with food: food is the fundamental need of all animals (*Memorabilia* II 1.1). In *Hiero* 7.3, where he hides his wisdom to a lesser degree than in the preceding sections, he does not call, as he did in 2.1, the pleasures of the body "small things."

13. Compare *Memorabilia* I 4.5 and IV 3.11.

14. Compare Plato, *Theatetus* 184c5–7 and 185e6–7.

15. *Hiero* 1.1. Compare the κάλλιον θεᾶσθαι in 2.5 with the ἥδιον θεᾶσθαι in 8.6.

16. *Hiero* 1.5. A remark which Simonides makes later on (9.10) might induce one to believe that he identified the good with the useful, and this might be thought to imply that the end for which the good things are useful, is pleasure. This interpretation would not take account of the facts which we discuss in the text. Simonides must therefore be presumed to have distinguished between the good which is good because it is useful for something else, and the good which is intrinsically good and not identical with the pleasant.

17. *Hiero* 1.22.

18. *Hiero* 1.9; 2.1; 7.3.

19. See the reference to the divine in *Hiero* 7.4.

20. *Hiero* 1.27; 3.3; 6.16.

21. The importance of the problem "fatherland-friendship" for the understanding of the *Hiero* is shown by the fact that that problem determines the plan of the bulk of the second section (ch. 3–6). This is the plan of ch. 3–6: I (a) friendship (3.1–9); (b) trust (4.1–2); (c) fatherland (4.3–5). II (a) possessions (4.6–11); (b) good men or the virtues (5.1–2); (c) fatherland (5.3–4). III (a) pleasures of private men (6.1–3); (b) fear, protection, laws (6.4–11); (c) helping friends and hurting enemies (6.12–15). The difference between "fatherland" and "trust" is not as clear-cut as that between either of them and "friendship": both fatherland and trust are good with regard to protection, or freedom from fear, whereas friendship is intrinsically pleasant. "Friendship" can be replaced by "possessions" for the reason given in *Hiero* 3.6, *Memorabilia* II 4.3–7 and *Oeconomicus* 1.14; "friendship" can be replaced by "pleasures of private men" for the reason given in *Hiero* 6.1–3. "Trust" can be replaced by "virtue" (cf. Plato, *Laws* 630b2–c6) as well as by "protection" (trustworthiness is the specific virtue of guards: *Hiero* 6.11). "Fatherland" can be replaced by "helping the friends and hurting the enemies" with a view to the fact that helping the friends, i.e., the fellow citizens, and hurting the enemies, i.e., the enemies of the city, is the essence of patriotism (cf. *Symposium* 8.38). The same distinction which governs the plan of ch. 3–6, governs the plan of ch. 8–11 as well: (a) friendship (ch. 8–9; see 10.1); (b) protection (guards) (ch. 10); (c) fatherland or city (ch. 11; see 11.1).

22. Compare *Hiero* 3.3 with 4.1 on the one hand, and with 4.3–5 on the other. Compare 4.2 and 6.11.

23. *Hiero* 4.3–4. Compare 6.6, 10. In what may best be called the repetition of the statement on the fatherland (5.3–4), Hiero says it is necessary to be patriotic because one cannot be preserved or be happy without the city. Compare the οὐκ ἄνευ in 5.3 with the (οὐκ) ἄνευ in 4.1. From 5.3–4 it appears that the power and renown of the fatherland is normally pleasant. When speaking of friendship, Hiero had not spoken of

the power and renown of friends: he had not implied that only powerful and renowned friends are pleasant (compare *Agesilaus* 11.3). Not
the fatherland, but power and renown are pleasant, and the power and
renown of one's city are pleasant because they contribute to one's own
power and renown. Compare *Hiero* 11.13. When speaking of the pleasures
which he enjoyed while being a private man, Hiero mentions friendship;
he does not mention the city or the fatherland (6.1–3).

24. *Hiero* 4.3–4 and 5.3.

25. Compare *Hiero* 4.3 and 10.4 with 6.10.

26. *Hiero* 9.2–4 (cf. 1.37; 5.2–3; 8.9). Compare also Hiero's emphasis
(in his statement on friendship: 3.7–9) on the relations within the family,
with the opposite emphasis in Xenophon's account of Socrates' character
(*Memorabilia* II 2–10): the blood relations are "necessary" (*Memorabilia*
II 1.14). *Cyropaedia* IV 2.11. *Anabasis* VII 7.29. *Memorabilia* II 1.18.
Compare Aristotle, *Rhetoric* 1370a8–17 and Empedocles fr. 116 (Diels,
Vorsokratiker, first ed.). See V, note 27 above.

27. Compare *Hiero* 5.3 and 4.9 with 3.1–9.

28. Observe that friendship and virtue occur in different columns of
the plan of ch. 3–6 (see note 21 above). Compare Hiero's praise of the
friend with Socrates' praise of the good friend (*Memorabilia* II 4 and 6).

29. *Hiero* 11.14.

30. *Hiero* 11.1, 5–6. Compare pp. 90 ff. above.

31. Compare *Hellenica* I 7.21.

32. Compare *Hiero* 4.3 with *Memorabilia* II 3.2 and 1.13–15.

33. Only the fairly short first part of the *Memorabilia* (I 1–2) deals
with "Socrates and the city," whereas the bulk of the work deals with
"Socrates' character"; see the two perorations: I 2.62–64 and IV 8.11.
As regards the plan of the *Memorabilia*, see Emma Edelstein, *Xeno-
phontisches und Platonisches Bild des Sokrates*, Berlin, 1935, 78–137.

34. Isocrates, *Antidosis* 155–56.

35. *Anabasis* III 1.4–9; V 6.15–37. Compare *ibid.* V 3.7 and VII 7.57.
The sentiment of Proxenus is akin to that expressed by Hermes in
Aristophanes' *Plutus* 1151 (*Ubi bene ibi patria*). (Compare *Hiero* 5.1
and 6.4 with *Plutus* 1 and 89.) Compare Cicero, *Tusc. disput.* V 37.106 ff.

36. *Anabasis* V 3.6 and *Hellenica* IV 3.15 (cf. IV 2.17).

37. B. G. Niebuhr, "Ueber Xenophons Hellenika," *Kleine historische
und philosophische Schriften*, I, Bonn, 1828, 467: "Wahrlich einen
ausgearteteren Sohn hat kein Staat jemals ausgestossen als diesen
Xenophon. Plato war auch kein guter Bürger, Athens wert war er nicht,
unbegreifliche Schritte hat er getan, er steht wie ein Sünder gegen die
Heiligen, Thukydides und Demosthenes, aber doch wie ganz anders als
dieser alte Tor!"

38. *Hiero* 4.3–5 and 5.3.

39. See pp. 77–78 above.

40. *Cyropaedia* II 2.24–26. Dakyns comments on the passage as follows: "Xenophon's breadth of view: virtue is not confined to citizens, but we have the pick of the whole world. Cosmopolitan Hellenism." Consider the conditional clauses in *Agesilaus* 7.4, 7. Compare *Hipparchicus* 9.6 and *De vectigalibus* 2.1–5.

41. Compare Burke, *Reflections on the Revolution in France*, Everyman's Library ed., p. 59, on the one hand, and Pascal, *Provinciales* XIII as well as Kant, "Über den Gemeinspruch: Das mag in der Theorie richtig sein, taugt aber nicht für die Praxis," on the other.

42. Socrates' statement that cities and nations are "the wisest of human things" (*Memorabilia* I 4.16) does not mean then that the collective wisdom of political societies is superior to the wisdom of wise individuals. The positive meaning of the statement cannot be established but by detailed interpretation of the conversation during which the statement is made.

43. The only special virtues of which Simonides speaks with some emphasis, are moderation and justice. Moderation may be produced by fear, the spoiler of all pleasures (*Hiero* 10.2–3 and 6.6; cf. IV, note 35 above), and it goes along with lack of leisure (9.8). As for justice, Simonides speaks once of a special kind of justice, the justice in business relations, and twice of "doing injustice" (9.6 and 10.8). Now, the term "justice" designates in Xenophon's works a variety of kindred phenomena which range from the most narrow legalism to the confines of pure and universal beneficence. Justice may be identical with moderation, it may be a subdivision of moderation, and it may be a virtue apart from moderation. It is certain that Simonides does not understand by justice legality, and there is no reason to suppose that he identified justice with beneficence. He apparently holds a considerably more narrow view of justice than does Hiero. (For Hiero's view of justice, see especially 5.1–2 and 4.11.) He replaces Hiero's "unjust men" by "those who commit unjust actions" (for the interpretation consider Aristotle, *Eth. Nic.* 1134a17 ff.). Whereas Hiero identifies justice and moderation by using ἀδικεῖν and ὑβρίζειν synonymously, Simonides distinguishes the two virtues from each other: he identifies ἀδικεῖν and κακουργεῖν and he distinguishes between κακουργεῖν and ὑβρίζειν (see 8.9; 9.8; 10.8, 2–4; cf. Aristotle, *Rhetoric* 1389b7–8 and 1390a17–18; Plato, *Protagoras* 326a4–5). It seems that Simonides understands by justice the abstaining from harming others (cf. *Agesilaus* 11.8 and *Memorabilia* IV 4.11–12; consider *Symposium* 4.15) and that he thus makes allowance for the problem inherent in benefiting "human beings" (as distinguished from "real men" or "men of excellence"). It is easy to see that justice thus understood, as distinguished from its motives and results, is not intrinsically pleasant.

44. *Memorabilia* II 1.23, 26, 29.

45. Diogenes Laertius II 65–66.

46. Compare *Memorabilia* II 1.34 with *ibid* I 6.13, *Symposium* 1.5 and 4.62 and *Cynegeticus* 13.

47. *Memorabilia* I 3.8–13.

48. Compare *Hiero* 11.15 with *Anabasis* VII 7.41. See *Anabasis* II 1.12 (cf. Simonides fr. 5 Bergk) and *Cyropaedia* I 5.8–10; also *Agesilaus* 10.3.

49. V. Brochard, *Études de philosophie ancienne et de philosophie moderne*, Paris (Vrin), 1926, 43.

50. Compare III a, note 27 and IV, note 25 above.

51. *Memorabilia* IV 6. 15.

52. *Memorabilia* IV 8.6–8 (cf. I 6.9 and IV 5.9–10). *Apol. Socr.* 5–6 and 32.

53. Compare Plato, *Republic* 357b4–358a3.

54. *Apol. Socr.* 5. Compare *Memorabilia* II 1.19. Regarding *sibi ipsi placere* see especially Spinoza, *Ethics* III, aff. deff. 25. As for the difference between Socrates and Simonides, compare also p. 97 above.

VII. Piety and Law

1. *De vectigalibus* 6.2–3. Compare p. 31 above.

2. When Simonides suggests to Hiero that he should spend money for the adornment of his city with temples *inter alia* (*Hiero* 11.1–2), he does not admonish him to practice piety; he merely advises him to spend his money in a way proper to a ruler. Aristotle's ethics which is silent about piety, mentions expenses for the worship of the gods under the heading "munificence." (*Eth. Nic.* 1122b19–23. Compare *Politics* 1321a35 ff. Cf. also J. F. Gronovius' note to Grotius' *De jure belli ac pacis*, Prolegg. §45: "Aristoteli ignoscendum, si inter virtutes morales non posuit religionem. . . . Nam illi ut veteribus omnibus extra Ecclesiam cultus deorum sub magnificentia ponitur.")

3. *Agesilaus* 1.34 and *Anabasis* III 2.13. Compare Plato, *Republic* 573c3–6.

4. *Politics* 1314b39 ff. No remark of this kind occurs in Aristotle's discussion of the preservation of the other régimes in the fifth book of the *Politics*. *Cyropaedia* VIII 1.23. Compare Isocrates, *To Nicocles* 20 and Machiavelli, *Principe* XVIII.

5. *Memorabilia* IV 6.2–4.

6. *Memorabilia* IV 8.11; I 4; IV 3.

7. *Hiero* 3.9. Compare *Oeconomicus* 7.16, 29–30 (cf. 7.22–28).

8. Cicero, *De natura deorum* I 22.60.

9. Φύσις and φύειν (or derivatives) occur in *Hiero* 1.22, 31, 33; 3.9; 7.3; 9.8. θεοὶ occurs in 3.5; 4.2; 8.5. Τò θεῖον occurs in 7.4. Compare the remarks on ἱερά in 4.5, 11 with *Hellenica* VI 4.30.

10. Compare *Anabasis* V 2.24–25 and Plato, *Laws* 709b7–8. Considering the relation between "nature" and "truth" (*Oeconomicus* 10.2 and *Memorabilia* II 1.22), the distinction between nature and law may imply the view that the law necessarily contains fictitious elements. In *Hiero* 3.3 Hiero says: "It has not even escaped the cities that friendship is a very great good and most pleasant to human beings. At any rate, many cities have a law (νομίζουσι) that only adulterers may be killed with impunity, evidently for this reason, because they believe (νομίζουσι) that they (the adulterers) are the destroyers of the wives' friendship with their husbands." The law that adulterers may be killed with impunity is based on the belief that the adulterers as distinguished from the wives are responsible for the wives' faithlessness. The question arises whether this belief is always sound. Xenophon alludes to this difficulty by making Hiero take up the question of the possible guilt of the wife in the subsequent sentence: "Since when the wife has been raped, husbands do not honor their wives any less on that account, provided the wives' love remains inviolate." It seems that the men's belief in the modesty of women is considered conducive to that modesty. Compare Montesquieu, *De l'esprit des lois* VI 17: "Parce que les hommes sont méchants, la loi est obligée de les supposer meilleurs qu'ils ne sont. Ainsi . . . on juge . . . que tout enfant conçu pendant le mariage est légitime; la loi a confiance en la mère comme si elle était la pudicité même." Cf. also Rousseau, *Emile* V (ed. Garnier, vol. 2, 147–48) Similarly, by considering (νομίζων) one's sons as the same thing as one's life or soul (*Hiero* 11.14), whereas in truth one's sons are not one's life or soul, one will be induced to act more beneficently than one otherwise would.

11. *Anabasis* II 6.19–20 (cf. Aristotle, *Eth. Nic.* 1179b4 ff.). *Symposium* 4.19.

ALEXANDRE KOJÈVE

Tyranny and Wisdom

◘ ◘ ◘

IN MY OPINION it is not only Xenophon who is of importance in this book that Strauss has devoted to him. Perhaps in spite of what its author thinks about it, this book of Strauss' is truly important not because it might reveal to us the authentic and uncomprehended thought of a contemporary and compatriot of Plato, but rather because of the problem it raises and discusses.

Xenophon's dialogue, as interpreted by Strauss, sets against a disillusioned tyrant, who claims to be discontented with his position as tyrant, a wise man who has come from afar to advise him on the way he ought to govern his state so that he himself may be satisfied by the exercise of tyranny. Xenophon makes these two characters speak, and he tells us between the lines what we should think of their words. Strauss presents the thought of Xenophon openly, and he tells us between the lines what we ought to think about it. More precisely, by presenting himself in his book not as a wise man possessing knowledge but as a philosopher seeking it, Strauss tells us not *what* we should think about all this but only what we should think *about* when we speak of the relations between

Translated from the French by Michael Gold.
Tyrannie et Sagesse (Paris: Editions Gallimard, 1954).

tyranny, or government in general, and wisdom or philosophy. In other words, he limits himself to raising the problems; but he raises them looking toward a solution.

It is regarding certain of these problems explicitly or implicitly raised by Strauss in the preceding pages that I should like to speak in these that follow.

To begin with, let us take the question of tyranny.

Note that it is not Hiero who asks Simonides for advice on the way he ought to exercise tyranny. Simonides gives it to him spontaneously. But it is the case nonetheless that Hiero listens to it (at a moment of leisure, it is true). And he does not say anything after having heard it; his silence shows us that he does not have anything to answer. We may conclude from this that he judges, indeed as we ourselves do, following Xenophon and Strauss, that Simonides' advice is full of wisdom. But as soon as he does not say so, and does not say that he is going to follow this advice, we assume that Hiero will not do anything about it. And such was probably the opinion of Simonides himself—who, according to Xenophon, does not even ask whether Hiero intends to use the advice he has just been given.

Confronted by this situation, we have a natural inclination to be shocked. We understand, to be sure, why Hiero would want to listen attentively to Simonides' advice, since, left to himself, he has, by his own admission, not been able to exercise his tyranny in a way that is satisfactory even to himself. But, "in his place," upon recognizing our incapacity we would have asked for advice spontaneously. We would even have done so "a long time ago"; and not in a moment of leisure, but "dropping everything." Above all, when we had discerned the excellence of the advice received, we would have loudly proclaimed it, and we would have done everything in our power to put it into use. And we would do this, once again, "dropping everything."

But before yielding to this natural impulse I believe we ought to reflect. Let us first ask ourselves if it is really true that "in Hiero's place" we would have been able to execute our noble intentions, "dropping everything." Hiero himself does not think so, since he says to Simonides (end of ch. vii): "That is exactly the greatest affliction of tyranny: one cannot get rid of it." And perhaps he is right. For the tyrant always has some "current business" which he cannot leave without properly winding it up. And it may very well be that the nature of this business is such that its pursuit proves to be incompatible with the measures that he would have to take in applying the wise man's advice, or more exactly, in establishing the ideal state of things which the latter demands. It may also be that the conclusion of "current business" requires more years than belong to the life of the tyrant himself. And who can say whether some of this business might not require centuries of effort to be completed?

Hiero draws Simonides' attention to the fact that in order to come to power, the tyrant must take certain measures which are, let us say, "unpopular" (in fact, Hiero considers them "criminal"). Simonides does not deny it, but he asserts that the tyrant could *maintain* himself in power without having recourse to violence, while gaining "popularity" by the appropriate measures. But Simonides does not say how the tyrant should set about abrogating the "unpopular" measures without immediately imperiling his life or power (and hence the very reforms which he was ready to introduce, following the wise man's intervention) or even the existence of the State as such. Nor does he explain how the "popular" nonviolent regime could have been established without the abolition of the measures in question.

Obviously this is what Simonides would have had to explain to Hiero if he had really wanted him to follow his advice. Not having done so, Simonides perhaps did not behave like a wise man but like a typical "intellectual," who criticizes the real world in which he lives from the standpoint of an "ideal" constructed in the universe of discourse: an "ideal" to which is attributed an "eternal" value, above all because it does not exist in the present and has not existed in the past. The fact is, Simonides presents his "ideal" in the form of a "utopia." For the "ideal" presented in the form of a "utopia" differs from this same ideal presented as an "active" (revolutionary) idea precisely because we cannot see, on the basis of the utopia, how the given concrete reality must be transformed in the present, to render it in the future conformable to the ideal in question.

Perhaps then Strauss is right in telling us that Simonides, who believes himself a wise man, is in reality only a poet. Confronted by a poetical vision, a dream, a utopia, Hiero reacts not like a "tyrant," but simply like a statesman—a "liberal" statesman at that. In order not to encourage his critics, he does not want to proclaim openly that he recognizes the "theoretical" value of the ideal that Simonides describes to him. He does not want to do so not only because he knows that he could not *realize* this ideal (in the actual state of things) but also, and above all, because nobody tells him what is the first step to be taken in order to approach it. So, as a good liberal, he limits himself to remaining *silent:* he *does* nothing, he *decides* nothing, and he allows Simonides to *speak* and to *go* in peace.

According to Strauss, Xenophon was perfectly well aware of the necessarily utopian character of the sort of advice given by Simonides. He thought that the "enlightened" and "popular" tyranny portrayed by the latter is an ideal which cannot be realized, and his dialogue has as its goal to convince us that, this being the case, it is better to give up any idea of tyranny before even having tried to establish it. Strauss and Xenophon thus seem to reject the very idea of "tyrannical" government. But that is altogether another question, an extremely complex one moreover. This would be advice which would no longer have anything to do with that which a wise man could give to a tyrant with a view to an "ideal" tyranny.

To evaluate the meaning and the true bearing of this new advice, it would be necessary to know if, in certain concrete cases, the renunciation of tyranny would not mean the renunciation of government in general, and imply either the ruin of a state or the abandonment of any real possibility of progress in a particular state or for mankind altogether (at least at a given historical moment). But before speaking of this, it would be necessary to see if Hiero, Simonides, Xenophon, and Strauss are really right in asserting that the "ideal" tyranny sketched by Simonides is only a utopia.

When one reads the last three chapters of the dialogue, where Simonides describes the "ideal" tyranny, one observes that what might appear utopian to Xenophon has today become an almost banal reality. What is said in those three chapters is this. To begin with, the tyrant ought to distribute "prizes" of all sorts, especially honorific, in order to establish in his State a stakhanovistic emulation in the fields of agriculture, industry, and commerce (ch. ix). Next, instead of maintaining a mercenary bodyguard, the tyrant should organize a state police (which will "always be needed"), and a permanent armed force which would serve as the nucleus of an army mobilized in case of war (ch. x). The tyrant, moreover, ought not to disarm his subjects, but introduce obligatory military service and turn to general mobilization, if necessary. Finally, he ought to spend a part of his "personal" fortune for the common good and construct public buildings rather than palaces. Generally speaking, the tyrant would gain the "affection" of his subjects by making them happier and by treating "his country as his household, his fellow citizens as his comrades" (ch. xi).

It can be understood that Xenophon might have considered all this utopian. The fact is, he knew only tyrannies exercised for the advantage of an already established social class, or for the sake of personal or familial ambitions, or with the vague idea of doing better than any others, though wanting the same thing as they did. He had not seen "tyrannies" exercised in the service of truly revolutionary political, social, or economic ideas (in the service, that is, of rational objectives, radically different from anything already existing) with a national, racial, imperial, or humanitarian grounding. But it is surprising to see our contemporary—Strauss—sharing, as it seems, this way of looking at things. Personally, I do not accept Strauss' position because in my opinion the utopia of Simonides-Xenophon has been *realized* by modern "tyrannies" (by Salazar, for example). And it is possible that what was utopian in the time of Xenophon could have been realized later precisely because the time necessary for the conclusion of the "current business" of which I spoke above has elapsed, business which one was obliged to conclude before one could even begin to take the measures prerequisite to the realization of the ideal suggested by Simonides. But does it follow that these tyrannies are [philosophically] justified by Xenophon's dialogue? Must one say that the modern "tyrant" has been able to realize the "philosophic" ideal of tyranny without having relied upon the advice of the wise man, or must it be admitted that he has been able to do so only because a Simonides once advised a Hiero?

I will try below to answer the second question. As for the first, to answer that we shall have to go to the heart of the matter.

At the culmination of the dialogue (ch. vii), Simonides explains to Hiero that his grievances against tyranny are worthless, since the supreme goal and ultimate motive of men is honor, and since, as far as honor goes, the tyrant is better off than all the others.

Let us stop for a moment to consider this way of arguing. Simonides adopts, with perfect self-awareness, the "pagan" or even "aristocratic" existential attitude, which Hegel will later call that of the "Master" (as opposed to the attitude of the Slave, which is that of the Judeo-Christian, i.e., bourgeois man). And Simonides develops this point of view in an extremely radical form. In fact, he does not limit himself to saying that "the desire to be honored makes one endure any labor and brave any danger," making us believe that it is exclusively for glory that man struggles and labors. He goes much further still, asserting that "what makes the difference between man and the other animals is the desire for honor." But like any consistent "pagan," "aristocrat," or "Master," Simonides does not believe that the quest for glory is the prerogative of *all* creatures with a human form. The quest belongs properly and necessarily only to those who are born Masters, and it is irremediably missing in "servile natures," who, by that very fact, are not truly human (and deserve to be treated accordingly). "Those to whom *nature* has given the love of honor and praise are the ones who differ most from animals; and they are regarded not as simple creatures [human in appearance], but as [real] men." And these "real" men who live for glory are to a certain extent "divine." For, "no human pleasure brings us closer to the divinity than the joy which comes from honors."

This profession of "pagan" and "aristocratic" faith would no doubt have shocked the "bourgeois" who lived (or live) in the Judeo-Christian world. In this world neither the philosophers nor the tyrants themselves *said* such things, and insofar as they wanted to *justify* tyranny, they used other arguments. It would be vain to enumerate all of them, for, in my opinion, only one is really valid. But this one deserves our complete attention. I think it would be false to say, with Simonides, that only the "desire to be honored" and the "joy which comes from honor" makes one "endure any labor and brave any danger." The *joy* that comes from labor itself and the desire to *succeed* in an undertaking can, by themselves, prompt a man to undertake painful and dangerous labors (as is already shown in the ancient myth of Heracles). A man can work hard, risking his life, for no other reason than to experience the joy which he always has in the *execution* of his plan or, what is the same thing, in the transformation of his "idea," or his "ideal," into a *reality* conditioned by his own *efforts*. A child, alone on a beach, makes sand-patties which he will, perhaps, never show anyone; and a painter may cover the cliffs of some desert isle with drawings, knowing all the while that he will never leave it. Thus—though it is an extreme case—a man can aspire to tyranny in the same way that a "conscientious" and "enthusiastic" workman can aspire to adequate conditions for his labor. Actually, a "legitimate" monarch who accedes to power and effortlessly maintains himself in it, and who would not be impressed by glory, need not sink into the life of pleasure, and he could actively devote himself to the government of the State. But this monarch, and in general the "bourgeois" states-man who in principle renounces glory, will exercise his hard political "trade" only if he has the mentality of a "laborer." And they will want to justify their tyranny solely by its being a necessary condition for success in their "labor."

In my opinion, this "bourgeois" way of looking at things and of justifying tyranny (a way which made the "Judeo-Christian" world, in which men were in theory asked to renounce glory, to a certain extent and for a certain time viable) must complete the "aristocratic" theory of which Simonides makes himself the spokesman and which gives an account *only* of the attitude of the *idle* "aristocrat" devoting the best of his powers to occasionally bloody struggles with other men for the sake of the *honor* victory will bring him.

But we ought not isolate the "bourgeois" point of view by forgetting or denying the "aristocratic" theory. It ought not be forgotten that, to return to our examples, the "desire to be honored" and the joy that arises from "honors" come into play, and become decisive, as soon as the child makes his sand-patties in the presence of adults or his comrades, and as soon as the painter returns home and shows the reproductions of his rupestrine drawings; generally, as soon as there appears among men this emulation, which is, in fact, never absent, and which, according to Simonides (ch. ix), is necessary even for the true prosperity of agriculture, industry, and commerce. But in order for this observation to be applicable to the statesman, there must be a *struggle* for power, and *emulation* in its exercise, in the precise sense of these terms. To be sure, in theory the statesman could have done away with his rivals without thinking of glory, just as a workman, absorbed in his work and indifferent to what surrounds him, almost unconsciously does away with the objects which disturb his labor. But in fact, and this is particularly true for those who aspire to "tyranny," they do away with their rivals because they do not want the goal attained, the job done, by *another*, even if this other could do it just as well. In the situation where there is "emulation" or "competition" they do in fact act for the sake of glory, and it is only to justify themselves from the "Christian" or "bourgeois" point of view that they claim or believe themselves to do it only because they are or imagine themselves to be more "capable" or "better equipped" than the others.

Be that as it may, Hiero, in his role as an authentic "pagan aristocrat," unreservedly accepts Simonides' point of view. Nonetheless, he rejects the latter's argument as a *justification* of tyranny; admitting that the highest goal of man is honor, he asserts that the tyrant never attains this goal.

Hiero explains to Simonides (ch. vii, second paragraph) that the tyrant rules by terror and that consequently the compliments he receives from his subjects are dictated only by the fear he inspires in them. Now, "compliments dictated by fear are not honors; . . . such compliments must be regarded as servile acts." And the acts of a Slave give no satisfaction to that aristocratic Master, the ancient tyrant.

In presenting his own situation, Hiero describes the tragedy of the Master analyzed by Hegel in the *Phenomenology of Mind* (ch. iv, section A). The Master engages in a death struggle in order to make his adversary recognize his exclusive human dignity. But if his adversary is himself a Master, he will be animated by the same desire for "recognition," and he will fight to the death: his or the other's. And if the adversary submits (through fear of death), he shows himself to be a Slave. His "recognition" is then of no value to the victorious Master, in whose eyes the Slave is not a truly human being. The victor in this bloody struggle for pure prestige will not then be "satisfied" by his victory. His situation is thus essentially tragic since there is no possible way out.

To tell the truth, Xenophon's text is less precise than Hegel's.

Hiero confuses spontaneously accorded "sexual love" with the "affection" of his subjects who "recognize" him. Simonides corrects him by making him see that the tyrant as such is interested not in his "lovers" but in his subjects taken as citizens. But Simonides maintains the idea of "affection" (ch. xi). Moreover, Hiero would like to be made happy by his tyranny and by "honors" in general, and Simonides tells him that he will be "happy" (the last sentence of the dialogue) if he follows his advice and thereby obtains the "affection" of his fellow citizens. Now it is quite clear that tyranny or political action in general can, as such, engender neither "love" nor "affection" nor "happiness," for these three phenomena imply elements which have nothing to do with politics: a mediocre politician can be the object of an intense and authentic "affection" on the part of his fellow citizens, just as a great statesman may be universally admired without arousing love of any kind, and the most complete political success is perfectly compatible with a profoundly unhappy private life. And so it is better to stick to the precise formula of Hegel, who talks not of "affection" or "happiness" but of "recognition" and of "satisfaction," which comes from "recognition." For the desire to be "recognized" in one's reality and in one's eminent human dignity (by those whom one "recognizes in return") is actually, as I believe, the ultimate motive of all *emulation* among men and hence of all political *struggle*, including that which leads to tyranny. And the man who has satisfied this desire by his own action is, by that very fact, "satisfied," whether he is happy or not, beloved or not.

We may acknowledge then that the tyrants (and Hiero himself) will seek, before anything else, Hegelian "recognition." We may likewise acknowledge that Hiero, not having obtained this recognition, is really not "satisfied" in the full sense of that word. We thus understand why he listens to the advice of the wise man who, by indicating the means of obtaining "recognition," promises him "satisfaction."

Moreover, Hiero and Simonides know very well what is involved. Hiero would like his subjects "willingly to yield him the right of way" (ch. vii, second paragraph) and Simonides promises him that if he follows his advice his subjects will "obey him *without being constrained*" (ch. xi, twelfth paragraph). This is to say that the two of them look to authority.[1] For to get oneself "recognized" by someone, while inspiring in him neither fear (in the final analysis, fear of violent death) nor love—this, in his eyes, is to have *authority*. To acquire authority in the eyes of someone is to make him recognize this authority. Now a man's authority (that is to say, in the final analysis, his eminently human value, though not necessarily his *superiority*), is *recognized* by another when his advice or his orders are followed or executed not because this other man cannot do otherwise (physically, or through fear, or as a result of any other "passion"), but because he spontaneously considers them worthy of being followed or executed—and this not because he himself recognizes their intrinsic value, but only because it is *that man* who tells him (like an oracle); that is to say, precisely because he recognizes the "authority" of him who tells him. We may thus acknowledge that Hiero, exactly like any political man, has actively sought his tyranny because he wanted (consciously or not) to impose his exclusive *authority* on his fellow citizens.

We can believe Hiero then when he says he is not "satisfied." His enterprise has indeed failed, since he confesses that he must have recourse to *force*, to the exploitation of his subjects' fear (of death). But Hiero certainly exaggerates (and, according to Strauss, he does so voluntarily, to discourage from tyranny any possible rivals, Simonides in particular) when he says that he does not get *any* "satisfaction" from his "tyranny" because he enjoys *no* authority and governs *solely* through terror. For, contrary to a rather common prejudice, such a situation is absolutely impossible. Pure terror presupposes force alone—in the final analysis, physical force. By his physical force alone a man can dominate children, old men, and

---

[1] Hiero (*ibid.*), it is true, would like his subjects to "crown him for his *virtue*" and he believes that at the present time they condemn him "on account of his *injustice*." But "injustice" disturbs him only to the extent that it prevents his being "recognized," and it is only in order to obtain "recognition" that he would practice "virtue." In other words, "virtue" and "justice" are for him only means of imposing his *authority* on his subjects; they are not ends in themselves. What follows shows that Simonides' attitude is exactly the same: the tyrant must be "virtuous" and "just" in order to win the "affection" of his subjects; in order, that is, to do the things that will make his subjects obey "without being constrained," and—finally—in order to be "happy without being envied." This attitude is hardly "Socratic." We may recognize, with Strauss, that Simonides, as an advisor to a tyrant, adopts Hiero's point of view only for pedagogical reasons, without himself as a wise man sharing it.

some women, at the outside two or three adults; but he cannot in this way impose himself for long on a group of able-bodied men, however small. This is to say that "despotism" in the precise sense is possible only within some isolated family, and that the head of any state always has recourse to something besides his own force. In fact, a political chief always has recourse to his *authority*, and it is by his authority that he holds his power. The whole question is: By *whom* is this authority recognized and who "obeys him without constraint"? Indeed, the authority of a chief of state may be recognized either by a more or less extensive majority of the citizens or by a more or less restricted minority. Until very recently, it was not believed possible to speak of tyranny in a pejorative sense except where a minority (guided by an authority that it alone recognizes) directs by force or by "terror" (exploiting, that is, the fear of death) the majority of the citizens. Of course, only those citizens recognized as such by the state were taken into account. For no one criticizes, even today, the governing of children or criminals or madmen by force, nor was the forcible governing of women, slaves, or metics, for example, ever criticized in the past. But this way of looking at things, while logically possible, does not in fact correspond to men's natural reactions. Men have finally become aware of this; and recent political experiences, such as the present polemic between "Western" and "Eastern" democrats, have made it possible to give a more adequate definition of tyranny.

In fact, it is tyranny (in the morally neutral sense of the word) when a fraction of the citizens (it matters little whether it be a majority or a minority) imposes its ideas and acts on all the other citizens, which are determined by an authority which it recognizes spontaneously but which it has not succeeded in making the others recognize; and where it does so without "coming to terms" with these others, without seeking any "compromises" with them, and without taking into account their ideas and desires (determined by another authority recognized by these others). Quite plainly this fraction can do this only through force or terror, by playing in the last analysis on the fear that the others have of the violent death which the former can inflict on them. One can say, then, that in this situation the others are "enslaved," since they behave in fact like slaves who are ready to do anything to save their lives. And it is to this situation that certain of our contemporaries give the name *tyranny* in the pejorative sense of the word.

Be that as it may, it is clear that Hiero is not fully "satisfied," not because he has *no* authority and governs *solely* by force, but because his authority, recognized by some, is not recognized by *all* of those whom he himself considers citizens—as men worthy of recognizing it and hence expected to do so. By behaving in this manner, Hiero, who symbolizes for us the ancient tyrant, is in full agreement with the analysis of "satisfaction" (obtained by emulation or by action which is "political" in the broadest sense) given by Hegel.

Hegel says that the political man acts at the prompting of the desire for "recognition" and that he can be fully "satisfied" only if he has completely satisfied *this* desire. Now this desire is by definition unlimited: a man wants to be actually "recognized" by *all* those he considers capable and hence worthy of "recognizing" him. To the extent that the citizens of a foreign state, animated by a "spirit of independence," successfully resist the chief of some given state, he must necessarily recognize their human worth. He will therefore want to extend his authority over them. And if they do not resist him, it is because they already recognize his authority, if only in the way in which the Slave recognizes the authority of his Master. Thus, in the last analysis, the chief of state will be fully "satisfied" only when his state encompasses all of mankind. But even within the state he will likewise want to extend his authority as far as possible, by reducing to a minimum the number of those who are only capable of a servile obedience. In order for him to be "satisfied" by their authentic "recognition," he will tend to "enfranchise" the slaves, "emancipate" the women, and reduce the authority of the family over its children by giving them "their majority" as soon as possible; he will reduce the number of criminals and of those who are in any way "unbalanced"; and he will raise to a maximum the "cultural" level (which evidently depends on the economic level) of all social classes.

At all events, he will want to be "recognized" by all those who oppose him with "disinterested" motives—motives, that is to say, which are "ideological" or "political" in the precise sense of these terms—because this very resistance is the mark of their human worth. This is what he will want as soon as such resistance comes to light, and he will give up this desire (regretfully, too) only when, for one reason or another, he finds himself forced to *kill* "the members of the resistance." The fact is that the political man acting consciously at the prompting of his desire for "recognition" (or for "glory") will be *fully* "satisfied" only when he is at the head of a State, not only *universal* but politically and socially homogeneous as well (taking account of irreducible physiological differences); of a State, that is, which is the end and the end product of the common labor of all and of each. If one acknowledges that this State is the realization of the supreme political ideal of mankind, one can say that the "satisfaction" of the chief of this state is a sufficient "justification" (not only subjective, but objective as well) of his activity. From this point of view, the modern tyrant, while actually applying Simonides' advice and obtaining thereby more satisfying results than those of which Hiero complained, is himself not *perfectly* "satisfied" either. This is because the state he directs is in fact neither universal nor homogeneous, so that his authority—like Hiero's—is not recognized by *all* those who, according to him, could have and should have recognized it.

Fully satisfied neither by his state nor by his own political acts, the modern tyrant thus has the same reasons as Hiero for lending an ear to the advice of the wise man. But in order that the tyrant not have the same reasons for failing to follow this advice, or for reacting with a "silence" which might be infinitely less "liberal" than Hiero's, the new Simonides would have to avoid the error of his "poetic" predecessor. He would have to avoid *utopia*.

The description, even the eloquent description, of an idyllic state of things which lacks real ties with any present situation will strike a tyrant, or a statesman in general, about as much as "utopian" advice which lacks any direct relation to day-to-day reality and current business. This kind of "advice" will interest the modern tyrant so much the less as, perhaps instructed by some wise man other than Simonides, he might very well know already the "ideal" that the "advisor" is ready to reveal to him and already be consciously working toward its realization. It would be quite as useless to choose to confront this ideal with the concrete measures that this tyrant is taking with a view to realizing it as to try to administer, on the basis of an "ideal," a concrete policy (tyrannical or not) which explicitly or tacitly rejects it.

If, on the other hand, the wise man—recognizing that the tyrant seeks "glory" and consequently could be fully "satisfied" only by the recognition of his authority in a universal and homogeneous State—would be willing to give "realistic" and "concrete" advice by explaining to the tyrant who consciously accepts the ideal of "universal recognition" how one could attain this ideal, taking as his point of departure the *existing* state of things, and attain it better and faster than would be possible by the measures which this tyrant is taking, the tyrant would then have been perfectly able to accept and follow his advice openly. In any case, the refusal of the tyrant would then be absolutely "unreasonable" or "unjustified" and would not raise any questions of principle.

The question that we must still resolve is whether or not the wise man as wise man *can* do anything but talk of a political "ideal," and whether or not he *wants* to leave the domain of "utopia" and "general or abstract ideas" and, by giving the tyrant some "realistic" advice, confront the concrete reality.

To be able to answer this question, it is necessary to distinguish carefully between the wise man properly so-called and the philosopher, for the situation is far from being the same in both cases. In order to simplify things, I will speak only of the latter. Anyway, neither Xenophon nor Strauss seems to admit the existence of the former. By definition, the philosopher does not possess Wisdom (the plenitude of self-consciousness—in fact omniscience); but (a Hegelian would have to qualify, at a given epoch) he is further advanced on the road which leads to Wisdom than any nonphilosopher, and "noninitiate," the tyrant included. Also by definition, the philosopher is supposed to "dedicate his life" to the quest for wisdom.

It is in taking this double definition as our point of departure that we must ask ourselves "*Can* the philosopher govern man or participate in his government, in particular by giving concrete political advice to the tyrant, and does he want to?"

Let us first ask ourselves whether he can—or, more exactly, if he has, as philosopher, any advantage over the "noninitiate" (and the tyrant is a noninitiate) when it comes to questions of government.

I believe that the negative response which is so habitually made is based on a misunderstanding, on a total misapprehension of what philosophy is and what the philosopher is.

For the purpose at hand it will be sufficient for me to recall three distinctive traits of the philosopher as opposed to the "uninitiate." In the first place, the philosopher is more expert in the art of *dialectic* or *discussion* in general: he sees better than his "uninitiate" interlocutor the insufficiencies of the other's argument, and he knows better how to make the most of his own arguments and how to refute the objections of others. In the second place, the art of dialectic enables the philosopher to free himself from *prejudices* further than the "uninitiate": he is thus more open to reality as it is, and he is less dependent on the way in which men, at a given historical moment, imagine that it is. In the third place, and finally, since he is more open to the real, he more closely approaches the concrete than the "uninitiate," who confines himself to abstractions, without, moreover, being aware of their abstract, even unreal, character.[2]

Now these three distinctive traits of the philosopher are so many advantages which he has in principle over the "uninitiate" when it comes to governing.

Strauss points out that Hiero, in recognizing Simonides' dialectical superiority, is suspicious of him, seeing in him a potential and formidable rival. And I think that Hiero is right. In point of fact, governmental action within an already constituted State is purely *discursive* in its origin, and the philosopher who is a past master of discourse or "dialectic" can just as well become master of the government. If Simonides was able to beat Hiero in their oratorical jousting, if he was able to "maneuver" him as he pleased, there is no reason at all why he could not beat him and outmaneuver him in the domain of politics; and, in particular, there is no reason why he could not

---

[2] This assertion appears paradoxical only if one does not bear in mind the precise sense of the words "concrete" and "abstract." One enters the "abstract" when one "neglects" or *abstracts* certain elements implied in the "concrete," that is, in the real. Thus, for example, one speaks of a tree abstracting from everything which is not it (the earth, the air, the planet Earth, the solar system, etc.), one is speaking of an abstraction which does not exist in reality (for the tree can exist only if there is the earth, the air, the rays of the sun, etc.). Hence all the particular sciences each have, in varying degrees, to do with abstractions. Similarly, an exclusively "national" political policy is necessarily abstract (exactly as a "pure" political policy which would, for example abstract from religion or art). The isolated "particular" is by definition *abstract*. It is precisely in seeking the *concrete* that the philosopher rises to the level of the "general ideas" which the "uninitiate" pretends to disdain.

replace him at the head of the government—should he ever feel the desire.

If the philosopher took power by means of his "dialectic," he would exercise it better than any "uninitiate" whatsoever—and this not only because of his greater dialectical facility: his government would be better on account of the relative absence of *prejudices* and because of the relatively more *concrete* character of his thought.

Of course, when it is simply a matter of preserving an established state of things, without proceeding to "structural reform" or to "revolution," the *unconscious* application of generally accepted prejudices does not present any major disadvantage. This is to say that in such situations one can, with no great harm, forego having philosophers in or near power. But where "structural reforms" or "revolutionary action" are objectively possible and hence necessary, the philosopher is particularly able to put them into operation or to give advice in this regard since, as opposed to the "uninitiate" ruler, he knows that what has to be reformed or combated are only prejudices; that is, something unreal and hence relatively unresistant.

Finally, in a "revolutionary" era as well as in a "conservative" period, it is always preferable for the rulers not to lose sight of the *concrete* reality. This reality, to be sure, offers extremely heavy going. This is why, in order to understand it with a view to its domination, the man of action is obliged (since he thinks and acts in time) to simplify it through abstractions: he makes cuts and isolates certain parts or certain aspects by "abstracting" them from the rest and treating them "in themselves"; but there is no reason to suppose that the philosopher would be unable to do as much. One could reproach him for his predilection for "general ideas," as is generally done, only if they prevented him from seeing the particular *abstractions* that the "uninitiate" wrongly calls "concrete cases." But such a reproach, if it were justified, could only be made against the contingent errors of the man, not against him as a philosopher. As such, the philosopher knows how to handle abstractions just as well as, if not better, than the "uninitiate." But since he is aware of the fact that he has proceeded to an *abstraction*, he will be able to handle the "particular case" better than the "uninitiate" who believes that what is involved is a *concrete* reality which really is isolated from the rest and can be treated as such. The philosopher will thus see the implications of the particular problem which escape the "uninitiate": he will see *farther* than the "uninitiate" in space as well as in time.

For all these reasons, to which many more could have been added, I believe, with Hiero, Xenophon, and Strauss, and contrary to a commonly accepted opinion, that the philosopher is perfectly capable of taking power and governing, or of participating in government—for example, by giving political advice to the tyrant.

The whole question then is whether or not he *wants* to. Now it is enough to ask this question (keeping in mind the *definition* of the philosopher) to perceive that it is extremely complex, in fact insoluble.

The complexity and the difficulty of this question consist in the banal fact that man *needs time* to think and to act and that the time he has at his disposal is in fact very limited.

It is this double fact—the essential temporality and finitude of man—which forces him to make a *choice* among his various existential possibilities (and gives *liberty* a *raison d'être,* rendering it, moreover, ontologically possible). In particular, it is on account of his own temporality and finitude that the philosopher is obliged to *choose* between the quest for wisdom, and (for example) political activity—even if this means only advising the tyrant. At first glance, in conformity to the very definition of the philosopher, he will devote "his whole time" to the quest for Wisdom, that being his supreme goal and value. He will renounce then not only "vulgar pleasures" but also all *action* properly so-called, including that of government, direct or indirect. Such was, at all events, the attitude taken by the "Epicurean" philosophers; and it is this "Epicurean" attitude which inspired the popular image of the philosophical existence. According to this image, the philosopher lives "outside the world": he retires into himself, isolates himself from other men, and has no interest in public life; he devotes all his time to the quest for "truth," which is pure "theory" or "contemplation" with no necessary ties to "action" of any kind. To be sure, a tyrant can get in the way of this philosopher. But such a philosopher would not get in the tyrant's way, for he does not have the slightest desire to meddle in the tyrant's affairs, even to the extent of merely advising him. All that this philosopher asks of the tyrant, the only thing that he "advises" him, is that he not concern himself with the life of the philosopher—which is entirely devoted to the quest for a purely *theoretical* "truth" or an "ideal" of a strictly isolated life.

In the course of history two principal variants of this "Epicurean" attitude can be discerned. The pagan or aristocratic Epicurean, who is more or less rich, or in any case does not work for a living (generally finding a Maecenas to support him), isolates himself in a garden, which he would like the government to treat as an inviolable castle—from which, moreover, he will not make a single "sortie." The Christian or bourgeois Epicurean, the more or less poor intellectual who must do something (write, teach, etc.) to assure his subsistence, cannot permit himself the luxury of the aristocratic Epicurean's "splendid isolation." So he replaces the private "garden" by what Pierre Bayle has so well described as the "Republic of Letters." Here the atmosphere is less serene than in the "garden"; the struggle for life, "economic competition," here reigns as master. But the enterprise remains essentially "peaceful" in the sense that the "bourgeois republican," exactly like the "aristocratic chatelain" is ready to renounce all *active* interference in public affairs, asking in exchange that he be "tolerated" by the tyrant or the government: it should leave him in peace and permit him to exercise without encumbrance his trade of thinker, orator, or writer, it being understood that his thoughts, speeches (lectures or seminars), and writings will remain purely "theoretical" and he will do nothing which could lead directly or indirectly to any *action* in the proper sense of the term, and in particular to any kind of *political* action.

Of course, it is practically impossible for the philosopher to keep this (generally sincere) promise of noninterference in affairs of state, and this is why rulers, tyrants first of all, are always suspicious of these Epicurean "republics" or "gardens." But this does not interest us at the moment. It is the attitude of the philosopher which does concern us, and that of the Epicurean appears to us at first sight irrefutable; implied, in fact, in the very definition of philosophy.

But at first sight only. For in fact the Epicurean attitude derives from the definition of philosophy as the quest for Wisdom or Truth only if one makes a supposition with regard to the latter which in no sense goes without saying, and which, from the point of view of the Hegelian conception, is even fundamentally erroneous. Actually, in order to justify the absolute *isolation* of the philosopher, it is necessary to maintain that Being is essentially immutable in itself, eternally identical with itself, and completely revealed for all eternity in and by an intelligence perfect from the outset—this sufficient revelation of the nontemporal totality of Being is the Truth. Man (the philosopher) can *at any moment* participate in this Truth: whether consequent to an action coming from the Truth itself (divine revelation), or by his own individual effort of comprehension (Platonic "intellectual intuition"), an effort conditioned by nothing but the innate "talent" of the man who undertakes it and which depends neither on the localization of this man in space (in the state) nor on his position in time (in history). If this is the case, the philosopher can and must isolate himself from the changing and tumultuous world (which is only pure appearance), and live in a tranquil "garden," or in case of real necessity, within a "Republic of Letters" where the intellectual disputes still are less "disturbing" than the political struggles outside. It is in the quietude of this isolation, in this total lack of interest in his fellows and in the whole of "society," that the absolutely *egoistic* philosopher has the greatest chance of attaining the truth, to the quest for which he has decided to dedicate his whole life.[3]

But if one does not accept this *theistic* conception of Truth (and of Being), if one accepts the radical Hegelian atheism according to which Being itself is essentially temporal (Being=Becoming) and creates itself insofar as it is discursively revealed in the course of history (or insofar as it *is* history: revealed Being=Truth=Man= History), and if one does not want to sink into skeptical relativism which ruins the very idea of Truth and thus ruins the quest for it or philosophy, it is necessary to flee the absolute solitude and isolation of the "garden" as well as the restricted society (relative solitude and isolation) of the "Republic of Letters," and, like Socrates, frequent not the "trees and cicadas" but the "citizens of the City" (cf. *Phaedrus*). If Being creates itself, ("becomes") in the course of history, it is not by isolating oneself from history that one can reveal it (transform it by discourse into Truth that man possesses in the form of Wisdom). To do this the philosopher must, on the contrary, participate in history, and then one cannot see why he ought

[3] Strauss, in agreement with Xenophon, seems to admit this radical egoism of the philosophical existence. He says in fact that "the wise man is as self-sufficient as is humanly possible." The wise man is thus absolutely "disinterested" *vis-à-vis* other men.

not participate in it *actively*, for example by giving advice to the tyrant, given that he is, as a philosopher, more able to govern than any "uninitiate." The only thing which could keep him from it is *lack of time*. And so we come to the fundamental problem of the philosophical life, which the Epicureans wrongly believed they had disposed of.

I shall return later to this Hegelian problem of the philosophical existence. For the moment we must take a somewhat closer look at the Epicurean attitude. For it is open to criticism, even allowing the theistic conception of Being and Truth. Indeed, it involves and presupposes a most contestable conception of *Truth* (although generally recognized by pre-Hegelian philosophy), according to which "subjective certainty" (*Gewissheit*) coincides everywhere and always with "objective truth" (*Wahrheit*): one is supposed actually to possess the Truth (or *a* truth) as soon as he is subjectively "sure and certain" that he has it (by having a "clear and distinct idea," for example).

In other words, the isolated philosopher must necessarily hold that the necessary and sufficient criterion of truth consists in the feeling of "evidentness" which is supposed to be given by the "intellectual intuition" of the real and of Being, or which accompanies "clear and distinct ideas" or "axioms," or which is associated from the beginning with divine revelation. This criterion of "evidentness" was accepted by all "rationalist" philosophers from Plato to Husserl, passing by way of Descartes. Unfortunately it is itself not in the least bit "evident," and I think that it is invalidated by the sole fact that there have always been on earth *illuminati* and "false prophets" who have never had the least doubt concerning the truth of their "intuitions" or of the authenticity of the "revelations" they have received in one form or another. In short, the subjective "evidentness" that an "isolated" thinker might sense is invalidated as a *criterion* for Truth by the sole fact of the existence of madness or lunacy, which, as correct deduction from subjectively "evident" first principles, can be "systematic" or "logical."

Strauss seems to follow Xenophon (and the ancient tradition in general) in justifying (explaining) the indifference (the "egoism") and the pride of the *isolated* philosopher by the fact that he knows something more—and something different—than the "uninitiate" he disdains. But the lunatic who believes that he is made out of glass, or who identifies himself with God the Father or Napoleon, also believes that he knows something more than anyone else. And we can assess his knowledge as lunacy or madness only because he is *entirely alone* in taking this knowledge (subjectively "evident," moreover) for a truth, the other lunatics themselves refusing to believe it. Likewise, it is only by seeing our ideas shared by others (or at least by *an* other) or accepted by them as debatable (even if only as erroneous ideas) that we can be sure of not finding ourselves in the domain of lunacy (though still not at all sure of being in the domain of Truth). Consequently, the Epicurean philosopher, entirely isolated in his "garden," could never know if he has attained Wisdom or sunk into lunacy, and as a philosopher he would then have to flee the "garden" and his solitude. In fact, recalling his Socratic origins, the Epicurean does not live in absolute solitude and receives into his "garden" certain philosophical *friends* in order to discuss things with them. From this point of view there is then no essential difference between the "Republic of Letters" of the bourgeois intellectual and the aristocratic "garden": the difference lies only in the number of the "elect." The "garden" and the "Republic," where one "discusses" from morning till night, both give a sufficient guarantee against the danger of lunacy. Although by taste, and as a result of their profession itself, the "lettered citizens" are never in agreement among themselves, they will always be unanimous when it comes to sending one of their number, properly, to an asylum. Thus, perhaps in spite of appearances, in the "garden" or in the "Republic," one can be sure of meeting only persons who are sometimes odd but essentially of sound mind (and only feigning madness on occasion to appear "original").

But the fact that one is never alone there is not the only thing the "garden" has in common with the "Republic." There is also the fact that the "mob" is excluded from it. To be sure, a "Republic of Letters" is generally more populated than an Epicurean "garden." But there is in either case a relatively small "elite" which has a marked tendency to withdraw into itself and to exclude the "uninitiated."

Here again Strauss seems to follow Xenophon (who is in agreement with the ancient tradition) and to justify this kind of behavior. The wise man, he says, "is satisfied with the approval of a small minority." He seeks only the approval of those who are

"worthy," and this cannot but be a very small number. Thus the
philosopher will have recourse to *esoteric* instruction (preferably
oral) which permits him, among other things, to choose the "better,"
while eliminating the "limited" who are incapable of understanding
the dissimulated allusions and tacit implications.

I must say that here again I differ from Strauss and the ancient
tradition that he would like to follow, and which rests, in my opinion, on an aristocratic *prejudice* (which characterizes, perhaps, a
conquering people). For I believe that the idea and the practice of
the "intellectual elite" involves a very serious danger that the
philosopher as such should want to avoid at any cost.

The danger run by dwellers in various "gardens," "academies,"
"lyceums," and "Republics of Letters" stems from what is called
the "cloistered mind." To be sure, the "cloister," which is a society,
does exclude *lunacy*—which is essentially asocial. But far from excluding *prejudices*, it tends on the contrary to cultivate them by
perpetuating them: it can easily happen that only those are admitted
to the intimacy of the cloister who accept the prejudices on which
the cloister prides itself. Now, philosophy is by definition something
other than Wisdom: it necessarily involves "subjective certainties"
which are not *the* Truth; or in other words are "prejudices." The
duty of the philosopher is to abandon these prejudices as quickly and
completely as possible. Any society which is closed upon itself and
adopts a doctrine, any elite selected on the grounds of the teaching
of some doctrine, tends to consolidate the prejudices involved in this
doctrine. The philosopher who shuns prejudices would, then, have
to try to live in the outside world (in the "market place" or "in the
street," like Socrates) rather than in a "sect" or "cloister," whether
"republican" or "aristocratic."[4]

Dangerous under any supposition, the sectarian or cloistered life
is completely unacceptable for the philosopher who recognizes, with
Hegel, that reality (at least *human* reality) is not given once and for
all, but creates itself in the course of time (at least in the course of
historical time). For if this is the case, sooner or later the members
of the cloister, isolated from the rest of the world and not really
taking part in public life in its historical evolution, will be "left

[4] As Queneau has recalled in *les Temps Modernes*, the philosopher is
essentially a "voyou." (The French "voyou," which means a thug or hooligan,
comes from the word "voie," meaning road or street. Hence anyone who
hangs out in the streets may be called a "voyou."—Trans. note.)

behind by events." Thus, even what was "true" at a given time can later on become "false"—that is, transformed into a "prejudice," and only those in the cloister will fail to notice it.

But the question of the philosophical "elite" can be treated fundamentally only in the context of the general problem of "recognition" as related to the philosopher. Indeed, it is in this perspective that the question is raised by Strauss himself. And it is from this point of view that I should now like to speak.

According to Strauss, the essential difference between Hiero, the tyrant, and Simonides, the philosopher, lies in this: Hiero would like "to be *loved* by *human beings* as such," while Simonides "is satisfied by the admiration, the praise, the approval of a *small minority*." It is to win his subjects' *love* that Hiero must become their *benefactor;* Simonides lets himself be admired without *doing* anything to gain this admiration. In other words, Simonides is admired solely for his own *perfection*, while Hiero would like to be loved for his benefactions, even without being himself perfect. This is why the desire for admiration, apart from the desire for love, is "the natural foundation of the predominance of the desire for one's own perfection," while the need for love does not encourage a desire for self-perfection and hence is not a "philosophical" desire.

This conception of the difference between the philosopher and the tyrant (which is, indeed, neither Strauss' nor, according to him, Xenophon's) does not seem to me to be satisfactory.

If one recognizes (with Goethe and Hegel) that a man is *loved* solely because he *is* independent of what he *does* (a mother loves her son in spite of his faults), while "admiration" or "recognition" are evoked only by the *actions* of him one "admires" or "recognizes," it is clear that the tyrant—and the statesman in general—seeks *recognition* and not *love: love* thrives in the family, and it is to seek not the love, but the *recognition* of the citizens in the state that the young man leaves his family and devotes himself to the public life. It is rather Simonides, who would seek love if he had truly wanted to have a positive (even absolute) value attributed, not to his *acts*, but to his (perfect) *being*. But in fact it is nothing like that. Simonides wants to be admired for his *perfection* and not for his *being*, pure and simple—whatever that may be. Now love is precisely characterized by the fact that it attributes, *without reason*, a positive value to the beloved or to the *being* of the beloved. It is just this recognition of his perfection and not the love of his being that Simonides is seeking: he would like to be recognized for his perfection and therefore he *desires* his perfection. Now *desire* is realized by *action* (negating action, since it involves the negation of existing imperfection, perfection being only desired and not yet acquired). Thus it is actually for his *acts* (of self-perfection) that Simonides is and wants to be recognized, just as Hiero is and wants to be for his.

It is not true that the tyrant and the statesman in general are *by definition* content with a "gratuitous" admiration or recognition: just like the philosopher, they wish to "merit" this admiration and this recognition by truly being or becoming such as they appear to others. Thus the tyrant who is seeking recognition will also make some effort to perfect himself, if only out of concern for his security, since any impostor or hypocrite always runs a risk of being sooner or later "unmasked."

From this viewpoint, then, there is no difference at all *in principle* between the statesman and the philosopher: they both seek *recognition*, and they both act with a view to meriting it (imposture can be found, in fact, in both cases).

There remains the problem of knowing whether or not it is true that the statesman seeks recognition by the "masses" while the philosopher wishes to make himself recognized only by a small number of "elect."

To begin with, this does not seem to apply necessarily to the statesman as such. As a matter of fact, it is generally true of "democratic" leaders who depend on the opinion of the majority. But "tyrants" have not always sought "popularity" (Tiberius, for example), and they have often had to be satisfied with the approval of a small circle of "political friends." Moreover, nothing says that the acclaim of the mob is incompatible with the approval of competent judges, and it is not in the least necessary that the statesman prefer the acclaim to the approval. On the other hand, I see no reason why the philosopher would have systematically to eschew the praise of the "masses" (which undoubtedly gives him pleasure). The important thing is that the philosopher not sacrifice the approval of the "elect" to "popular" acclaim and that he not adapt his conduct to the exigencies of the "worse." But the statesman (tyrant or not) who behaved in this matter otherwise than the philosopher would im-

mediately be called a "demagogue"; and nothing says that by definition all statesmen are "demagogues."

The fact is that a man is fully satisfied only by the recognition of
those he himself recognizes as worthy of recognizing him. And this
is as true for the statesman as for the philosopher.

To the extent that a man seeks recognition, he must do everything
in his power to make the number of "worthy" men as great as
possible. Consciously or not, statesmen have often taken upon themselves this task of political pedagogy (the "enlightened despot," the
"pedagogical" tyrant). And philosophers have generally done quite
the same, by devoting a part of their time to philosophical pedagogy.
It is not clear why the number of adepts or disciples of the philosopher must necessarily be restricted, or in any case smaller than the
number of *competent* admirers of the political man. If a philosopher
limited this number artificially, asserting that in any case he would
not *want* to have many adepts, he would prove thereby that he is
less self-conscious than the "uninitiated" political man who consciously tends to an unlimited extension of his recognition by competent judges. And if he should maintain *a priori*, without having
made the experiment, that the number of people to whom philosophy
is accessible falls short of the number of those who can knowledge-
ably judge a political doctrine or a political action, he would then
be speaking on the basis of an undemonstrated opinion, and he
would thus be prey to a "prejudice," at best valid only under certain
social conditions and at a particular historical moment. In either
case he would not be truly a philosopher.

Moreover, this prejudice of the "elite" is so much the more
serious since it can lead to a total reversal of the situation. In
principle the philosopher ought to seek only the admiration or
approval of those he deems *worthy* of "recognizing" him. But if he
never leaves the intentionally restricted circle of a purposefully
recruited elite or of judiciously chosen "friends," he runs the risk
of considering "worthy" all those, and only those, who admire or
agree with him. And it must be admitted that this particularly disagreeable form of reciprocal and restricted recognition has always
prevailed in the Epicurean "gardens" and intellectual "cloisters."

Be that as it may, if one holds, with Simonides, that the philosopher seeks recognition (or admiration), and if one recognizes with
Hegel that the statesman does the same, one must say that from this

viewpoint there is no essential difference between the tyrant and the philosopher. It is probably for this reason that Xenophon (according to Strauss) and Strauss himself do not align themselves with Simonides. According to Strauss, Xenophon opposes to Simonides Socrates, who is not in the least interested in "the admiration or the praise of others," while Simonides is interested only in that. And one has the impression that Strauss agrees with this Socratic attitude: to the extent that the philosopher seeks recognition and admiration, he is supposed to consider only his own recognition of his own value and his own admiration for himself.

As for me, I confess that I do not understand this very well, and I do not see how this could make it possible to find an *essential* difference between the philosopher (or the wise man) and the tyrant (or the statesman in general).

If one takes the attitude of Xenophon-Strauss' Socrates literally, one falls back again to the case of the *isolated* philosopher who is completely disinterested in the opinion that other men have of him. This attitude is not in itself contradictory ("absurd"), if the philosopher believes that he may attain the Truth by some direct personal revelation of Being or by an individual revelation proceeding from a transcendent God. But if he does believe this, he will have no philosophically valid reason for *communicating* his knowledge (orally or in writing) to others (unless it be for the purpose of obtaining their "recognition" or admiration, which is excluded by definition). Hence if he is truly a philosopher, he will not do so (the philosopher does not act "without a reason"). Hence we will know nothing about him; we will not even know whether or not he exists and, consequently, we will not know whether he is a philosopher or simply a lunatic. In my opinion, moreover, he will not even know it himself, since he will be deprived of any sort of social testing or criticism which alone is capable of weeding out "pathological" cases. In any event, his "solipsist" attitude, which excludes discussion, would be fundamentally anti-Socratic.

Let us grant then that "Socrates," who "discusses" with others, is in the highest degree interested in the opinion that others hold or will hold about what he says and does, at least to the extent to which they are, according to him, "competent." If "Socrates" is a true philosopher, he progresses toward wisdom (which implies knowledge and "virtue") and he is aware of his progress. If he is not perverted by the prejudice of Christian humility to the point of being hypocritical with himself, he will be more or less *satisfied* with this progress, which is to say with himself: let us say, without being afraid of the word, that he will, more or less *admire* himself (above all if he considers himself more "advanced" than the *others*). If those who express opinions about him are "competent," they will appreciate him in the same way he appreciates himself (supposing that he is not deluding himself). That is to say, if they are not blinded by envy they will admire him to the same extent he admires himself. And if "Socrates" is not a "Christian," he will acknowledge (to himself and to others) that the admiration of others brings (a certain) "satisfaction" and (a certain) "pleasure." To be sure, this does not mean that the fact of his having (consciously) made progress on the road to Wisdom does not bring "Socrates" pleasure and satisfaction independent of that brought by the admiration of others and his right to admire himself: everyone is aware of the "pure" joy that comes from the acquisition of knowledge, and they are all aware of the "disinterested satisfaction" that comes from the feeling of "duty done." And neither can one say that it is *in principle* impossible to seek knowledge and do one's duty without having as the motive the pleasure which results from it. Is it really impossible to devote oneself to sport just for "the love of it," and without especially seeking, in a *competition,* the "pleasure" which comes from the "glory of the victor"?

On the contrary, it can be said that all of these things are in fact inseparable. Certainly "in theory" all sorts of subtle distinctions are possible, but "in practice" there is no way of eliminating one of these elements while retaining the others. This is to say that there can be no verifying experiment in this area and hence, in the scientific sense of the term, nothing can be *known* about the question.

It is known that there are pleasures which have nothing to do with knowledge or virtue. It is also known that men have at times renounced these pleasures to devote themselves fully to the quest for truth or the exercise of virtue. But since this quest and this exercise are in fact inseparably linked with *sui generis* "pleasures," there is absolutely no way of knowing if in fact it is a choice between different "pleasures" which makes them act this way, or a choice between "pleasure" and "duty" or between "pleasure" and "knowledge." Now these *sui generis* "pleasures" are in turn *inseparably* linked with the specific "pleasure" which comes from self-satisfaction or self-admiration: whatever the Christians say, one cannot be wise and virtuous (that is, in fact wiser and more virtuous than others, or at least certain others) without deriving therefrom a certain "satisfaction" and a sort of "pleasure."[5] Thus one cannot know whether in fact the "primary motive" of conduct is the "pure" joy which comes from Wisdom (knowledge + virtue), or whether it is the "pleasure," at times condemned, which comes from the Wise Man's self-admiration (conditioned or not by the admiration in which he is held by others).

The same ambiguity appears when one considers "Socrates" in his relations with others. We have accepted the fact that he is interested in the opinion others have of him to the extent that it enables him to test whether or not the opinion he has of himself is well founded. But all the rest is ambiguous. One can maintain, as Xenophon-Strauss seem to, that Socrates is interested only in the "theoretical" judgments made about him by others and is completely indifferent to the *admiration* they may have for him: he derives his "pleasure" only from *self*-admiration (which determines, or only accompanies, his philosophical activity). But one might just as well say that the self-admiration of a man who is not mad implies and necessarily presupposes the admiration of others; that a "normal" man cannot be truly "satisfied" with himself without being not merely judged, but also "recognized" by the others or at least by certain others. One might even go so far as to say that the pleasure involved in self-admiration is relatively valueless when compared with that derived from the admiration of others. These are some of the *possible* psychological analyses of the phenomenon of "recognition," but since there is no possibility of making experiments in separating

[5] Moreover, the Christians only succeeded in "spoiling this pleasure" by playing on the disagreeable sentiment which appears in the form of "jealousy" or "envy," among others: one is discontent with himself (at times he even despises himself) when he is "worse than another." Now the Christian always has at his disposal Another Who is better than he, this Other being God Himself, Who, to facilitate the comparison, made Himself man. To the extent that this man to whom he compares himself and whom he tries in vain to imitate is for him a God, the Christian feels neither "envy" nor "jealousy" toward him, but limits himself to the pure and simple "inferiority complex" which is nonetheless sufficient to prevent him from recognizing his own wisdom or virtue and rejoicing in it.

them, it is impossible to come to any definite decision in favor of any one of them.

Certainly it would be quite wrong to suppose that "Socrates" seeks knowledge and exercises virtue *solely* for the sake of the recognition of others. For experience shows that science may be pursued out of pure love even on a desert isle with no hope of return, and that "virtue" may be practiced without witness (human or even divine), simply from fear of falling in one's own estimation. But nothing prevents us from asserting that, when "Socrates" *communicates* with others and exercises his virtue *publicly*, he does so not only for the purpose of testing himself but also (and perhaps even above all) for the sake of outward "recognition." By what right can we say that he does not seek this "recognition," since in fact he *necessarily* finds it?

To tell the truth, all these distinctions make sense only if one accepts the existence of a God who sees clearly into the hearts of men and judges them according to their intentions (which may, moreover, be unconscious). If one is truly an atheist, none of this makes sense. For, evidently, only introspection could then provide the elements of an answer. Now, as long as a man is alone in knowing something, he can never be sure that he truly *knows* it. If, as a consistent atheist, one replaces God (taken as consciousness and will surpassing individual human consciousness and will) by Society (the State) and History, one must say that whatever is, in fact, out of the range of social and historical verification is forever relegated to the domain of *opinion* (*doxa*).

This is why I do not agree with Strauss when he says that Xenophon posed the problem of the relationship between pleasure and virtue in a radical way. I do not agree for the simple reason that I do not think that (from the atheistic point of view) there is a problem there which could be resolved by some form of knowledge (*epistēmē*). More exactly, this problem could be solved in several possible ways, none of which is truly *certain*. It is impossible to know whether the philosopher (wise man) seeks knowledge and practices virtue "for themselves" (or "out of duty") or whether he does it for the sake of the "pleasure" (joy) he derives from doing so, or—finally—whether he acts in this way in order to feel admiration for himself (conditioned or not by admiration on the part of others). This question obviously cannot be settled "from outside," and thus there is no way of verifying the "subjective certainty" given by introspection; nor will there be any way of deciding between these "certainties" if they are discordant.[6]

What should be remembered in all that has gone before is that the "Epicurean" conception of certain philosophers is in no way warranted by a total and consistent system of thought. This conception becomes contestable as soon as one takes account of the problem of "recognition," as I have just done, and it is unreliable even when one limits oneself to the problem of the criterion of truth, as I did at first.

To the extent that the philosopher sees in "discussion" (dialogue, dialectic) a method of investigation and a criterion of truth, he must necessarily "educate" his interlocutors. And we have seen that he has no reason to limit a priori the number of his possible interlocutors. This is to say that the philosopher must be a pedagogue and try to extend his pedagogical activity without limit (directly or indirectly). In so doing, he will sooner or later encroach on the field of action of the statesman or tyrant who are themselves, more or less consciously, also "educators."

As a general rule, the interference of the philosopher's pedagogical activity with that of the tyrant takes the form of a more-or-less acute conflict. "Corruption of the youth" was the principal charge in Socrates' indictment. The philosopher-pedagogue thus will naturally be inclined to try to influence the tyrant (or government

---

[6] Observation of "conduct" cannot *settle* the question. But the fact remains that in observing philosophers (for want of wise men) one does not really have the impression that they are insensitive to praise, or even to flattery. One can even say that they are, like all intellectuals, more vain on the whole than men of action. And, moreover, one can readily see why. Men do a particular thing in order to *succeed* or "to win success" (and not to fail). Now, the success of an undertaking based on action may be measured by its objective "good results" (a bridge which does not collapse, a business that makes money, a war won, a state that is strong and prosperous, etc.), independent of the opinion that others have of it, while the success of a book or of an intellectual discourse is nothing but the recognition of its value by others. The intellectual depends then very much more than the man of action (the tyrant included) on the admiration of others, and he is more sensitive than the latter to the absence of this admiration. Without it, it is absolutely impossible for him to admire himself with any valid reason, while the man of action can admire himself on account of his objective—even solitary—"successes." And this is why, as a general rule, the intellectual who does nothing but talk and write is more vain than the man who, in the full sense of the word, acts.

in general) with a view to obtaining from him the creation of conditions which permit the exercise of philosophical pedagogy. But in fact the state is itself a pedagogical institution. The pedagogy exercised and controlled by the government constitutes an integral part of governmental activity in general, and it is determined by the very structure of the state. Consequently, to want to influence the government with a view to the establishment or toleration of a philosophical pedogogy is to want to influence the government in general—to want to determine or codetermine its policy as such. The philosopher cannot give up pedagogy; in fact, the "success" of his philosophical pedagogy is the sole "objective" criterion of the truth of the philosopher's doctrine: the fact of his having disciples (in a broad or narrow sense) is his guarantee against the danger of lunacy, and the "success" of his disciples in private and public life is the "objective" proof of the (relative) "truth" of his doctrine, at least in the sense of its adequacy to the given historical reality.

If one wants something more than the subjective criteria of "evidentness" and "revelation" (which do not exclude the danger of lunacy), then it is impossible to be a philosopher without at the same time wanting to be a philosophical *pedagogue*. And if the philosopher does not want artificially or unduly to restrict the extent of his pedagogical activity (and thereby risk being subject to the prejudices of the cloister), he will necessarily have a marked tendency to participate, one way or another, in government as a whole, so that the state may be organized and governed in such a way that his philosophical pedagogy is possible and effectual.

It is probably for this reason (more or less consciously acknowledged) that most philosophers, the greatest included, have given up their "Epicurean" isolation and undertaken some sort of political activity, either by personal interventions or by means of their writings. Plato's voyages to Syracuse and the collaboration between Spinoza and DeWitt are well-known examples of direct intervention. And it is well known that nearly all philosophers have published works dealing with the State and with government.[7]

But it is here that there appears the conflict determined by the temporality and finitude of man of which I spoke above. On the one hand, the supreme goal of the philosopher is the quest for Wisdom or Truth; and this quest, by definition never completed by a philoso-

---

[7] The case of Descartes is too complicated to discuss here.

pher, is supposed to take *all of his time*. On the other hand, the governing of a State, however small it may be, also requires time— and a great deal of it. To tell the truth, the governing of a state also takes *all of a man's time*.

Not being able to devote *all their time* to philosophy and government together, philosophers have generally sought a compromise solution. While wishing to concern themselves with politics, they did not relinquish their strictly philosophical concern and consented only to limit a little the time that they devoted to it. This being the case, they gave up the idea of taking the government of the State in hand and satisfied themselves with devoting the small amount of time which they took away from philosophy to the *advice* they gave (orally or in writing) to the rulers of the day.

Unfortunately, this compromise proved unworkable. To be sure, philosophy did not greatly suffer from the political "distractions" of philosophers. But the direct and immediate effect of their political advice was exactly nil.

To tell the truth, the philosophers who were satisfied with giving written—indeed "bookish"—advice did not take their setback as a tragedy. Generally speaking, they had enough good sense not to expect that the powers of their world would read their writings, and even less that they would be inspired by them in their daily tasks. In resigning themselves to a purely scriptural activity they were already resigned to seeing this activity for the time being politically ineffectual. But those who deigned to take the trouble of giving political advice personally may have taken rather badly the lack of eagerness with which their advice was followed, and they may have had the impression of having truly "wasted their time."

Of course, we do not know Plato's reactions after his Sicilian failure. The fact that he renewed his abortive attempt seems to show that, in his opinion, the blame had to be shared and that he himself, acting differently, could have done better and had better results. But the common opinion of more-or-less philosophical intellectuals generally heaps opprobrium and contempt on these reticent rulers. I persist in believing that they are entirely wrong in so doing.

To begin with, there is a tendency to blame the "tyrannical" character of the government which is not sensitive to philosophical advice. It seems to me that the philosopher is in a particularly bad position to criticize tyranny as such. On the one hand the philos-opher-advisor is, by definition, in a great rush: he would like very much to contribute to the reform of the state, but he would like to do so while losing the least possible amount of time. If he wants to succeed *quickly* he will have to address himself to the tyrant in preference to the democratic leader. Actually, philosophers who want to *act* in the political present have, through all time, been drawn to tyranny. When there was a powerful and effective tyrant contemporary with the philosopher, it is precisely on him that the latter lavished his advice, even if the tyrant lived in a foreign land. On the other hand, one can scarcely imagine a philosopher himself becoming a statesman (*per impossibile*) except in the shape of some sort of "tyrant." In a hurry to get politics "over with" and return to more noble occupations, he will scarcely be endowed with any exceptional political patience. Despising the "great mass," indifferent to its praises, he will not want patiently to play the role of a "democratic" ruler, attentive to the opinions and desires of the "mob" and the "active partisans." Moreover, how could he *rapidly* fulfill his program of reforms (which is necessarily radical and op-posed to the commonly accepted ideas) without having recourse to political procedures which have always been burdened with the name of "tyranny"? In fact, as soon as a philosopher, not occupying him-self with affairs of state, so oriented one of his disciples, this latter— Alcibiades, for example—immediately had recourse to typically "tyrannical" methods. Inversely, when a statesman openly attached himself to a philosophy, it was as a "tyrant" that he acted in ac-cordance with it, just as energetic "tyrants" have generally had philosophical origins, more or less direct, and more or less conscious and avowed.

In short, of all possible statesmen, it is the tyrant who is incon-testably the most apt to receive and apply the advice of the philos-opher. If, having received the advice, he does not apply it, then it must be that he has very good reasons for not doing so. In my opinion these reasons would be, moreover, even more valid in the case of a "nontyrannical" ruler.

I have already indicated what these reasons are. A statesman, who-ever he may be, is intrinsically unable to follow "utopian" advice: since he can *act* only in the *present* he cannot take ideas into con-sideration which have no direct ties with the given concrete situation.

In order to obtain a hearing, then, it has been necessary for the philosopher to have given his advice by connecting it with "current business." But in order to do so, he must follow this business from day to day and thus devote *all* his time to it. And it is just this that the philosopher does not *want* to do. As philosopher he *cannot* do it: if he did, he would have to abandon that very quest for truth which makes him a philosopher, and which is, in his eyes, his only authentic title to his position as the tyrant's *philosophical* advisor: a position which gives him the right to advise the tyrant regarding more and different things than lie within the competence of the "uninitiate" advisor, however intelligent and capable the latter may be. To devote all his time to government is to cease being a philosopher and thus to lose all advantage over the tyrant and his "uninitiate" advisors.

Moreover, this is not the only reason which makes the philosopher's every attempt at direct action on the tyrant necessarily ineffective. Let us suppose, for example, that Plato had remained in Syracuse till the end of his days, that he had climbed (rapidly, of course) the various echelons leading to a position whose holder could make decisions and hence influence the general political orientation. It is practically sure and certain that, *in this case*, Plato would have had the ear of the tyrant and could actually have guided his policy. But what would happen then? On the one hand, being anxious to carry out the "radical" reforms indicated by Plato, Dionysius would certainly have had to intensify the "tyrannical" nature of his government more and more. His philosophical advisor would then find himself very quickly faced with a "case of conscience": his quest for an "objective truth," incarnate in the "ideal" State, coming into conflict with his notion of a "virtue" opposed to the "violence" whose exercise he would nevertheless like to continue. On the other hand, conscious of the limits of his own knowledge, as opposed to Dionysius, Plato would soon have become aware that he had reached these limits: he would then begin to hesitate in his advice and hence he would be unable to give it in time. Now, against the background of the "guilty conscience" provoked by the fact that he has no more time to spend on philosophy, these theoretical uncertainties and these moral conflicts will soon make the philosopher lose his taste for all direct and concrete political action. And, having in the meantime understood that it is either ridiculous or hypocritical to submit "general ideas" to the tyrant and to give him "utopian" advice, the philosopher, resigning, would leave the tyrant "in peace" and would spare him any further advice *and any further criticism:* especially in the case in which he knows that the tyrant is pursuing the same goal that he himself pursued during his career as advisor—a career he voluntarily ruined.

This is to say that the conflict of the philosopher faced with the tyrant is nothing else than the conflict of the intellectual faced with action or, more exactly, faced with the inclination, or even the necessity, of acting. This conflict is, according to Hegel, the only authentic tragedy that is played in the Christian or bourgeois world: the tragedy of Hamlet and of Faust. It is a *tragic* conflict because it is a conflict with no way out, a problem with no possible solution.

Faced with the impossibility of acting politically without giving up philosophy, the philosopher gives up political action. But has he reasons for doing it?

The preceding considerations can by no means be used to "justify" this choice. By definition the philosopher ought not make up his mind without "sufficient reason," nor take a position which is "un-justifiable" within the context of a system of coherent thought. It thus remains for us to see how the philosopher could, in his own eyes, "justify" his renunciation of political *action* in the precise sense of the term.

The first "justification" one would be tempted to make is easy: the fact that he has not solved a problem need not disturb the philosopher. Unlike a wise man, who possesses Wisdom, the philos-opher lives in a world of questions which, for him, remain open. To be a philosopher, it is enough if he is aware of the existence of these questions and if he . . . *tries* to solve them. The best method to use (according to the Platonists, at least) is that of "dialectic"— "meditation" tested and stimulated by "dialogue." In other words, the best method is "discussion." In our case, instead of giving political advice to the tyrant of the day or, on the contrary, giving up all criticism of the existing government, the philosopher could then be satisfied with "discussing" the question of knowing whether he himself ought to govern or whether he ought only to advise the tyrant; or whether he ought not rather abstain from all political action, and even give up all concrete criticism of the government, devoting all his time to theoretical pursuits of a more "elevated" and less "mundane" character. What philosophers have forever been doing is discussing this question. In particular, it is what Xenophon has done in his dialogue, Strauss in his book, and I myself in the present critical essay. Thus everything seems to be going along very nicely.

All the same, one cannot help being a bit disappointed by the fact that this "discussion" of the problem which engrosses us, having gone on for more than two thousand years, has not led to any *solution* whatever.

Perhaps one could try to *resolve* the question, going beyond *discussion* with philosophers and employing the "objective" method used by Hegel, in order to arrive at "indisputable" solutions.

This is the method of *historical verification*.

For Hegel, the outcome of the classical "dialectic" of the "dialogue," that is, the victory gained in a purely *verbal* "discussion," is not a sufficient criterion of the truth. In other words, discursive "dialectic" as such cannot, according to him, lead to any *definitive* solution of a problem (any solution, that is, which remains invariable for *all* time to come). This is for the simple reason that if one is content to *talk* one will never be able definitively to "eliminate" either the contradictor or, consequently, the contradiction itself, for to *refute* someone is not necessarily to *convince* him. "Contradiction" or "controversy" (between Man and Nature on the one hand, between men, or rather between a man and his social and historical milieu, on the other) can be "dialectically done away with" (that is, *done away with* insofar as they are "false," but *preserved* insofar as they are "true," and *raised* to a higher level of "discussion") only to the extent that they are played out on the *historical* terrain of *active social* life where one argues by *acts* of Labor (against Nature) and Struggle (against men). To be sure, Truth emerges from this active "dialogue," this historical dialectic, only at the moment when the latter is completed, that is to say, at the moment when history comes to its final conclusion in and by the universal and homogeneous state which, implying the "satisfaction" of the citizens, excludes all possibility of any negating *action* and hence of all *negation* in general and, consequently, of any new "discussion" of what has already been established. But, even without wishing to assume with the author of the *Phenomenology of Mind* that history is today already virtually "over," one can say that if the "solution" to a problem has in fact been historically or socially "valid" for the whole duration of time up to the present, one has the *right*, until (historical) *proof* to the contrary, to consider it philosophically "valid," in spite of the philosophers' continuance of the "discussion." In doing so, it can be assumed that history, at the opportune moment, will take it upon itself to put an end to the indefinite continuation of the "philosophical discussion" of a problem that it has already virtually "resolved."

Let us see then if the comprehension of our past history permits us to resolve the problem of the relation between wisdom and tyranny and to determine thus the "reasonable," that is to say "philosophical," conduct which the philosopher ought to maintain toward government.

A priori it seems plausible that history should be able to resolve the question or conflict that the *individual* meditations of philosophers (mine included) have been unable to decide up until now. Indeed, we have seen that this conflict itself, as well as its "tragic" character, has its source in the fact of *finitude*, the fact, that is, of the *finite temporality* of man in general and of the philosopher in particular. If he were *eternal*, in the sense that he did not need time to act and think, or had an unlimited amount of time at his disposal in which to do it, the question would never even arise (just as it never arises for God). Now, history *transcends* the finite duration of man's individual existence. To be sure, it is not "eternal" in the classical sense of the term, since it is only the integration with respect to time of *temporal* acts and thoughts. But if one holds, with Hegel (and anyone who would like to be able to hold, as he does, that there is a meaning and direction to history, and that there is such a thing as historical progress, ought to have agreed with him on this point), that history can be completed in and by itself, and that "absolute knowledge" (= wisdom or discursive truth) results from the "comprehension" or "explanation" of history as integral (or integrated in and by this very knowledge) by a "coherent discourse" (*Logos*) which is "circular" or "uni-total" in the sense that it exhausts all the possibilities (assumed to be *finite*) of "rational" thought (that is, thought which is not in itself contradictory)—if one grants all this, I say, one can equate history (completed and integrated in and by "absolute" discursive knowledge) and *eternity*, understanding by this word the *totality of time* (historical time, that is to say human time, that is to say time which can contain a "discussion" of some sort, active or verbal) beyond which no particular man could pass, nor could Man as such. In short, if the individual properly so-called has as yet been unable to resolve the problem which interests us because this problem is insoluble on the level of the individual, there is no reason to suppose *a priori* that the "great individual" of whom Pascal speaks (who will not *always* learn, but who *learns* certain things in the strict sense of the word) has not solved it a long time ago and in a "definitive" manner (even if not a single *individual* has noticed it yet).

Let us see then what history teaches us about the relations between tyrants and philosophers (admitting that there has not yet been a wise man on earth).

At first sight history confirms the current opinion. Not only has no philosopher ever yet actually governed a state, but all political men, "tyrants" in the first rank, have always despised the "general ideas" of the philosophers, and they have always turned up their noses at the philosophers' political advice. The political action of philosophers seems then to have been nil, and the lesson which they could draw from history would seem to encourage them to devote themselves to "contemplation" or "pure theory" without troubling themselves with what the "men of action," and in particular "rulers," are doing in the meantime.

But when one looks more closely, the lesson that can be drawn from history appears wholly different.

In the geographic domain of Western philosophy, perhaps the greatest statesman—in any case the one whom the great tyrants of our world have imitated through the ages (and who has been imitated more recently in the imitation of Napoleon who imitated Caesar, himself an imitator)—was Alexander the Great. Now Alexander had perhaps read the dialogues of Xenophon. He was certainly a student of Aristotle, himself a student of Plato, a student of Socrates. There is no doubt then that Alexander profited indirectly from the same instruction of which Alcibiades had had the benefit. Politically more gifted than Alcibiades, or simply come "at the right time," Alexander succeeded where Alcibiades had failed. But they both wanted the same thing, and they both tried to pass beyond the rigid and narrow compass of the ancient city. Nothing prevents our assumption that these two political undertakings—only one of which met with failure—may be traced back to the philosophical teaching of Socrates.

Of course, this is only a simple historical hypothesis. But an analysis of the facts relating to Alexander renders this hypothesis plausible.

What characterizes the political action of Alexander, distinguishing it from that of all his Greek predecessors and contemporaries, is the fact that it was directed by the idea of *empire*, that is, a *universal* state, in the sense at least that this state would have no limits (geographic, ethnic, or otherwise) *given a priori*, nor any *pre-established* "capital," that is, a geographically and ethnically *fixed* nucleus destined to dominate politically its periphery. To be sure, there have at all times been conquerors ready to extend indefinitely the domain of their conquests. But they were generally interested in the establishment, between the conquering and conquered, of a relation like that existing between master and slave. Alexander, on the contrary, was obviously ready to dissolve Macedonia and Greece entirely into a new political unity created by his conquest, and govern this unity from a geographic point freely (rationally) chosen by him in relation to the new *whole*. Moreover, by obliging the Macedonians and the Greeks to enter into mixed marriages with the "barbarians," he certainly had in mind the creation of a new ruling class which would be independent of all rigid and *given* ethnic support.

Now how is it that it was precisely the chief of a *national* state (and not of a "city" or a *polis*), who, having at his disposal an ethnic and geographic foundation sufficient to enable him to exercise over Greece and the Orient a unilateral political domination of the traditional type, had conceived the idea of a truly *universal* State or of an *Empire*, in the proper sense of the word, in which were fused conqueror and conquered? This, of all political ideas, is a new one, one which started toward *actualization* only with the edict of Caracalla and which even today has nowhere been actualized in all its purity, having undergone in the meantime (and quite recently) some spectacular eclipses and being still a subject for "discussion." How is it that it was a hereditary monarch who consented to expatriate himself and who wanted to fuse the victorious nobility of his native land with the newly vanquished? Instead of establish-

ing the domination of his *race* and letting his *Fatherland* reign over
the rest of the world, he chose to dissolve the race and do away
politically with the *Fatherland* itself.

It is here that one is tempted to give the credit to the education
he had from Aristotle and to the general influence of the "Socratic-
Platonic" *philosophy* (which is likewise at the root of the properly
political teaching of the Sophists whose benefits Alexander also
enjoyed). It is the student of Aristotle who could believe it necessary to create (by mixed marriages) a *biological* foundation for the
unity of the empire. But it is only the disciple of Socrates-Plato who
could conceive of this unity, taking as his point of departure the
"idea" or the "general notion" of Man brought forward by Greek
philosophy. All men can become citizens of one and the same State
(= empire) because they *have* (or acquire as a result of *biological*
union) one and the same "essence." And this single "essence" common to all men, is, in the last analysis, "*Logos*" (language-science),
that is to say, what we today call (Greek) "civilization" or
"culture." The empire planned by Alexander is not the political
expression of a *people* or a *caste*. It is the political expression of a
"civilization": it is the material actualization of a "logical" entity,
universal and one, just as *Logos* itself is universal and one.

A long time before Alexander, the Pharaoh Ikhnaton also probably
conceived the idea of empire in the sense of a political transethnic
(transnational) unity. An Amarnian bas-relief actually represents
the traditional Asiatic, Nubian, and Libyan not as enslaved by the
Egyptian but as worshiping with him, as equals, one and the same
god—Aton. Only here the unity of the Empire had a *religious*
(theistic), not philosophical (anthropological) origin: the foundation of the unity was a single *god* and not the "essential" unity of
men taken as human (= reasonable) beings. It was not the unity of
their reason and their culture (*Logos*), but the unity of their god
and the community of their worship which united the citizens.

Since Ikhnaton, who failed woefully, the idea of an empire on a
unitary *transcendent* (religious) foundation has often been taken
up again. Through the Hebrew prophets it was adopted by St.
Paul and the Christians, on the one hand, and by Islam on the other
(to speak only of the most spectacular political attempts). But it is
not the Moslem *theocracy* or the Germanic *Holy* Empire or even
the secular power of the Pope which has stood the test of time and

lasted to the present, but the universal *Church,* which is an entirely different thing from a *state,* properly speaking. One can say then that it is only the *philosophical* idea going back to Socrates which, when all is said and done, acts *politically* on earth and which continues today to determine the political acts and entities aiming at the actualization of the *universal* state or empire.

But the political goal that humanity is at present pursuing (or combating) is not only that of the politically universal state; it is just as much the socially *homogeneous* state or "classless society."

Here again the remote origins of the political idea are found in the *religious* universalist conception which is already found in Ikhnaton and culminates in St. Paul. It is the idea of the *fundamental equality* of all those who believe in a single God. This transcendent conception of social equality differs radically from the Socratic-Platonic conception of the identity of beings having the same *immanent* "essence." For Alexander, a disciple of the Greek philosophers, the Hellene and the barbarian have the same title to political citizenship in the Empire, to the extent that they HAVE the same human (moreover, rational, logical, discursive) "nature" (= essence, idea, form, etc.) or are "essentially" *identified* with each other as the result of a direct (= "immediate") "mixture" of their innate qualities (realized by means of biological union). For St. Paul there is no "essential" (irreducible) difference between the Greek and the Jew because they both can BECOME Christians, and this not by "mixing" their Greek and Jewish "qualities" but by *negating* them both and "synthesizing" them in and by this very negation into a homogeneous unity not innate or given, but (freely) *created* by "conversion." Because of the *negating* character of the Christian "synthesis," there are no longer any incompatible "qualities" or "contradictory" (= mutually exclusive) "qualities." For Alexander, a Greek philosopher, there was no possible "mixture" of Masters and Slaves, for they were "opposites." Thus his *universal* state, which did away with *race,* could not be *homogeneous* in the sense that it would equally do away with "class." For St. Paul, on the contrary, the negation (*active* to the extent that "faith" is an *act,* being "dead" without "acts") of the opposition between pagan mastery and servitude could engender an "essentially" *new* Christian unity (which is, moreover, active or acting, or "emotional," and not purely rational or discursive, that is, "logical") which could serve as the basis not only for political *universality* but also for the social *homogeneity* of the state.

But in fact, universality and homogeneity on a transcendent, theistic, religious foundation did not and could not engender a State, properly speaking. They served as the foundation only for the "mystical body" of the universal and homogeneous *Church*, and they are supposed to be fully actualized only in the *beyond* (in the "Kingdom of Heaven," provided one abstracts from the *permanent* existence of hell). Guided solely by the double influence of ancient pagan *philosophy* and Christian *religion*, politics has in fact pursued only the goal of the *universal* State, without, moreover, ever having attained it up to now.

But in our time the universal and *homogeneous* state has also become a *political* goal. Now here again, politics is a tributary of *philosophy*. To be sure, this philosophy (being the *negation* of religious Christianity) is in turn a tributary of St. Paul (who, since "negated," must have been presupposed). But it is only from the moment when modern philosophy could *secularize* (= rationalize, transform into coherent discourse) the religious Christian idea of human homogeneity that this idea could have a real *political* bearing.

In the case of social homogeneity, the relations between philosophy and politics are less direct than in the case of political universality, but they are, on the other hand, absolutely certain. In the case of universality, we know only that the statesman who actualized the first effective step had been educated by a disciple at the second remove from the theoretical initiator and we can only assume the filiation of ideas. In the case of homogeneity, we know, on the other hand, that there was a filiation of ideas in spite of the absence of a direct oral tradition. The tyrant who here inaugurated the *real* political movement consciously followed the instruction of the intellectual who deliberately transformed, with an eye to its political application, the idea of the philosopher in such a way that it ceased to be a "utopian" ideal (wrongly conceived, moreover, as describing an already existing political reality: the empire of Napoleon) and became a political theory on the basis of which one could give concrete advice to tyrants, advice which they could follow. Thus, while recognizing that the tyrant "deformed" (*verkehrt*) the philosophical idea, we know that he did so only in order to "transpose it (*verkehren*) from the realm of abstraction into that of reality."

I should like to cite only these two historical examples, although it would be easy to multiply their number. But these two fundamentally exhaust the great political themes of history. And if one acknowledges that in these two cases the "tyrannical" king and the tyrant properly so-called limited themselves to putting into political practice the teaching of philosophers (duly "prepared" in the meantime by intellectuals), then one can say that in essence the political advice of philosophers has been followed.

To be sure, the teaching of philosophers, even when it had a political aspect, could never be *directly* or "immediately" applied. One can therefore consider this teaching as by definition *inapplicable* because it lacked *direct* or "immediate" ties with what was concrete political reality on the day of its appearance. But the "intellectual mediators" have always seized on this teaching and they have confronted it with contemporary reality, trying to find or construct a bridge between the two. This labor of bringing about a purely intellectual reconciliation between the philosophical idea and the political reality may go on for some time. But sooner or later a tyrant always comes along to be inspired in his day-to-day affairs by the *applicable* advice which emanates (orally and in writing) from these "mediators." In this light, history appears a continuous succession of political events guided more or less directly by the evolution of philosophy.

Therefore, from the Hegelian point of view, based on the understanding of history, the relations between tyranny and Wisdom may be described as follows.

As long as man has not, by discursive *philosophical* reflection, become completely conscious of a given political situation at some moment in history, he has no "distance" on that situation. He cannot "take a position," he cannot consciously and freely come to any decision for or against. He simply "submits" to the political world, like an animal submits to the natural world in which it lives. But, once having come to philosophical consciousness, man can distinguish between the *given* political reality and the idea he has of it "in his head"; this idea can then serve as an "ideal." All the same, if man is satisfied with philosophically *understanding* (= explaining or justifying) the given political reality, he will never be able to *go beyond* either this reality itself or the philosophical idea which corresponds to it. In order that there be "going beyond" or philosophical *progress* toward Wisdom (= Truth), the political given (which *can* be negated) must be actually *negated* by action (Struggle and Labor), so that a new historical or political (that is to say human) reality may, in the first place, be *created* in and by this same active negation of the already existing and philosophically comprehended real, and, afterward, comprehended within the framework of a new philosophy. This new philosophy will preserve only that part of the old which has survived the test of the creative political negation of the historical reality which corresponded to it; and it will transform or "sublimate" the part preserved, synthesizing it (in and by a coherent discourse) with its own revelation of the new historical reality. It is only by proceeding in this way that philosophy will make its way toward absolute knowledge or Wisdom: which it will be able to attain only when it has accomplished all possible active (political) negations.

In short, if philosophers gave no political advice at all to statesmen, in the sense that it would be impossible to draw from their ideas (directly or indirectly) any political teaching whatsoever, there would be no historical *progress*, and hence no history in the proper sense of the word. But if the statesmen did not, by daily political action, at some time actualize this "advice," grounded in philosophy, there would be no philosophical *progress* (toward Wisdom or Truth) and hence no philosophy in the precise sense of this term. *Any* number of books called "philosophical" would of course be written but there would never be *the* book ("bible") of Wisdom which could *definitively* replace the one with that title which we have had for some two thousand years. Now, wherever it has been a matter of actively negating a given political reality in its very "essence," we have in the course of history always seen the appearance of political *tyrants*. One can say then that if the appearance of the reforming tyrant is inconceivable without the prior existence of the philosopher, the coming of the wise man must necessarily be preceded by the revolutionary political action of the tyrant (who will realize the universal and homogeneous State).

Be that as it may, when I confront the reflections inspired by Xenophon's dialogue and by Strauss' interpretation with the lessons which emerge from history, I have the impression that the relations between the philosopher and the tyrant have always, in the course of historical evolution, been "reasonable": on the one hand the "reasonable" advice of philosophers has always been *sooner or later* actualized by the tyrants; on the other hand, the philosophers and the tyrants have always behaved toward each other "conformably to reason."

The tyrant is perfectly right in not trying to apply a utopian philosophical theory, that is, a philosophical theory without direct ties to the political reality with which the tyrant has to deal: for the tyrant has no time to fill up the *theoretical* lacunae between utopia and reality. As for the philosopher, he too is right when he refuses to push his theories to the point where they meet the questions raised by current political affairs: if he did, he would have no more time for philosophy; he would cease to be a philosopher and then he would no longer have any right to give *politico-philosophical* advice to the tyrant. The philosopher is right in leaving the responsibility for reconciling his philosophical ideas and the political reality on the theoretical level to a pleiad of intellectuals of all tendencies (more or less spread out in time and space); the intellectuals are right in harnessing themselves to this task and, should the case arise, in giving advice to tyrants when they have reached the level of the concrete problems posed by current political affairs with their theories; the tyrant is right in following this advice (and in listening to it) only when it has reached this level. In short, in historical *reality* all behave in a *reasonable* way, and it is by behaving in a *reasonable* way that they all at last obtain, directly or indirectly, *real* results.

It would, on the other hand, be perfectly *unreasonable* for the statesman to want to deny the philosophical value of a theory only because it cannot be applied to a given political situation (which, of course, does not mean that the statesman may not have politically valid reasons for forbidding this theory within the context of that situation). It would be just as *unreasonable* for the philosopher to condemn tyranny "on principle," since a "tyranny" can be "condemned" or "justified" only within the context of a concrete political situation. Speaking generally, it would be *unreasonable* if the philosopher should, in terms of his philosophy alone, wish to criticize in any way whatsoever the concrete political measures taken by the statesman, tyrant or not, especially in the case in which he takes them so that the very ideal recommended by the philosophers may be actualized in the future. In either case the judgments passed on the philosophy or the policy would be *incompetent* judgments. Now, as such, this judgment would be more excusable (but not more justified) in the mouth of the "uninitiate" statesman or tyrant, "unreasonable" by definition, than in that of the philosopher. As for the "mediating" intellectuals, they would be *unreasonable* if they did not recognize the right of the philosopher to judge the philosophical value of their theories or the right of the statesman to select those of them which he judges actualizable under the given circumstances and discard the rest—even "tyrannically."

Speaking generally, it is history itself which attends to "judging" (by "results" or "success") the acts which statesmen or tyrants perform (consciously or not) in terms of the ideas of philosophers, adapted for practice by intellectuals.

RESTATEMENT ON

XENOPHON'S

HIERO

◻ ◻ ◻

A SOCIAL SCIENCE that cannot speak of tyranny with the same confidence with which medicine speaks, for example, of cancer, cannot understand social phenomena as what they are. It is therefore
not scientific. Present-day social science finds itself in this condition.
If it is true that present-day social science is the inevitable result of
modern social science and of modern philosophy, one is forced to
think of the restoration of classical social science. Once we have
learned again from the classics what tyranny is, we shall be enabled
and compelled to diagnose as tyrannies a number of contemporary
regimes which appear in the guise of dictatorships. This diagnosis
can only be the first step toward an exact analysis of present-day
tyranny, for present-day tyranny is fundamentally different from
the tyranny analyzed by the classics.

But is this not tantamount to admitting that the classics were
wholly unfamiliar with tyranny in its contemporary form? Must
one not therefore conclude that the classical concept of tyranny is
too narrow and hence that the classical frame of reference must
be radically modified, i.e., abandoned? In other words, is the

From Leo Strauss, *What Is Political Philosophy?* (New York: The Free
Press of Glencoe, 1959).

attempt to restore classical social science not utopian since it implies that the classical orientation has not been made obsolete by the triumph of the biblical orientation?

This seems to be the chief objection to which my study of Xenophon's *Hiero* is exposed. At any rate, this is the gist of the only criticisms of my study from which one could learn anything. Those criticisms were written in complete independence of each other and their authors, Professor Eric Voegelin and M. Alexandre Kojève, have, so to speak, nothing in common. Before discussing their arguments, I must restate my contention.

The fact that there is a fundamental difference between classical tyranny and present-day tyranny, or that the classics did not even dream of present-day tyranny, is not a good or sufficient reason for abandoning the classical frame of reference. For that fact is perfectly compatible with the possibility that present day tyranny finds its place within the classical framework, i.e., that it cannot be understood adequately except within the classical framework. The difference between present-day tyranny and classical tyranny has its root in the difference between the modern notion of philosophy or science and the classical notion of philosophy or science. Present-day tyranny, in contradistinction to classical tyranny, is based on the unlimited progress in the "conquest of nature" which is made possible by modern science, as well as on the popularization or diffusion of philosophic or scientific knowledge. Both possibilities—the possibility of a science that issues in the conquest of nature and the possibility of the popularization of philosophy or science—were known to the classics. (Compare Xenophon, *Memorabilia* I 1.15 with Empedocles, fr. 111; Plato, *Theaetetus* 180c7-d5.) But the classics rejected them as "unnatural," i.e., as destructive of humanity. They did not dream of present-day tyranny because they regarded its basic presuppositions as so preposterous that they turned their imagination in entirely different directions.

Voegelin, one of the leading contemporary historians of political thought, seems to contend (*The Review of Politics*, 1949, pp. 241–44) that the classical concept of tyranny is too narrow because it does not cover the phenomenon known as Caesarism: when calling a given regime tyrannical, we imply that "constitutional" government is a viable alternative to it; but Caesarism emerges only after "the final breakdown of the republican constitutional order";

hence Caesarism or "postconstitutional" rule cannot be understood as a subdivision of tyranny in the classical sense of tyranny. There is no reason to quarrel with the view that genuine Caesarism is not tyranny, but this does not justify the conclusion that Caesarism is incomprehensible on the basis of classical political philosophy: Caesarism is still a subdivision of absolute monarchy as the classics understood it. If in a given situation "the republican constitutional order" has completely broken down, and there is no reasonable prospect of its restoration within all the foreseeable future, the establishment of permanent absolute rule cannot, as such, be justly blamed; therefore it is fundamentally different from the establishment of tyranny. Just blame could attach only to the manner in which that permanent absolute rule that is truly necessary is established and exercised; as Voegelin emphasizes, there are tyrannical as well as royal Caesars. One has only to read Coluccio Salutati's defense of Caesar against the charge that he was a tyrant—a defense which in all essential points is conceived in the spirit of the classics— in order to see that the distinction between Caesarism and tyranny fits perfectly into the classical framework.

But the phenomenon of Caesarism is one thing; the current concept of Caesarism is another. The current concept of Caesarism is certainly incompatible with classical principles. The question thus arises whether the current concept or the classical concept is more nearly adequate. More particularly, the question concerns the validity of the two implications of the current concept which Voegelin seems to regard as indispensable, and which originated in nineteenth-century historicism. In the first place, he seems to believe that the difference between "the constitutional situation" and "the postconstitutional situation" is more fundamental than the difference between the good king or the good Caesar on the one hand and the bad king or the bad Caesar on the other. But is not the difference between good and bad the most fundamental of all practical or political distinctions? Secondly, Voegelin seems to believe that "postconstitutional" rule is not per se inferior to "constitutional" rule. But is not "postconstitutional" rule justified by necessity or, as Voegelin says, by "historical necessity"? And is not the necessary essentially inferior to the noble or to what is choiceworthy for its own sake? Necessity excuses: what is justified by necessity is in need of excuse. The Caesar, as Voegelin conceives of him, is "the avenger of the misdeeds of a corrupt people." Caesarism is then essentially related to a corrupt people, to a low level of political life, to a decline of society. It presupposes the decline, if not the extinction, of civic virtue or of public spirit, and it necessarily perpetuates that condition. Caesarism belongs to a degraded society, and it thrives on its degradation. Caesarism is just, whereas tyranny is unjust. But Caesarism is just in the way in which deserved punishment is just. It is as little choiceworthy for its own sake as is deserved punishment. Cato refused to see what his time demanded because he saw too clearly the degraded and degrading character of what his time demanded. It is much more important to realize the low level of Caesarism (for, to repeat, Caesarism cannot be divorced from the society which deserves Caesarism) than to realize that under certain conditions Caesarism is necessary and hence legitimate.

While the classics were perfectly capable of doing justice to the merits of Caesarism, they were not particularly concerned with elaborating a doctrine of Caesarism. Since they were primarily concerned with the best regime, they paid less attention to "postconstitutional" rule or to late kingship, than to "preconstitutional" rule or to early kingship: rustic simplicity is a better soil for the good life than is sophisticated rottenness. But there was another reason which induced the classics to be almost silent about "postconstitutional" rule. To stress the fact that it is just to replace constitutional rule by absolute rule, if the common good requires that change, means to cast a doubt on the absolute sanctity of the established constitutional order. It means encouraging dangerous men to confuse the issue by bringing about a state of affairs in which the common good requires the establishment of their absolute rule. The true doctrine of the legitimacy of Caesarism is a dangerous doctrine. The true distinction between Caesarism and tyranny is too subtle for ordinary political use. It is better for the people to remain ignorant of that distinction and to regard the potential Caesar as a potential tyrant. No harm can come from this theoretical error which becomes a practical truth if the people have the mettle to act upon it. No harm can come from the political identification of Caesarism and tyranny: Caesars can take care of themselves.

The classics could easily have elaborated a doctrine of Caesarism or of late kingship if they had wanted, but they did not want to do it. Voegelin however contends that they were forced by their historical situation to grope for a doctrine of Caesarism, and that they failed to discover it. He tries to substantiate his contention by referring to Xenophon and to Plato. As for Plato, Voegelin was forced by considerations of space to limit himself to a summary reference to the royal ruler in the *Statesman*. As for Xenophon, he rightly asserts that it is not sufficient to oppose "the *Cyropaedia* as a mirror of the perfect king to the *Hiero* as a mirror of the tyrant," since the perfect king Cyrus and the improved tyrant who is described by Simonides "look much more opposed to each other than they really are." He explains this fact by suggesting that "both works fundamentally face the same historical problem of the new [*sc*. postconstitutional] rulership," and that one cannot solve this problem except by obliterating at the first stage the distinction between king and tyrant. To justify this explanation he contends that "the very motivation of the *Cyropaedia* is the search for a stable rule that will make an end to the dreary overturning of democracies and tyrannies in the Hellenic polis." This contention is not supported by what Xenophon says or indicates in regard to the intention of the *Cyropaedia*. Its explicit intention is to make intelligible Cyrus' astonishing success in solving the problem of ruling human beings. Xenophon conceives of this problem as one that is coeval with man. Like Plato in the *Statesman,* he does not make the slightest reference to the particular "historical" problem of stable rule in "the postconstitutional situation." In particular, he does not refer to "the dreary overturning of democracies and tyrannies in the Hellenic polis": he speaks of the frequent overturning of democracies, monarchies, and oligarchies and of the essential instability of all tyrannies. As for the implicit intention of the *Cyropaedia*, it is partly revealed by the remark, toward the end of the work, that "after Cyrus died, his sons immediately quarrelled, cities and nations immediately revolted, and all things turned to the worse." If Xenophon was not a fool, he did not intend to present Cyrus' regime as a model. He knew too well that the good order of society requires stability and continuity. (Compare the opening of the *Cyropaedia* with the parallel in the *Agesilaus*, I. 4.) He rather used Cyrus' meteoric success and the way in which it was brought about as an example for making intelligible the nature of political things. The work, which describes Cyrus' whole life, is entitled

The Education of Cyrus: the education of Cyrus is the clue to his whole life, to his astonishing success, and hence to Xenophon's intention. A very rough sketch must here suffice. Xenophon's Cyrus was the son of the king of Persia, and until he was about twelve years old he was educated according to the laws of the Persians. The laws and the polity of Xenophon's Persians, however, are an improved version of the laws and polity of the Spartans. The Persia in which Cyrus was raised was an aristocracy superior to Sparta. The political activity of Cyrus—his extraordinary success—consisted in transforming a stable and healthy aristocracy into an unstable "Oriental despotism" whose rottenness showed itself at the latest immediately after his death. The first step in this transformation was a speech which Cyrus addressed to the Persian nobles and in which he convinced them that they ought to deviate from the habit of their ancestors by practicing virtue no longer for its own sake, but for the sake of its rewards. The destruction of aristocracy begins, as one would expect, with the corruption of its principle. (*Cyropaedia* I 5.5–14; compare Aristotle, *Eudemian Eehics* 1248b 38 ff., where the view of virtue which Xenophon's Cyrus instills into the minds of the Persian gentlemen is described as the Spartan view.) The quick success of Cyrus' first action forces the reader to wonder whether the Persian aristocracy was a genuine aristocracy; or more precisely, whether the gentleman in the political or social sense is a true gentleman. This question is identical with the question which Plato answers explicitly in the negative in his story of Er. Socrates says outright that a man who has lived in his former life in a well-ordered regime, participating in virtue by habit and without philosophy, will choose for his next life "the greatest tyranny," for "mostly people make their choice according to the habits of their former life" (*Republic* 619b6–620a3). There is no adequate solution to the problem of virtue or happiness on the political or social plane. Still, while aristocracy is always on the verge of declining into oligarchy or something worse, it is the best possible political solution of the human problem. It must here suffice to note that Cyrus' second step is the democratization of the army, and that the end of the process is a regime that might seem barely distinguishable from the least intolerable form of tyranny. But one must not overlook the essential difference between Cyrus' rule and tyranny, a distinction that is never obliterated. Cyrus is and remains a legitimate ruler. He is born as the legitimate heir to the reigning king, a scion of an old royal house. He becomes the king of other nations through inheritance or marriage and through just conquest, for he enlarges the boundaries of Persia in the Roman manner: by defending the allies of Persia. The difference between Cyrus and a Hiero educated by Simonides is comparable to the difference between William III and Oliver Cromwell. A cursory comparison of the history of England with the history of certain other European nations suffices to show that this difference is not unimportant to the well-being of peoples. Xenophon did not even attempt to obliterate the distinction between the best tyrant and the king because he appreciated too well the charms, nay, the blessings of legitimacy. He expressed this appreciation by subscribing to the maxim (which must be reasonably understood and applied) that the just is identical with the legal.

Voegelin might reply that what is decisive is not Xenophon's conscious intention, stated or implied, but the historical meaning of his work, the historical meaning of a work being determined by the historical situation as distinguished from the conscious intention of the author. Yet opposing the historical meaning of Xenophon's work to his conscious intention implies that we are better judges of the situation in which Xenophon thought than Xenophon himself was. But we cannot be better judges of that situation if we do not have a clearer grasp than he had of the principles in whose light historical situations reveal their meaning. After the experience of our generation, the burden of proof would seem to rest on those who assert rather than on those who deny that we have progressed beyond the classics. And even if it were true that we could understand the classics better than they understood themselves, we would become certain of our superiority only after understanding them exactly as they understood themselves. Otherwise we might mistake our superiority to our notion of the classics for superiority to the classics.

According to Voegelin, it was Machiavelli, as distinguished from the classics, who "achieved the theoretical creation of a concept of rulership in the postconstitutional situation," and this achievement was due to the influence on Machiavelli of the Biblical tradition. He refers especially to Machiavelli's remark about the "armed prophets" (*Prince* VI). The difficulty to which Voegelin's contention is exposed is indicated by these two facts: he speaks on the one hand of "the apocalyptic [hence thoroughly non-classical] aspects of the 'armed prophet' in the *Prince*," whereas on the other hand he says that Machiavelli claimed "for [the] paternity" of the "armed prophet" "besides Romulus, Moses and Theseus, precisely the Xenophontic Cyrus." This amounts to an admission that certainly Machiavelli himself was not aware of any non-classical implication of his notion of "armed prophets." There is nothing unclassical about Romulus, Theseus, and Xenophon's Cyrus. It is true that Machiavelli adds Moses; but, after having made his bow to the Biblical interpretation of Moses, he speaks of Moses in exactly the same manner in which every classical political philosopher would have spoken of him; Moses was one of the greatest legislators or founders (*fondatori: Discorsi* I 9) who ever lived. When reading Voegelin's statement on this subject, one receives the impression that in speaking of armed prophets, Machiavelli put the emphasis on "prophets" as distinguished from nonprophetic rulers like Cyrus, for example. But Machiavelli puts the emphasis not on "prophets," but on "armed." He opposes the armed prophets, among whom he counts Cyrus, Romulus, and Theseus as well as Moses, to unarmed prophets like Savonarola. He states the lesson which he intends to convey with remarkable candor: "All armed prophets succeed and the unarmed ones come to ruin." It is difficult to believe that in writing this sentence Machiavelli should have been completely oblivious of the most famous of all unarmed prophets. One certainly cannot understand Machiavelli's remark on the "unarmed prophets" without taking into consideration what he says about the "unarmed heaven" and "the effeminacy of the world" which, according to him, are due to Christianity. (*Discorsi* II 2 and III 1.) The tradition which Machiavelli continues, while radically modifying it, is not, as Voegelin suggests, that represented by Joachim of Floris, for example, but the one which we still call, with pardonable ignorance, the Averroistic tradition. Machiavelli declares that Savonarola, that unarmed prophet, was right in saying that the ruin of Italy was caused by "our sins," "but our sins were not what he believed they were," namely, religious sins, "but those which I have narrated," namely, political or military sins (*Prince* XII). In the same vein Maimonides declares that the ruin of the Jewish kingdom was caused by the "sins of our fathers," namely, by their idolatry; but idolatry worked its effect in a perfectly natural manner: it led to astrology and thus induced the Jewish people to devote themselves to astrology instead of to the practice of the arts of war and the conquest of countries. But apart from all this, Voegelin does not give any indication of what the armed prophets have to do with "the postconstitutional situation." Certainly Romulus, Theseus, and Moses were "preconstitutional" rulers. Voegelin also refers to "Machiavelli's complete drawing of the savior prince in the *Vita di Castruccio Castracani*" which, he says, "is hardly thinkable without the standardized model of the *Life of Timur*." Apart from the fact that Voegelin has failed to show any connection between the *Castruccio* and the *Life of Timur* and between the *Life of Timur* and the Biblical tradition, the *Castruccio* is perhaps the most impressive document of Machiavelli's longing for classical *virtù* as distinguished from, and opposed to, Biblical righteousness. Castruccio, that idealized condottiere who preferred in so single-minded a manner the life of the soldier to the life of the priest, is compared by Machiavelli himself to Philip of Macedon and to Scipio of Rome.

Machiavelli's longing for classical *virtù* is only the reverse side of his rejection of classical political philosophy. He rejects classical political philosophy because of its orientation by the perfection of the nature of man. The abandonment of the contemplative ideal leads to a radical change in the character of wisdom: Machiavellian wisdom has no necessary connection with moderation. Machiavelli separates wisdom from moderation. The ultimate reason why the *Hiero* comes so close to the *Prince* is that in the *Hiero* Xenophon experiments with a type of wisdom which comes relatively close to a wisdom divorced from moderation: Simonides seems to have an inordinate desire for the pleasures of the table. It is impossible to say how far the epoch-making change that was effected by Machiavelli is due to the indirect influence of the Biblical tradition, before that change has been fully understood in itself.

The peculiar character of the *Hiero* does not disclose itself to cursory reading. It will not disclose itself to the tenth reading, however painstaking, if the reading is not productive of a change of orientation. This change was much easier to achieve for the eighteenth-century reader than for the reader in our century who has been brought up on the brutal and sentimental literature of the last five generations. We are in need of a second education in order to accustom our eyes to the noble reserve and the quiet grandeur of the classics. Xenophon, as it were, limited himself to cultivating exclusively that character of classical writing which is wholly foreign to the modern reader. No wonder that he is today despised or ignored. An unknown ancient critic, who must have been a man of uncommon discernment, called him most bashful. Those modern readers who are so fortunate as to have a natural preference for Jane Austen rather than for Dostoievski, in particular, have an easier access to Xenophon than others might have; to understand Xenophon, they have only to combine the love of philosophy with their natural preference. In the words of Xenophon, "it is both noble and just, and pious and more pleasant to remember the good things rather than the bad ones." In the *Hiero*, Xenophon experimented with the pleasure that comes from remembering bad things, with a pleasure that admittedly is of doubtful morality and piety.

For someone who is trying to form his taste or his mind by studying Xenophon, it is almost shocking to be suddenly confronted by the more than Machiavellian bluntness with which Kojève speaks of such terrible things as atheism and tyranny and takes them for granted. At least on one occasion he goes so far as to call "unpopular" certain measures which the very tyrant Hiero had declared to be criminal. He does not hesitate to proclaim that present-day dictators are tyrants without regarding this in the least as an objection to their rule. As for reverence for legitimacy, he has none. But the nascent shock is absorbed by the realization, or rather the knowledge of long standing, that Kojève belongs to the very few who know how to think and who love to think. He does not belong to the many who today are unabashed atheists and more than Byzantine flatterers of tyrants for the same reason for which they would have been addicted to the grossest superstitions, both religious and legal, had they lived in an earlier age. In a word, Kojève is a philosopher and not an intellectual.

Since he is a philosopher, he knows that the philosopher is, in principle, more capable of ruling than other men and hence will be regarded by a tyrant like Hiero as a most dangerous competitor for tyrannical rule. It would not occur to him for a moment to compare the relationship between Hiero and Simonides with the relationship, say, between Stefan George or Thomas Mann and

Hitler. For, to say nothing of considerations too obvious to be mentioned, he could not overlook the obvious fact that the *hypothesis* of the *Hiero* demanded a tyrant of whom it was at least imaginable that he could be taught. In particular, he knows without having to be reminded of the *Seventh Letter* that the difference between a philosopher who is a subject of the tyrant and a philosopher who merely visits the tyrant is immaterial as far as the tyrant's fear of philosophers is concerned. His understanding does not permit him to rest satisfied with the vulgar separation of theory from practice. He knows too well that there never was and there never will be reasonable security for sound practice except after theory has overcome the powerful obstacles to sound practice which originate in theoretical misconceptions of a certain kind. Finally, he brushes aside in sovereign contempt the implicit claim of current, i.e., running or heedless thought to have solved the problems that were raised by the classics—a claim that is only implicit because current thought is unaware of the existence of those problems.

Yet while admitting and even stressing the absolute superiority of classical thought to current thought, Kojève rejects the classical solution of the basic problems. He regards unlimited technological progress and universal enlightenment as essential for the genuine satisfaction of what is human in man. He denies that present-day social science is the inevitable outcome of modern philosophy. According to him, present-day social science is merely the inevitable product of the inevitable decay of that modern philosophy which has refused to learn the decisive lesson from Hegel. He regards Hegel's teaching as the genuine synthesis of Socratic and Machiavellian (or Hobbian) politics, which, as such, is superior to its component elements. In fact, he regards Hegel's teaching, as in principle, the final teaching.

Kojève directs his criticism in the first place against the classical notion of tyranny. Xenophon reveals an important part of that notion by making Hiero answer with silence to Simonides' description of the good tyrant. As Kojève rightly judges, Hiero's silence signifies that he will not attempt to put into practice Simonides' proposals. Kojève suggests, at least provisionally, that this is the fault of Simonides, who did not tell Hiero what the first step is which the tyrant must take in order to transform bad tyranny into good tyranny. But would it not have been up to Hiero if he seriously desired to become a good tyrant, to ask Simonides about the first step? How does Kojève know that Simonides was not waiting in vain for this very question? Or perhaps Simonides has answered it already implicitly. Yet this defense of Simonides is insufficient. The question returns, for, as Kojève again rightly observes, the attempt to realize Simonides' vision of a good tyrant is confronted with an almost insurmountable difficulty. The only question which Hiero raises while Simonides discusses the improvement of tyranny concerns the mercenaries. Hiero's imperfect tyranny rests on the support of his mercenaries. The improvement of tyranny would require a shift of part of the power from the mercenaries to the citizens. By attempting such a shift, the tyrant would antagonize the mercenaries without being at all certain that he could regain by that concession, or by any concession, the confidence of the citizens. He would end by sitting between two chairs. Simonides seems to disregard this state of things and thus to reveal a poor understanding of Hiero's situation or a lack of wisdom. To save Simonides' reputation, one seems compelled to suggest that the poet himself did not believe in the viability of his improved tyranny, that he regarded the good tyranny as a utopia, or that he rejected tyranny as a hopelessly bad regime. But, Kojève continues, does this suggestion not imply that Simonides' attempt to educate Hiero is futile? And a wise man does not attempt futile things.

This criticism may be said to be based on an insufficient appreciation of the value of utopias. The utopia in the strict sense describes the simply good social order. As such it merely makes explicit what is implied in every attempt at social improvement. There is no difficulty in enlarging the strict meaning of utopia in such a manner that one can speak of the utopia of the best tyranny. As Kojève emphasizes, under certain conditions the abolition of tyranny may be out of the question. The best one could hope for is that the tyranny be improved, i.e., that the tyrannical rule be exercised as little inhumanely or irrationally as possible. Every specific reform or improvement of which a sensible man could think, if reduced to its principle, forms part of the complete picture of the maximum improvement that is still compatible with the continued existence of tyranny, it being understood that the maximum improvement is possible only under the most favorable conditions. The maximum improvement of tyranny would require, above all, the shift of part of the power from the mercenaries to the citizens. Such a shift is not absolutely impossible, but its actualization is safe only in circumstances which man cannot create or which no sensible man would create (e.g., an extreme danger threatening equally the mercenaries and the citizens, like the danger of Syracuse being conquered, and all its inhabitants being put to the sword, by barbarians). A sensible man like Simonides would think that he had deserved well of his fellow men if he could induce the tyrant to act humanely or rationally within a small area, or perhaps even in a single instance, where, without his advice, the tyrant would have continued an inhuman or irrational practice. Xenophon indicates an example: Hiero's participating at the Olympian and Pythian games. If Hiero followed Simonides' advice to abandon this practice, he would improve his standing with his subjects and in the world at large, and he would indirectly benefit his subjects. Xenophon leaves it to the intelligence of his reader to replace that particular example by another one which the reader, on the basis of his particular experience, might consider to be more apt. The general lesson is to the effect that the wise man who happens to have a chance to influence a tyrant should use his influence for benefiting his fellow men. One may say that the lesson is trivial. It would be more accurate to say that it was trivial in former ages, for today such little actions like that of Simonides are not taken seriously because we are in the habit of expecting too much. What is not trivial is what we learn from Xenophon about how the wise man has to proceed in his undertaking, which is beset with great difficulties and even with dangers.

Kojève denies our contention that the good tyranny is a utopia. To substantiate his denial, he mentions one example by name: the rule of Salazar. I have never been to Portugal, but from all that I have heard about that country, I am inclined to believe that Kojève is right, except that I am not quite certain whether Salazar's rule should not be called "postconstitutional" rather than tyrannical. Yet one swallow does not make a summer, and we never denied that good tyranny is possible under very favorable circumstances. But Kojève contends that Salazar is not an exception. He thinks that circumstances favorable to good tyranny are easily available today. He contends that all present-day tyrants are good tyrants in Xenophon's sense. He alludes to Stalin. He notes in particular that the tyranny improved according to Simonides' suggestions is characterized by Stakhanovistic emulation. But Stalin's rule would live up to Simonides' standards only if the introduction of Stakhanovistic emulation had been accompanied by a considerable decline in the use of the NKVD or of "labor" camps. Would Kojève go so far as to say that Stalin could travel outside of the Iron Curtain wherever he liked in order to see sights without having anything to fear? (*Hiero* 11.10 and 1.12.) Would Kojève go so far as to say that everyone living behind the Iron Curtain is an ally of Stalin, or that Stalin regards all citizens of Soviet Russia and the other "people's democracies" as his comrades? (*Hiero* 11.11 and 11.14.)

However this may be, Kojève contends that present-day tyranny, and perhaps even classical tyranny, cannot be understood on the basis of Xenophon's principles, and that the classical frame of reference must be modified radically by the introduction of an element of Biblical origin. He argues as follows. Simonides maintains that honor is the supreme or sole goal of the tyrant in particular and of the highest type of human being (the Master) in general. This shows that the poet sees only half of the truth. The other half is supplied by the Biblical morality of Slaves or Workers. The actions of men, and hence also the actions of tyrants, can be, and frequently are, prompted by desire for the pleasure deriving from the successful execution of their work, their projects, or their ideals. There is such a thing as devotion to one's work, or to a cause, "conscientious" work, into which no thought of honor or glory enters. But this fact must not induce us to minimize hypocritically the essential contribution of the desire for honor or prestige to the completion of man. The desire for prestige, recognition, or authority is the primary motive of all political struggles, and in particular of the struggle that leads a man to tyrannical power. It is perfectly unobjectionable for an aspiring statesman or a potential tyrant to try for no other reason than for the sake of his preferment to oust the incumbent ruler or rulers although he knows that he is in no way better equipped for the job than they are. There is no reason to find fault with such a course of action, for the desire for recognition necessarily transforms itself, in all cases which are of any consequence, into devotion to the work to be done or to a cause. The synthesis of the morality of Masters with the morality of Slaves is superior to its component elements.

Simonides is very far from accepting the morality of Masters or from maintaining that honor is the supreme goal of the highest human type. In translating one of the crucial passages (the last sentence of *Hiero* 7.4), Kojève omits the qualifying *dokei* ("no human pleasure *seems* to come closer to what is divine than the joy concerning honors"). Nor does he pay attention to the implication of the fact that Simonides declares the desire for honor to be the dominating passion of *andres* (whom Kojève calls Masters) as distinguished from *anthropoi* (whom he calls Slaves). For, according to Xenophon, and hence according to his Simonides, the *anēr* is by no means the highest human type. The highest human type is the wise man. A Hegelian will have no difficulty in admitting that, since the wise man is distinguished from the Master, he will have something important in common with the Slave. This was certainly Xenophon's view. In the statement of the Master's principle, which he entrusted to Simonides, the poet cannot help admitting implicitly the unity of the human species which his statement explicitly denies. And the unity of the human species is thought to be more easily seen by the Slave than by the Master. One does not characterize Socrates adequately by calling him a Master. Xenophon contrasts him with Ischomachus, who is the prototype of the *kalos te kagathos anēr*. Since the work and the knowledge which is best for the type represented by Ischomachus is agriculture and Socrates was not an agriculturist, Socrates was not a *kalos te kagathos anēr*. As Lycon explicitly says, Socrates was a *kalos te kagathos anthropos* (*Symposium* 9.1; *Oeconomicus* 6.8, 12). In this context we may note that in the passage of the *Hiero* which deals with gentlemen living under a tyrant (10.3), Simonides characteristically omits *andres: kaloi te kagathoi andres* could not live happily under a tyrant however good (compare *Hiero* 9.6 and 5.1–2). Xenophon indicates his view most succinctly by failing to mention manliness in his two lists of Socrates' virtues. He sees in Socrates' military activity a sign not of his manliness, but of his justice (*Memorabilia* IV 4.1).

Since Xenophon or his Simonides did not believe that honor is the highest good, or since they did not accept the morality of Masters, there is no apparent need for supplementing their teaching by an element taken from the morality of Slaves or Workers. According to the classics, the highest good is a life devoted to wisdom or to virtue, honor being no more than a very pleasant, but secondary and dispensable, reward. What Kojève calls the pleasure deriving from doing one's work well or from realizing one's projects or one's ideals was called by the classics the pleasure deriving from virtuous or noble activity. The classical interpretation would seem to be truer to the facts. Kojève refers to the pleasure which a solitary child or a solitary painter may derive from executing his projects well. But one can easily imagine a solitary safecracker deriving pleasure from executing his project well, and without a thought of the external rewards (wealth or admiration of his competence) which he reaps. There are artists in all walks of life. It does make a difference what kind of a "job" is the source of disinterested pleasure: whether the job is criminal or innocent, whether it is mere play or serious, and so on. By thinking through this observation one arrives at the view that the highest kind of job, or the only job that is truly human, is noble or virtuous activity, or noble or virtuous work. If one is fond of this manner of looking at things, one may say that noble work is the synthesis effected by the classics between the morality of workless nobility and the morality if ignoble work (cf. Plato, *Meno* 81d3 ff.).

Simonides is therefore justified in saying that the desire for honor is the supreme motive of men who aspire to tyrannical power. Kojève seems to think that a man may aspire to tyrannical power chiefly because he is attracted by "objective" tasks of the highest order, by tasks whose performance requires tyrannical power, and that this motive will radically transform his desire for honor or recognition. The classics denied that this is possible. They were struck by the similarity between Kojève's tyrant and the man who is more attracted to safecracking by its exciting problems than by its rewards. One cannot become a tyrant and remain a tyrant without stooping to do base things; hence, a self-respecting man will not aspire to tyrannical power. But, Kojève might object, this still does not prove that the tyrant is motivated chiefly or exclusively by a desire for honor or prestige. He may be motivated, e.g., by a misguided desire to benefit his fellow men. This defense would hold good if error in such matters were difficult to avoid. But it is easy to know that tyranny is base; we all learn as children that one must not give others bad examples and that one must not do base things for the sake of the good that may come out of them. The potential or actual tyrant does not know what every reasonably well-bred child knows, because he is blinded by passion. By what passion? The most charitable answer is that he is blinded by desire for honor or prestige.

Syntheses effect miracles. Kojève's or Hegel's synthesis of classical and Biblical morality effects the miracle of producing an amazingly lax morality out of two moralities both of which made very strict demands on self-restraint. Neither Biblical nor classical morality encourages us to try, solely for the sake of our preferment or our glory, to oust from their positions men who do the required work as well as we could. (Consider Aristotle, *Politics* 1271a10–19.) Neither Biblical nor classical morality encourages all statesmen to try to extend their authority over all men in order to achieve universal recognition. It does not seem to be sound that Kojève encourages others by his speech to a course of action to which he himself would never stoop in deed. If he did not suppress his better knowledge, it would be given him to see that there is no need for having recourse to a miracle in order to understand Hegel's moral and political teaching. Hegel continued, and in a certain respect radicalized, the modern tradition that emancipated the passions and hence "competition." That tradition was originated by Machiavelli and perfected by such men as Hobbes and Adam Smith. It came into being through a conscious break with the strict moral demands made by both the Bible and classical philosophy; those demands were explicitly rejected as too strict. Hegel's moral or political teaching is indeed a synthesis: it is a synthesis of Socratic and Machiavellian or Hobbian politics. Kojève knows as well as anyone living that Hegel's fundamental teaching regarding master and slave is based on Hobbes' doctrine of the state of nature. If Hobbes' doctrine of the state of nature is abandoned *en pleine connaissance de cause* (as indeed it should be abandoned), Hegel's fundamental teaching will lose the evidence which it apparently still possesses for Kojève. Hegel's teaching is much more sophisticated than Hobbes', but it is as much a construction as the latter. Both doctrines construct human society by starting from the untrue assumption that man as man is thinkable as a being that lacks awareness of sacred restraints or as a being that is guided by nothing but a desire for recognition.

But Kojève is likely to become somewhat impatient with what, as I fear, he might call our Victorian or pre-Victorian *niaiseries*.

He probably will maintain that the whole previous discussion is irrelevant because it is based on a dogmatic assumption. We assume indeed that the classical concept of tyranny is derived from an adequate analysis of the fundamental social phenomena. The classics understand tyranny as the opposite of the best regime, and they hold that the best regime is the rule of the best or aristocracy. But, Kojève argues, aristocracy is the rule of a minority over the majority of citizens or of adult residents of a given territory, a rule that rests, in the last resort, on force or terror. Would it then not be more proper to admit that aristocracy is a form of tyranny? Yet Kojève apparently thinks that force or terror are indispensable in every regime, while he does not think that all regimes are equally good or bad and hence equally tyrannical. If I understand him correctly, he is satisfied that "the universal and homogeneous state" is the simply best social order. Lest we get entangled in a merely verbal difficulty, I shall state his view as follows: the universal and homogeneous state is the only one which is essentially just; the aristocracy of the classics in particular is essentially unjust.

To see the classical view in the proper light, let us make the assumption that the wise do not desire to rule. The unwise are very unlikely to force the wise to rule over them. For the wise cannot rule as wise if they do not have absolute power or if they are in any way responsible to the unwise. No broil in which the unwise may find themselves could be great enough to induce them to surrender absolute control to the wise, whose first measure would probably be to expel everyone above the age of ten from the city (Plato, *Republic* 540d–541a). Hence, what pretends to be absolute rule of the wise will in fact be absolute rule of unwise men. But if this is the case, the universal state would seem to be impossible. For the universal state requires universal agreement regarding the fundamentals, and such agreement is possible only on the basis of genuine knowledge or of wisdom. Agreement based on opinion can never become universal agreement. Every faith that lays claim to universality, i.e., to be universally accepted, of necessity provokes a counter-faith which raises the same claim. The diffusion among the unwise of genuine knowledge that was acquired by the wise would be of no help, for through its diffusion or dilution, knowledge inevitably transforms itself into opinion, prejudice, or mere belief. The utmost in the direction of universality that one could expect is, then, an absolute rule of unwise men who control about half of the globe, the other half being ruled by other unwise men. It is not obvious that the extinction of all independent states but two will be a blessing. But it is obvious that absolute rule of the unwise is less desirable than their limited rule: the unwise ought to rule under law. In addition, it is more probable that in a situation that is favorable to radical change, the citizen body will for once follow the advice of a wise man or a founding father by adopting a code of laws which he has elaborated, than that they will ever submit to perpetual and absolute rule of a succession of wise men. Yet laws must be applied or are in need of interpretation. The full authority under law should therefore be given to men who, thanks to their good upbringing, are capable of "completing" the laws (*Memorabilia* IV 6.12) or of interpreting them equitably. "Constitutional" authority ought to be given to the equitable men (*epieikeis*), i.e., to gentlemen—preferably an urban patriciate which derives its income from the cultivation of its landed estates. It is true that it is at least partly a matter of accident—of the accident of birth—whether a given individual does or does not belong to the class of gentlemen and has thereby had an opportunity of being brought up in the proper manner. But in the absence of absolute rule of the wise on the one hand, and on the other hand of a degree of abundance which is possible only on the basis of unlimited technological progress with all its terrible hazards, the apparently just alternative to aristocracy open or disguised will be permanent revolution, i.e., permanent chaos in which life will be not only poor and short but brutish as well. It would not be difficult to show that the classical argument cannot be disposed of as easily as is now generally thought, and that liberal or constitutional democracy comes closer to what the classics demanded than any alternative that is viable in our age. In the last analysis, however, the classical argument derives its strength from the assumption that the wise do not desire to rule.

In discussing the fundamental issue which concerns the relation of wisdom to rule or to tyranny, Kojève starts from the observation that at least up to now there have been no wise men but at best men who strove for wisdom, i.e., philosophers. Since the philosopher is the man who devotes his whole life to the quest for wisdom, he has no time for political activity of any kind: the philosopher cannot possibly desire to rule. His only demand on the political men is that they leave him alone. He justifies his demand by honestly declaring that his pursuit is purely theoretical and does not interfere in any way with the business of the political men. This simple solution presents itself at first glance as the strict consequence from the definition of the philosopher. Yet a short reflection shows already that it suffers from a fatal weakness. The philosopher cannot lead an absolutely solitary life because legitimate "subjective certainty" and the "subjective certainty" of the lunatic are indistinguishable. Genuine certainty must be "inter-subjective." The classics were fully aware of the essential weakness of the mind of the individual. Hence their teaching about the philosophic life is a teaching about friendship: the philosopher is as philosopher in need of friends. To be of service to the philosopher in his philosophizing, the friends must be competent men: they must themselves be actual or potential philosophers, i.e., members of the natural "elite." Friendship presupposes a measure of conscious agreement. The things regarding which the philosophic friends must agree cannot be known or evident truths. For philosophy is not wisdom but quest for wisdom. The things regarding which the philosophic friends agree will then be opinions or prejudices. But there is necessarily a variety of opinions or prejudices. Hence there will be a variety of groups of philosophic friends: philosophy, as distinguished from wisdom, necessarily appears in the form of philosophic schools or of sects. Friendship as the classics understood it offers then no solution to the problem of "subjective certainty." Friendship is bound to lead to, or to consist in, the cultivation and perpetuation of common prejudices by a closely knit group of kindred spirits. It is therefore incompatible with the idea of philosophy. The philosopher must leave the closed and charmed circle of the "initiated" if he intends to remain a philosopher. He must go out to the market place; the conflict with the political men cannot be avoided. And this conflict by itself, to say nothing of its cause or its effect, is a political action.

The whole history of philosophy testifies that the danger eloquently described by Kojève is inevitable. He is equally right in saying that that danger cannot be avoided by abandoning the sect in favor of what he regards as its modern substitute, the Republic of Letters. The Republic of Letters indeed lacks the narrowness of the sect: it embraces men of all philosophic persuasions. But precisely for this reason, the first article of the constitution of the Republic of Letters stipulates that no philosophic persuasion must be taken too seriously or that every philosophic persuasion must be treated with as much respect as any other. The Republic of Letters is relativistic. Or if it tries to avoid this pitfall, it becomes eclectic. A certain vague middle line, which is perhaps barely tolerable for the most easy-going members of the different persuasions if they are in their drowsiest mood, is set up as The Truth or as Common Sense; the substantive and irrepressible conflicts are dismissed as merely "semantic." Whereas the sect is narrow because it is passionately concerned with the true issues, the Republic of Letters is comprehensive because it is indifferent to the true issues: it prefers agreement to truth or to the quest for truth. If we have to choose between the sect and the Republic of Letters, we must choose the sect. Nor will it do that we abandon the sect in favor of the party or more precisely—since a party which is not a mass party is still something like a sect—of the mass party. For the mass party is nothing but a sect with a disproportionately long tail. The "subjective certainty" of the members of the sect, and especially of the weaker brethren, may be increased if the tenets of the sect are repeated by millions of parrots instead of by a few dozens of human beings, but this obviously has no effect on the claim of the tenets in question to "objective truth." Much as we loathe the snobbish silence or whispering of the sect, we loathe even more the savage noise of the loudspeakers of the mass party. The problem stated by Kojève is not then solved by dropping the distinction between those who are able and willing to think and those who are not. If we must choose between the sect and the party, we must choose the sect.

But must we choose the sect? The decisive premise of Kojève's argument is that philosophy "implies necessarily 'subjective certainties' which are not 'objective truths' or, in other words, which are prejudices." But philosophy in the original meaning of the term is nothing but knowledge of one's ignorance. The "subjective certainty" that one does not know coincides with the "objective truth" of that certainty. But one cannot know that one does not know without knowing what one does not know. What Pascal said with antiphilosophic intent about the impotence of both dogmatism and skepticism, is the only possible justification of philosophy which as such is neither dogmatic nor skeptic, and still less "decisionist," but zetetic (or skeptic in the original sense of the term). Philosophy as such is nothing but genuine awareness of the problems, i.e., of the fundamental and comprehensive problems. It is impossible to think about these problems without becoming inclined toward a solution, toward one or the other of the very few typical solutions. Yet as long as there is no wisdom but only quest for wisdom, the evidence of all solutions is necessarily smaller than the evidence of the problems. Therefore the philosopher ceases to be a philosopher at the moment at which the "subjective certainty" of a solution becomes stronger than his awareness of the problematic character of that solution. At that moment the sectarian is born. The danger of succumbing to the attraction of solutions is essential to philosophy which, without incurring this danger, would degenerate into playing with the problems. But the philosopher does not necessarily succumb to this danger, as is shown by Socrates, who never belonged to a sect and never founded one. And even if the philosophic friends are compelled to be members of a sect or to found one, they are not necessarily members of one and the same sect: *Amicus Plato.*

At this point we seem to get involved in a self-contradiction. For, if Socrates is the representative *par excellence* of the philosophic life, the philosopher cannot possibly be satisfied with a group of philosophic friends but has to go out to the market place where, as everyone knows, Socrates spent much or most of his time. However, the same Socrates suggested that there is no essential difference between the city and the family, and the thesis of Friedrich Mentz, *Socrates nec officiosus maritus nec laudandus paterfamilias* (Leipzig 1716), is defensible: Xenophon goes so far as not to count the husband of Xanthippe among the married men (*Symposium in fine*).

The difficulty cannot be discussed here except within the context of a limited exegetic problem. Xenophon indicates in the *Hiero* that the motivation of the philosophic life is the desire for being honored or admired by a small minority, and ultimately the desire for "self-admiration," whereas the motivation of the political life is the desire for love, i.e., for being loved by human beings irrespective of their qualities. Kojève rejects this view altogether. He is of the opinion that the philosopher and the ruler or tyrant are equally motivated by the desire for satisfaction, i.e., for recognition (honor) and ultimately for universal recognition, and that neither of the two is motivated by a desire for love. A human being is loved because he is and regardless of what he does. Hence love is at home within the family rather than in the public spheres of politics and of philosophy. Kojève regards it as particularly unfortunate that Xenophon tries to establish a connection between the "tyrannical" desire and sexual desire. He is equally averse to the suggestion that whereas the tyrant is guided by the desire for recognition by others, the philosopher is concerned exclusively with "self-admiration"; the self-satisfied philosopher is as such not distinguishable from the self-satisfied lunatic. The philosopher is then necessarily concerned with approval or admiration by others and he cannot help being pleased with it when he gets it. It is practically impossible to say whether the primary motive of the philosopher is the desire for admiration or the desire for the pleasures deriving from understanding. The very distinction has no practical meaning unless we gratuitously assume that there is an omniscient God who demands from men a pure heart.

What Xenophon indicated in the *Hiero* about the motivations of the two ways of life is admittedly incomplete. How can any man in his senses ever have overlooked the role played by ambition in political life? How can a friend of Socrates ever have overlooked the role played by love in the philosophic life? Simonides' speech on honor alone, to say nothing of Xenophon's other writings, proves abundantly that what Xenophon indicates in the *Hiero* about the motivations of the two ways of life is deliberately incomplete. It is incomplete because it proceeds from a complete disregard of everything but what one may call the most fundamental difference between the philosopher and the ruler. To understand this difference, one must start from the desire which the philosopher and the ruler have in common with each other and indeed with all men. All men desire "satisfaction." But satisfaction cannot be identified with recognition and even universal recognition. The classics identified satisfaction with happiness. The difference between the philosopher and the political man will then be a difference with respect to happiness. The philosopher's dominating passion is the desire for truth, i.e., for knowledge of the eternal order, or the eternal cause or causes of the whole. As he looks up in search for the eternal order, all human things and all human concerns reveal themselves

to him in all clarity as paltry and ephemeral, and no one can find
solid happiness in what he knows to be paltry and ephemeral. He
has then the same experience regarding all human things, nay, regarding man himself, which the man of high ambition has regarding
the low and narrow goals, or the cheap happiness, of the general
run of men. The philosopher, being the man of the largest views,
is the only man who can be properly described as possessing *mega-
loprepreia* (which is commonly rendered by "magnificence") (Plato,
Republic 486a). Or, as Xenophon indicates, the philosopher is the
only man who is truly ambitious. Chiefly concerned with eternal
beings, or the "ideas," and hence also with the "idea" of man, he
is as unconcerned as possible with individual and perishable human
beings and hence also with his own "individuality," or his body, as
well as with the sum total of all individual human beings and their
"historical" procession. He knows as little as possible about the way
to the market place, to say nothing of the market place itself, and
he almost as little knows whether his very neighbor is a human
being or some other animal (Plato, *Theaetetus* 173c8–d1, 174b1–6).
The political man must reject this way altogether. He cannot toler-
ate this radical depreciation of man and of all human things (Plato,
Laws 804b5–c1). He could not devote himself to his work with all
his heart or without reservation if he did not attach absolute importance to man and to human things. He must "care" for human beings
as such. He is essentially attached to human beings. This attachment
is at the bottom of his desire to rule human beings, or of his ambition. But to rule human beings means to serve them. Certainly an
attachment to beings which prompts one to serve them may well
be called love of them. Attachment to human beings is not peculiar
to the ruler; it is characteristic of all men as mere men. The difference between the political man and the private man is that in the case
of the former, the attachment enervates all private concerns; the
political man is consumed by erotic desire, not for this or that human
being, or for a few, but for the large multitude, for the *demos*
(Plato, *Gorgias* 481d1–5, 513d7–8; *Republic* 573e6–7, 574e2, 575a1–
2), and in principle, for all human beings. But erotic desire craves
reciprocity: the political man desires to be loved by all his subjects.
The political man is characterized by the concern with being loved
by all human beings regardless of their quality.

Kojève will have no difficulty in granting that the family man

can be characterized by "love" and the ruler by "honor." But if, as
we have seen, the philosopher is related to the ruler in a way
comparable to that in which the ruler is related to the family man,
there can be no difficulty in characterizing the ruler, in contradistinction to the philosopher, by "love" and the philosopher by
"honor." Furthermore, prior to the coming of the universal state,
the ruler is concerned with, and cares for, his own subjects as distinguished from the subjects of other rulers, just as the mother is
concerned with, and cares for, her own children as distinguished
from the children of other mothers; and the concern with, or care
for, what is one's own is what is frequently meant by "love." The
philosopher on the other hand is concerned with what can never
become private or exclusive property. We cannot then accept Kojève's doctrine regarding love. According to him, we love someone
"because he *is* and independently of what he *does*." He refers to
the mother who loves her son in spite of all his faults. But, to
repeat, the mother loves her son, not because he is, but because he
is her own, or because he has the quality of being her own. (Compare Plato, *Republic* 330c3–6.)

But if the philosopher is radically detached from human beings
as human beings, why does he communicate his knowledge, or his
questionings, to others? Why was the same Socrates, who said that
the philosopher does not even know the way to the market place,
almost constantly in the market place? Why was the same Socrates,
who said that the philosopher barely knows whether his neighbor
is a human being, so well informed about so many trivial details
regarding his neighbors? The philosopher's radical detachment from
human beings must then be compatible with an attachment to human
beings. While trying to transcend humanity (for wisdom is divine)
or while trying to make it his sole business to die and to be dead
to all human things, the philosopher cannot help living as a human
being who as such cannot be dead to human concerns, although
his soul will not be in these concerns. The philosopher cannot devote his life to his own work if other people do not take care of
the needs of his body. Philosophy is possible only in a society in
which there is "division of labor." The philosopher needs the services of other human beings and has to pay for them with services
of his own if he does not want to be reproved as a thief or fraud.
But man's need for other men's services is founded on the fact that

man is by nature a social animal or that the human individual is not self-sufficient. There is therefore a natural attachment of man to man which is prior to any calculation of mutual benefit. This natural attachment to human beings is weakened in the case of the philosopher by his attachment to the eternal beings. On the other hand, the philosopher is immune to the most common and the most powerful dissolvent of man's natural attachment to man, the desire to have more than one has already and in particular to have more than others have; for he has the greatest self-sufficiency which is humanly possible. Hence the philosopher will not hurt anyone. While he cannot help being more attached to his family and his city than to strangers, he is free from the delusions bred by collective egoisms; his benevolence or humanity extends to all human beings with whom he comes into contact. (*Memorabilia* I 2.60–61; 6.10; IV 8.11.) Since he fully realizes the limits set to all human action and all human planning (for what has come into being must perish again), he does not expect salvation or satisfaction from the establishment of the simply best social order. He will therefore not engage in revolutionary or subversive activity. But he will try to help his fellow man by mitigating, as far as in him lies, the evils which are inseparable from the human condition. (Plato, *Theaetetus* 176a5–b1; *Seventh Letter* 331c7–d5; Aristotle, *Politics* 1301a39–b2.) In particular, he will give advice to his city or to other rulers. Since all advice of this kind presupposes comprehensive reflections which as such are the business of the philosopher, he must first have become a political philosopher. After this preparation he will act as Simonides did when he talked to Hiero, or as Socrates did when he talked to Alcibiades, Critias, Charmides, Critobulus, the younger Pericles and others.

The attachment to human beings as human beings is not peculiar to the philosopher. As philosopher, he is attached to a particular type of human being, namely to actual or potential philosophers or to his friends. His attachment to his friends is deeper than his attachment to other human beings, even to his nearest and dearest, as Plato shows with almost shocking clarity in the *Phaedo*. The philosopher's attachment to his friends is based in the first place on the need which arises from the deficiency of "subjective certainty." Yet we see Socrates frequently engaged in conversations from which he cannot have benefited in any way. We shall try to explain what this means in a popular and hence unorthodox manner. The philosopher's attempt to grasp the eternal order is necessarily an ascent from the perishable things which as such reflect the eternal order. Of all perishable things known to us, those which reflect that order most, or which are most akin to that order, are the souls of men. But the souls of men reflect the eternal order in different degrees. A soul that is in good order or healthy reflects it to a higher degree than a soul that is chaotic or diseased. The philosopher who as such has had a glimpse of the eternal order is therefore particularly sensitive to the difference among human souls. In the first place, he alone knows what a healthy or well-ordered soul is. And secondly, precisely because he has had a glimpse of the eternal order, he cannot help being intensely pleased by the aspect of a healthy or well-ordered soul, and he cannot help being intensely pained by the aspect of a diseased or chaotic soul, without regard to his own needs or benefits. Hence he cannot help being attached to men of well-ordered souls: he desires "to be together" with such men all the time. He admires such men not on account of any services which they may render to him but simply because they are what they are. On the other hand, he cannot help being repelled by ill-ordered souls. He avoids men of ill-ordered souls as much as he can, while trying of course not to offend them. Last but not least, he is highly sensitive to the promise of good or ill order, or of happiness or misery, which is held out by the souls of the young. Hence he cannot help desiring, without any regard to his own needs or benefits, that those among the young whose souls are by nature fitted for it, acquire good order of their souls. But the good order of the soul is philosophizing. The philosopher therefore has the urge to educate potential philosophers simply because he cannot help loving well-ordered souls.

But did we not surreptitiously substitute the wise man for the philosopher? Does the philosopher of whom we have spoken not possess knowledge of many most important things? Philosophy, being knowledge of our ignorance regarding the most important things, is impossible without some knowledge regarding the most important things. By realizing that we are ignorant of the most important things, we realize at the same time that the most important thing for us, or the one thing needful, is quest for knowledge of the most important things, or philosophy. In other words, we realize that only by philosophizing can man's soul become well-ordered. We know how ugly or deformed a boaster's soul is; but everyone who thinks that he knows, while in truth he does not, is a boaster. Still, observations of this kind do not prove the assumption, for example, that the well-ordered soul is more akin to the eternal order, or to the eternal cause or causes of the whole, than is the chaotic soul. And one does not have to make that assumption in order to be a philosopher, as is shown by Democritus and other pre-Socratics, to say nothing of the moderns. If one does not make the assumption mentioned, one will be forced, it seems, to explain the philosopher's desire to communicate his thoughts by his need for remedying the deficiency of "subjective certainty" or by his desire for recognition or by his human kindness. We must leave it open whether one can thus explain, without being forced to use *ad hoc* hypotheses, the immediate pleasure which the philosopher experiences when he sees a well-ordered soul or the immediate pleasure which we experience when we observe signs of human nobility.

We may have explained why the philosopher is urged, not in spite of but because of his radical detachment from human beings as such, to educate human beings of a certain kind. But cannot exactly the same be said of the tyrant or ruler? May a ruler not likewise be penetrated by a sense of the ultimate futility of all human causes? It is undeniable that detachment from human beings, or what is popularly known as the philosophic attitude toward all things which are exposed to the power of chance, is not a preserve of the philosopher. But a detachment from human concerns which is not constantly nourished by genuine attachment to eternal things, i.e., by philosophizing, is bound to wither or to degenerate into lifeless narrowness. The ruler too tries to educate human beings and he too is prompted by love of some kind. Xenophon indicates his view of the ruler's love in the *Education of Cyrus*, which is, at any rate at first glance, his description of the greatest ruler. Xenophon's Cyrus is a cold or unerotic nature. That is to say, the ruler is not motivated by true or Socratic *eros* because he does not know what a well-ordered soul is. The ruler knows political virtue, and nothing prevents his being attracted by it; but political virtue, or the virtue of the nonphilosopher, is a mutilated thing; therefore it cannot elicit more than a shadow or an imitation of true love. The ruler is in fact dominated by love based on need in the common meaning of need, or by mercenary love; for "all men by nature believe they love those things by which they believe they are benefited" (*Oeconomicus* 20.29). In the language of Kojève, the ruler is concerned with human beings because he is concerned with being recognized by them. This explains incidentally why the indications of the *Hiero* about love are so strikingly incomplete; the purpose of the work required the disregard of nonmercenary love just as it required that wisdom be kept in its ordinary ambiguity.

We cannot agree then with Kojève's contention that the educative tendency of the ruler has the same character or scope as that of the philosopher. The ruler is essentially the ruler of all his subjects; his educative effort must therefore be directed toward all his subjects. If every educative effort is a kind of conversation, the ruler is forced by his position to converse with every subject. Socrates, however, is not compelled to converse with anyone except those with whom he likes to converse. If the ruler is concerned with universal recognition, he must be concerned with enlarging universally the class of competent judges of his merits. But Kojève does not seem to believe that all men are capable of becoming competent judges in political matters. He limits himself to contending that the number of men of philosophic competence is not smaller than the number of men of political competence. Yet contrary to what he seems to say in the text of his essay as distinguished from his note number five, many more men are capable of judging competently of the greatness of a ruler than of the greatness of a philosopher. This is the case not merely because a much greater intellectual effort is required for competent judgment of a philosophic achievement than for competent judgment of a political achievement. Rather is it true because philosophy requires liberation from the most potent natural charm whose undiminished power in no way obstructs political competence as the ruler understands political competence: from that charm that consists in unqualified attachment to human things as such. If the philosopher addresses himself, therefore, to a small minority, he is not acting on the basis of an a priori judgment. He is following the constant experience of all times and countries and, no doubt, the experience of Kojève himself. For try as one may to expel nature with a hayfork, it will always come back. The philosopher will certainly not be compelled, either by the need to remedy the deficiency of "subjective certainty" or by ambition, to strive for universal recognition. His friends alone suffice to remedy that deficiency, and no shortcomings in his friends can be remedied by having recourse to utterly incompetent people. And as for ambition, as a philosopher, he is free from it.

According to Kojève, one makes a gratuitous assumption in saying that the philosopher as such is free from ambition or from the desire for recognition. Yet the philosopher as such is concerned with nothing but the quest for wisdom and kindling or nourishing the love of wisdom in those who are by nature capable of it. We do not have to pry into the heart of any one in order to know that, insofar as the philosopher, owing to the weakness of the flesh, becomes concerned with being recognized by others, he ceases to be a philosopher. According to the strict view of the classics he turns into a sophist. The concern with being recognized by others is perfectly compatible with, and in fact required by, the concern essential to the ruler who is the ruler of others. But concern with being recognized by others has no necessary connection with the quest for the eternal order. Therefore, concern with recognition necessarily detracts from the singleness of purpose which is characteristic of the philosopher. It blurs his vision. This fact is not at variance with the other fact that high ambition is frequently a sign by which one can recognize the potential philosopher. But to the extent to which high ambition is not transformed into full devotion to the quest for wisdom, and to the pleasures which accompany that quest, he will not become an actual philosopher. One of the pleasures accompanying the quest for truth comes from the awareness of progress in that quest. Xenophon goes so far as to speak of the self-admiration of the philosopher. This self-admiration or self-satisfaction does not have to be confirmed by the admiration of others in order to be reasonable. If the philosopher, trying to remedy the deficiency of "subjective certainty," engages in conversation with others and observes again and again that his interlocutors, as they themselves are forced to admit, involve themselves in self-contradictions or are unable to give any account of their questionable contentions, he will be reasonably confirmed in his estimate of himself without necessarily finding a single soul who admires him. (Consider Plato, *Apology of Socrates* 21d1–3.) The self-admiration of the philosopher is in this respect

akin to "the good conscience" which as such does not require con-
firmation by others.

The quest for wisdom is inseparable from specific pleasures just
as the quest for these pleasures is inseparable from the quest for
wisdom. Thus it might seem possible to understand the quest for
wisdom in terms of the quest for pleasure. That this is in fact possible is asserted by all hedonists. In the *Hiero*, Xenophon (or his
Simonides) is forced to argue on the basis of the hedonistic thesis.
Hence the argument of the *Hiero* implies the question whether
the philosophic life can be understood in hedonistic terms. It implies the answer that it cannot be so understood because the rank
of the various kinds of pleasure ultimately depends upon the rank
of the activities to which the pleasures are related. Neither the
quantity nor the purity of the pleasures determines in the last resort
the rank of human activities. The pleasures are essentially secondary;
they cannot be understood but with reference to the activities. The
question as to whether the activities or the pleasures are in themselves
primary has nothing to do with the question as to whether someone
who engages in an activity is prompted to do so primarily by the
intrinsic value of the activity or by the pleasure which he expects to
enjoy as a consequence of the activity. Kojève may be perfectly right
in saying that the latter question does not permit a responsible
answer and is unimportant from the point of view of philosophy.
But the consideration is irrelevant to Xenophon's argument, which
is concerned exclusively with the former question.

While I must disagree with a considerable part of Kojève's reasoning, I agree with his conclusion that the philosopher has to go to the
market place, or in other words, that the conflict between the
philosopher and the city is inevitable. The philosopher must go to
the market place in order to fish there for potential philosophers. His
attempts to convert young men to the philosophic life will necessarily be regarded by the city as an attempt to corrupt the young.
The philosopher is therefore forced to defend the cause of philosophy. He must therefore act upon the city or upon the ruler.
Up to this point Kojève is in perfect agreement with the classics.
But does the final consequence mean, as he maintains, that the philosopher must desire to determine or codetermine the politics of the
city or of the rulers? Must the philosopher desire "to participate, in
one way or another, in the total direction of public affairs, so that

the State be organized and governed in such a manner that the philosopher's philosophic pedagogy be possible and effectual"? Or must we conceive of philosophic politics, i.e., of the philosopher's action on behalf of philosophy, in entirely different terms?

Contrary to what Kojève apparently implies, it seems to us that there is no necessary connection between the philosopher's indispensable philosophic politics and the efforts which he might or might not make to contribute toward the establishment of the best regime. For philosophy and philosophic education are possible in all kinds of more or less imperfect regimes. One may illustrate this by an example taken from the eighth book of Plato's *Republic*. There Plato contends that the Spartan regime is superior to the Athenian, although he knows that the Athenian is more favorable than the Spartan regime to the possibility and the survival of philosophic education (consider 557c6 and d4). It is true that it was in Athens that Socrates was compelled to drink the hemlock. But he was permitted to live and engage in philosophic education until he was seventy: in Sparta he would have been exposed as an infant. Plato could not have decided, however provisionally, in favor of the Spartan regime, if the philosopher's concern with a good political order were absolutely inseparable from the concern guiding his philosophic politics. In what then does philosophic politics consist? In satisfying the city that the philosophers are not atheists, that they do not desecrate everything sacred to the city, that they reverence what the city reverences, that they are not subversives, in short, that they are not irresponsible adventurers but good citizens and even the best of citizens. This is the defense of philosophy which was required always and everywhere, whatever the regime might have been. For, as the philosopher Montesquieu says, "*dans tous les pays du monde, on veut de la morale*" and "*les hommes, fripons en détail, sont en gros de très honnêtes gens; ils aiment la morale.*" This defense of philosophy before the tribunal of the city was achieved by Plato with a resounding success (Plutarch, *Nicias* ch. 23). The effects have lasted down to the present throughout all ages except the darkest ones. What Plato did in the Greek city and for it was done in and for Rome by Cicero, whose political action on behalf of philosophy has nothing in common with his actions against Catiline and for Pompey, for example. It was done in and for the Islamic world of Fārābī and in and for Judaism by Maimonides. Contrary to what Kojève seems to suggest, the political action of the philosophers on behalf of philosophy has achieved full success. One sometimes wonders whether it has not been too successful.

Kojève, I said, fails to distinguish between philosophic politics and that political action which the philosopher might undertake with a view to establishing the best regime or to the improvement of the actual order. He thus arrives at the conclusion that on the one hand the philosopher does not desire to rule, and on the other hand he must desire to rule, and that this contradiction involves a tragic conflict. The classics did not regard the conflict between philosophy and the city as tragic. Xenophon at any rate seems to have viewed that conflict in the light of Socrates' relation to Xanthippe. At least in this point there appears then something like an agreement between Xenophon and Pascal. For the classics, the conflict between philosophy and the city is as little tragic as the death of Socrates.

Kojève's argument continues as follows: Since the philosopher does not desire to rule because he has no time for ruling, but on the other hand is forced to rule, he has been satisfied with a compromise solution; with devoting a little time to giving advice to tyrants or rulers. Reading the chronicles, one receives the impression that this action of the philosophers has been wholly ineffectual—as ineffectual as Simonides' action that consisted in his conversation with Hiero. This conclusion does not entitle one, however, to infer that the philosopher should abstain from mingling in politics, for the strong reason for mingling in politics remains in force. The problem of what the philosopher should do in regard to the city remains, therefore, an open question, the subject of an unfinishable discussion. But the problem which cannot be solved by the dialectics of discussion may well be solved by the higher dialectics of History. The philosophic study of our past shows that philosophy, far from being politically ineffectual, has radically revolutionized the character of political life. One is even entitled to say that philosophic ideas alone have had significant political effect. For what else is the whole political history of the world except a movement toward the universal and homogeneous state? The decisive stages in the movement were actions of tyrants or rulers (Alexander the Great and Napoleon, e.g.). But these tyrants or rulers were and are pupils of philosophers. Classical philosophy created the idea of the universal state. Modern philosophy, which is the secularized form of Christianity, created the idea of the universal and homogeneous state. On the other hand, the progress of philosophy and its eventual transmutation into wisdom requires the "active negation" of the previous political states, i.e., requires the action of the tyrant: only when "all possible active [political] negations" have been effected and thus the final stage of the political development has been reached, can and will the quest for wisdom give way to wisdom.

I need not examine Kojève's sketch of the history of the Western world. That sketch would seem to presuppose the truth of the thesis which it is meant to prove. Certainly the value of the conclusion which he draws from his sketch depends entirely on the truth of the assumption that the universal and homogeneous state is the simply best social order. The simply best social order, as he conceives of it, is the state in which every human being finds his full satisfaction. A human being finds his full satisfaction if his human dignity is universally recognized and if he enjoys "equality of opportunity," i.e., the opportunity, corresponding to his capacities, of deserving well of the state or of the whole. Now if it were true that in the universal and homogeneous state, no one has any good reason for being dissatisfied with that state, or for negating it, it would not yet follow that everyone will in fact be satisfied with it and never think of actively negating it, for men do not always act reasonably. Does Kojève not underestimate the power of the passions? Does he not have an unfounded belief in the eventually rational effect of the movements instigated by the passions? In addition, men will have very good reasons for being dissatisfied with the universal and homogeneous state. To show this, I must have recourse to Kojève's more extensive exposition in his *Introduction à la lecture de Hegel*. There are degrees of satisfaction. The satisfaction of the humble citizen, whose human dignity is universally recognized and who enjoys all opportunities that correspond to his humble capacities and achievements, is not comparable to the satisfaction of the Chief of State. Only the Chief of State is "*really* satisfied." He alone is "truly free" (p. 146). Did Hegel not say something to the effect that the state in which one man is free is the Oriental despotic state? Is the universal and homogeneous state then merely a planetary Oriental despotism? However this may be, there is no guarantee that the incumbent Chief of State deserves his position to a higher degree than others. Those others then have very good reason for dissatisfaction: a state which treats equal men unequally is not just. A change from the universal-homogeneous monarchy into a universal-homogeneous aristocracy would seem to be reasonable. But we cannot stop here. The universal and homogeneous state, being the synthesis of the Masters and the Slaves, is the state of the working warrior or of the war-waging worker. In fact, all its members are warrior workers (pp. 114, 146). But if the state is universal and homogeneous, "wars and revolutions are henceforth impossible" (pp. 145, 561). Besides, work in the strict sense, namely the conquest or domestication of nature, is completed, for otherwise the universal and homogeneous state could not be the basis for wisdom (p. 301). Of course, work of a kind will still go on, but the citizens of the final state will work as little as possible, as Kojève notes with explicit reference to Marx (p. 435). To borrow an expression which someone used recently in the House of Lords on a similar occasion, the citizens of the final state are only so-called workers, workers by courtesy. "There is no longer fight nor work. History has come to its end. There is nothing more to *do*" (pp. 385, 114). This end of History would be most exhilarating but for the fact that, according to Kojève, it is the participation in bloody political struggles as well as in real work or, generally expressed, the negating action, which raises man above the brutes (pp. 490–492, 560, 378n.). The state through which man is said to become reasonably satisfied is, then, the state in which the basis of man's humanity withers away, or in which man loses his humanity. It is the state of Nietzsche's "last man." Kojève in fact confirms the classical view that unlimited technological progress and its accompaniment, which are the indispensable conditions of the universal and homogeneous state, are destructive of humanity. It is perhaps possible to say that the universal and homogeneous state is fated to come. But it is certainly impossible to say that man can reasonably be satisfied with it. If the universal and homogeneous state is the goal of History, History is absolutely "tragic." Its completion will reveal that the human problem, and hence in particular the problem of the relation of philosophy and politics, is insoluble. For centuries and centuries men have unconsciously done nothing but work their way through infinite labors and struggles and agonies, yet ever again catching hope, toward the universal and homogeneous state, and as soon as they have arrived at the end of their journey, they realize that through arriving at it they have destroyed their humanity and thus returned, as in a cycle, to the prehuman beginnings of History. *Vanitas vanitatum. Recognitio recognitionum.* Yet there is no reason for despair as long as human nature has not been conquered completely, i.e., as long as sun and man still generate man. There will always be men (*andres*) who will revolt against a state which is destructive of humanity or in which there is no longer a possibility of noble action and of great deeds. They may be forced into a mere negation of the universal and homogeneous state, into a negation not enlightened by any positive goal, into a nihilistic negation. While perhaps doomed to failure, that nihilistic revolution may be the only action on behalf of man's humanity, the only great and noble deed that is possible once the universal and homogeneous state has become inevitable. But no one can know whether it will fail or succeed. We still know too little about the workings of the universal and homogeneous state to say anything about where and when its corruption will start. What we do know is only that it will perish sooner or later (see Friedrich Engels' *Ludwig Feuerbach*, ed. by Hans Hajek, p. 6). Someone may object that the successful revolt against the universal and homogeneous state could have no other effect than that the identical historical process which has led from the primitive horde to the final state will be repeated. But would such a repetition of the process—a new lease of life for man's humanity—not be preferable to the indefinite continuation of the inhuman end? Do we not enjoy every spring although we know the cycle of the seasons, although we know that winter will come again? Kojève does seem to leave an outlet for action in the universal and homogeneous state. In that state the risk of violent death is still involved in the struggle for political leadership (p. 146). But this opportunity for action can exist only for a tiny minority. And besides, is this not a hideous prospect: a state in which the last refuge of man's humanity is political assassination in the particularly sordid form of the palace revolution? Warriors and workers of all countries, unite, while there is still time, to prevent the coming of "the realm of freedom." Defend with might and main, if it needs to be defended, "the realm of necessity."

But perhaps it is not war nor work but thinking that constitutes the humanity of man. Perhaps it is not recognition (which for many men may lose in its power to satisfy what it gains in universality) but wisdom that is the end of man. Perhaps the universal and homogeneous state is legitimated by the fact that its coming is the necessary and sufficient condition for the coming of wisdom: in the final state all human beings will be reasonably satisfied, they will be truly happy, because all will have acquired wisdom or are about to acquire it. "There is no longer fight nor work; History is completed; there is nothing more to *do*": man is at last free from all drudgery and for the highest and most divine activity, for the contemplation of the unchangeable truth (Kojève, *op. cit.*, p. 385). But if the final state is to satisfy the deepest longing of the human soul, every human being must be capable of becoming wise. The most relevant difference among human beings must have practically disappeared. We understand now why Kojève is so anxious to refute the classical view according to which only a minority of men are capable of the quest for wisdom. If the classics are right, only a few men will be truly happy in the universal and homogeneous state and hence only a few men will find their satisfaction in and through it. Kojève himself observes that the ordinary citizens of the final state are only "potentially satisfied" (p. 146). The actual satisfaction of all human beings, which allegedly is the goal of History, is impossible. It is for this reason, I suppose, that the final social order, as Kojève conceives of it, is a State and not a stateless society: the State, or coercive government, cannot wither away because it is impossible that all human beings should ever become actually satisfied.

The classics thought that, owing to the weakness or dependence of human nature, universal happiness is impossible, and therefore they did not dream of a fulfillment of History and hence not of a meaning of History. They saw with their mind's eye a society within which that happiness of which human nature is capable would be possible in the highest degree: that society is the best regime. But because they saw how limited man's power is, they held that the actualization of the best regime depends on chance. Modern man, dissatisfied with utopias and scorning them, has tried to find a guarantee for the actualization of the best social order. In order to succeed, or rather in order to be able to believe that he could succeed, he had to lower the goal of man. One form in which this was done was to replace moral virtue by universal recognition, or to replace happiness by the satisfaction deriving from universal recognition. The classical solution is utopian in the sense that its actualization is improbable. The modern solution is utopian in the sense that its actualization is impossible. The classical solution supplies a stable standard by which to judge of any actual order. The modern solution eventually destroys the very idea of a standard that is independent of actual situations.

It seems reasonable to assume that only a few, if any, citizens of the universal and homogeneous state will be wise. But neither the wise men nor the philosophers will desire to rule. For this reason alone, to say nothing of others, the Chief of the universal and homogeneous state, or the Universal and Final Tyrant will be an unwise man, as Kojève seems to take for granted. To retain his power, he will be forced to suppress every activity which might lead people into doubt of the essential soundness of the universal and homogeneous state: he must suppress philosophy as an attempt to corrupt the young. In particular he must in the interest of the homogeneity of his universal state forbid every teaching, every suggestion, that there are politically relevant natural differences among men which cannot be abolished or neutralized by progressing scientific technology. He must command his biologists to prove that every human being has, or will acquire, the capacity of becoming a philosopher or a tyrant. The philosophers in their turn will be forced to defend themselves or the cause of philosophy. They will be obliged, therefore, to try to act on the Tyrant. Everything seems to be a re-enactment of the age-old drama. But this time, the cause of philosophy is lost from the start. For the Final Tyrant presents himself as a philosopher, as the highest philosophic authority, as the supreme exegete of the only true philosophy, as the executor and hangman authorized by the only true philosophy. He claims therefore that he persecutes not philosophy but false philosophies. The experience is not altogether new for philosophers. If philosophers were confronted with claims of this kind in former ages, philosophy went underground. It accommodated itself in its explicit or exoteric teaching to the unfounded commands of rulers who believed they knew things which they did not know. Yet its very exoteric teaching undermined the commands or dogmas of the rulers in such a way as to guide the potential philosophers toward the eternal and unsolved problems. And since there was no universal state in existence, the philosophers could escape to other countries if life became unbearable in the tyrant's dominions. From the Universal Tyrant, however, there is no escape. Thanks to the conquest of nature and to the completely unabashed substitution of suspicion and terror for law, the Universal and Final Tyrant has at his disposal practically unlimited means for ferreting out, and for extinguishing, the most modest efforts in the direction of thought. Kojève would seem to be right although for the wrong reason: the coming of the universal and homogeneous state will be the end of philosophy on earth.

□ □ □

INDEX